CHRIST, LORD, SON OF GOD

STUDIES IN BIBLICAL THEOLOGY · 50

CHRIST, LORD, SON OF GOD

WERNER KRAMER

SCM PRESS LTD
BLOOMSBURY STREET LONDON

Translated by Brian Hardy from the German
Christos Kyrios Gottessohn
(Abhandlungen zur Theologie des Alten und Neuen Testaments 44)
(Zwingli-Verlag, Zürich, 1963)

FIRST PUBLISHED IN ENGLISH 1966
© SCM PRESS LTD 1966
PRINTED IN GREAT BRITAIN BY
W. & J. MACKAY & CO LTD, CHATHAM

SUSANNAE UXORI MEAE

CONTENTS

7

Contents

Contents

9

PREFACE

This book represents the thesis of mine which was approved by the theological faculty of the University of Zürich in February 1962. It is decidedly a specialist essay, in which my concern has been to examine the letters of the apostle Paul in order to gain a clearer understanding both of the way in which the christological titles are used and also of the ideas which lie behind those titles. Thus it aspires to be, before anything else, a contribution to New Testament research. All the same, I believe that I have not indulged in theological 'art for art's sake' but hope that this book will ultimately serve the true end of all theology, namely the preaching of the gospel.

Obviously the book itself is not a piece of direct evangelism, but my hope is that to some degree it may help to illuminate one particular aspect of the basic text of all preaching, the New Testament. And since the subject of investigation is the christology of the early Church, as illustrated in the thinking of the theologian Paul, then every step of the enquiry is an exciting one.

In keeping with the character of the book I have avoided making any references to the present time. Nevertheless, at many points the attentive reader will be able to see how particular developments in the early Church's christology, or particular elements in Paul's way of thinking, have direct relevance to our own situation. For what matters in the end, in the Church of our day as much as in the early Pauline Church, is that we believe in the crucified and risen Christ and therefore also that we confess Jesus as Lord. However different our historical situation may be, we have to take our bearings on the faith and confession of the first witnesses.

Here I would like to draw attention to a book which appeared at about the same time as the German edition of the present book, and which I therefore could not take into account. It is by Ferdinand Hahn, *Christologische Hoheitstitel. Ihre Geschichte im frühen*

Christentum (*FRLANT* 83), 1963. He deals with questions which are similar to those which I have discussed in the present book, only he draws his material from the synoptic Gospels. Thus the two books are complementary and make interesting comparisons possible.

With regard to the technical organization of the present book I should mention that in the text and notes I normally refer to other literature by giving simply the surname of the author and the first noun in the title. This noun is printed in bold type in the bibliography, where full details may be found. References to the present book are made by giving the appropriate paragraph number and sub-section letter. May I ask authors who quote my book to make references to it in the same way? A list of the abbreviations used is given on p. 223.

I am very happy that the SCM Press has decided to publish my book in English and I am grateful for the honour done to me. I am grateful, too, to the translator of my book, the Reverend Brian Hardy of Downing College, Cambridge, for his rendering into English of what at many places in the original is typically German terminology. If English readers find pleasure in reading my book, it will be in large measure as the result of his work.

My hope for the English edition as for the German edition of my book is that it may serve to open up a way to the plentiful land of the New Testament itself.

WERNER KRAMER

Zürich
1 September 1965

1. The Problem

a. The present essay, in common with all academic work, has limits which we need not lament, once we have become aware of them and taken them into account from the outset. For here, limitation means simply that we make a selection from all the material available and from the variety of methods of enquiry which might be adopted.

It has become the custom to approach the problem of the christological titles by asking historical questions. We do not wish to belittle the importance or the competence of this method in any way, but nevertheless its uncertainties and dangers are apparent. A frequent result of the historical method of inquiry, which deals with the wider perspectives, is that when applied to the New Testament it overlooks or blurs the particular accents and nuances of the NT texts. Furthermore, there is no point in opening up the question of titles from the historical angle unless new material on the subject is to hand. But such material is either unknown to me or inaccessible. [1]

For these reasons the present work takes the New Testament material as its starting point, and its object is primarily to examine, by means of a critical analysis of text, tradition and 'themes', [2] the places at which the christological titles occur within the strata of the NT tradition. From the results gained in this way we shall then have to go back again and again to inquire into historical contexts. It is this sense that historical questions are taken up, but they form neither the starting point nor the centre of the present work.

At the centre of the material examined is the Pauline corpus, i.e. the letters which are generally agreed to be Pauline. It became necessary to limit the scope in this way because a survey of the

---

[1] On the title *Kyrios* see Schulz, 'Maranatha und Kyrios Jesus', *ZNW* 53, 1962, 125–44.
[2] On the term 'theme-criticism' see Schulz, *Untersuchungen zur Menschensohn-Christologie im Johannesevangelium*, 1957, 87–93.

whole NT material showed that the Pauline epistles are by far the most fertile in the kind of contexts which are examined here. Besides this, the Pauline corpus offers a relatively broad yet unified basis for drawing standards of judgement which are relevant. Of course comparisons with non-Pauline writings are frequently necessary and useful, but that does not alter the fact that it is the Pauline material which gives the clearest, most vivid picture. In the post-Pauline writings the indiscriminate use of the christological titles quickly sets in on the one hand, whilst on the other hand each particular author increasingly favours a particular title which he then inserts into the most varied contexts, without stopping to consider whether the particular title originally belonged to that context or not.[3]

b. The choice of procedure in the narrower sense is decisive for the success of the work. Merely to compile in statistical fashion a list of the christological titles which occur in a particular context, without first analysing the stages of the tradition, would be to lose the path to a clear understanding of each individual title, for such statistics lead to the conclusion that each title can occur in any context.[4]

But it is just as misleading to classify and handle the christological titles on the basis of the position which they occupied in early Christian orthodoxy, for thus we would foist upon the individual titles in the Pauline period meanings which they took on only later as a result of all kinds of additions and harmonizing.[5] Equally little justice is done to the titles by arranging them individually within a systematic framework devised by a particular investigator to accord with his own understanding, for this means that they are interpreted in terms of their position within the framework and not in terms of themselves.[6]

Bearing in mind these dangers and false paths, we shall take

[3] See for instance the *Didache*, where (except for passages taken from elsewhere like 7.1; 92f.; 102f.) the *Kyrios* title occurs almost without exception. Ignatius, on the other hand, prefers *Jesus Christ*.

[4] Foerster's 'Exkurs I, Der urchristliche Gebrauch von Κύριος, 'Ιησοῦς und Χριστός', in *Herr ist Jesus*, 1924, 237–63, is a typical example of this procedure and corresponding result. The impression is given that in 'early Christianity' the christological titles were used entirely indiscriminately.

[5] The effects of this procedure are easily observable in Cerfaux, *Christ in the Theology of St Paul*, ET 1959.

[6] This danger becomes apparent in Cullmann, *Christology of the New Testament*, ET 1959.

care to establish for the present work a basis which is secure and appropriate to our task. This can be obtained only from the texts themselves. Fortunately there are in the Pauline corpus early (i.e. pre-Pauline) and relatively small units, distinguishable by their literary form, in each of which we find one of the christological titles firmly rooted. If we begin with these short pre-Pauline formulae, which normally have liturgical associations, we shall have in all respects firm ground under our feet, giving a sound basis on which to examine both the development of the tradition and larger historical questions. If we observe that the statements of the formulae determine the content of the titles associated with them, we shall then be able to recognize in those statements the elements of the original understanding of *Christ, Lord,* and *Son of God*. By comparing these statements with other pre-Pauline expressions, noting their content and the way in which they are used, we shall have a means of distinguishing what is accidental from what is characteristic. We can then go on to examine certain fixed combinations in which particular key words figure, and thus we shall have yet another bearing from which to test our own results.

With this as the foundation we shall then be able to tackle specifically Pauline language, and we shall find to what extent Paul follows usage already to hand and to what extent he deviates from it. This should reveal clearly what is Paul's own contribution with regard to the christological titles, or 'christology'.

Connected with the christological titles is a whole series of special problems which as a rule are not confined simply to one stratum of the tradition. Part Three of this book is devoted to these problems.

As befits the problem we have set ourselves and the procedure we have adopted, our main concern will be to analyse and compare a multitude of individual passages. We shall insist on making this as complete as possible, in order to avoid the danger of taking only those passages which 'fit the theory'.[7]

[7] See the preface for the technical organization of the present book and the method of reference.

PART ONE
The Pre-Pauline Material

I · CHRIST (JESUS)

A. The Traditional Pistis-formula

2. The Starting Point: I Cor. 15.3b–5

a. I Cor. 15.3b–5 is, according to Paul's own words, a piece which he took over from the tradition.[8] If we remove from it the syntactical links with its present context,[9] it runs:

> 'Christ died for our sins, in accordance with the scriptures; and he was buried;
> and he was raised to life on the third day, according to the scriptures; and he appeared to Cephas, and afterwards to the Twelve.'

This formula, made up of the two parts, 'Christ died—he was raised', has almost been extended to four parts by mentioning the facts, 'he was buried' and 'he appeared'.[10] Similarly the exactly parallel reference to scripture, 'according to the scriptures', show that this is an already developed form. The semitisms[11] indicate that it originates in a Jewish-Christian environment.[12] What is important for our purpose is that this pre-Pauline formula about

---

[8] παρέλαβον and παρέδωκα correspond to the rabbinical technical terms *qibbēl min* and *māsar lᵉ* which indicate an objective traditional precedent. Cf. I Cor. 11.23 and Jeremias, *The Eucharistic Words of Jesus*, ET 1955, 129. Full bibliography on the formula in Wilckens, *Die Missionsreden der Apostelgeschichte*, 1961, 73 n. 4.

[9] The introductory ὅτι is a normal stylistic feature in formulae connected with πιστεύειν, etc. See Wilckens, *Missionsreden* 76 n. 1. However, this is not so when ὅτι is repeated within the formula. To conclude, as Wilckens does, that the repeated ὅτι must introduce an originally independent formula contradicts all form-critical examination of the pistis-formula. Its occurrence here does not reflect an earlier stage, but is introduced *ad hoc* in order to emphasize each separate statement in turn. Its function is similar to our 'first', 'second', etc. If we wish to look at the formula on its own, we must therefore delete ὅτι.

[10] Cf. Oepke, *Die Missionspredigt des Apostels Paulus*, 1920, 59.

[11] Cf. Jeremias, *Eucharistic Words* 129f.

[12] Against Heitmüller, 'Zum Problem Paulus und Jesus', ZNW 13, 1912, 331f.; with Lietzmann, *An die Korinther I u. II*, ed. Kümmel, 1949, *ad loc.*, who invokes in support Jeremias, *Eucharistic Words* 129.

the death and the resurrection of Christ, i.e. saving acts of the past, is associated with '*Christ*'. For the present we defer the question whether *Christ* was originally rooted in this formula, or whether we are to ascribe its presence here to Paul's authorship.[13] This question will have to be answered when our investigation is further advanced.

So we turn now to those passages in the Pauline correspondence which similarly speak of the saving acts of the past.

Considerations of method suggest that we should not begin with the full two-part formula, for the passages in which this occurs are relatively few and the variations in form are relatively great. We shall do better to start by analysing the passages in which only one of the saving acts is mentioned. This will enable us to establish the form and the content of the single statements in the tradition, and then we shall return to the complete formula.

3. The Resurrection as a Statement in the Pistis-formula

a. Rom. 10.9b mentions only one saving act which is to be believed in the heart: 'God raised him from the dead.' Comparing this with I Cor. 15.4b, we note the following differences: First, God is explicitly the agent in the resurrection.[14] Secondly, the verb ἤγειρεν is aorist, emphasizing the once-for-all character of the resurrection as a past event.[15] Thirdly, the resurrection is a resurrection 'from the dead'. There is no mention of 'the third day'. Fourthly, the christological title to which this sentence relates might at first sight appear to be '*Lord Jesus*' in v. 9a, for it is to this that the personal pronoun 'him' seems to refer. But we can show that *Lord Jesus*, together with the rest of v. 9a, clearly belongs to a different range of christological ideas.[16] So the pronoun, even though grammatically it might be taken to refer to

---

[13] Seeberg, *Der Katechismus der Urchristenheit*, 1903, 57 and 60–65, considers it to be Paul's work, but his arguments turn out to be irrelevant, for they relate to the formula about 'sending'.

[14] This is implied in I Cor. 15.4b, as the passive form of the verb shows.

[15] The aorist, rather than the perfect tense, is the more original, preserving simply an event which happened once and now lies in the past. But the perfect tense indicates that the event as such has been left behind, and it expresses Christ's 'being raised' as a continuing state.

[16] See 15.

Lord Jesus, cannot be related to the ideas which underlie that title. But whether the presence of the personal pronoun in this context is typical, or whether a particular christological title is concealed behind it, can only be decided when we have examined other similar passages in Paul's writings.

But the verse does give a decisive clue, for it links the statement about the resurrection with the key word 'believe' (πιστεύειν). It is no mere accident that these should appear side by side, for the resurrection statement defines what is believed.[17] For this reason Conzelmann has given the name 'Credo' to these formulae which speak of the saving acts.[18] In order to stress the difference between these formulae and the credal formulae of the later Church, and in order to keep as close as possible to the NT πίστις, we shall be well advised to speak of these formulae within the NT as '*pistis*-formulae'. This is why we introduce here the term 'pistis-formula' as a name for the formula which has as its content the saving acts of death and resurrection.

The three main features of the pistis-formula, as established from Rom. 10.9b, (i.e. God as the subject, the verb in the aorist, and 'from the dead' qualifying 'raised') are found together or separately in several other places within the Pauline corpus.

b. In I Thess. 1.10b, which contains a traditional (i.e. Jewish or Jewish-Christian) formula, Paul has added the clause, 'whom he raised from the dead, (Jesus)'. The purpose of the addition is to give a more precise christological definition, and it comes very close to the wording of Rom. 10.9b.[19] Whether *Jesus* formed part

---

[17] See Wilckens, *Missionsreden* 76 n. 1.

[18] Conzelmann, 'Was glaubte die frühe Christenheit?', *Schweizerische Theologische Umschau* 25, 1955, 64. Seeberg, *Katechismus* 56, had already used the term 'formula of faith' (*Glaubensformel*) in this specific sense.

[19] Whereas Rom. 10.9b has ἐκ νεκρῶν, I Thess. 1.10b has ἐκ τῶν νεκρῶν. On text-critical grounds the article is uncertain, but since the majority of similar passages have no article its occurrence here might be defined as *lectio difficilior* and thus taken to be original. But the very passages which interest us here bring to light an inadequacy of the conventional text-critical method, particularly with regard to the christological titles. For when we find a textually uncertain variation in the use of certain christological titles, running counter to relatively constant Pauline usage, are we really to ascribe this to Paul himself as *lectio difficilior*, or are we not rather to see it as the work of a copyist in a period when indiscriminate use of the titles had become general? We cannot decide here for all passages, but must wait until individual passages have been examined; but these reflections surely mean that in the passages with which we are concerned *lectio difficilior* as a criterion loses its *a priori* conclusiveness. Thus, in practical terms, our arguments can neither be confirmed nor disproved by passages here and there which contain such variants. Applying this to the question of the article in I Thess. 1.10b, we must ask whether it is more likely

of the original confession, or whether it belongs to the inserted pistis-formula, cannot be decided at this point.

c. We can see how vividly God is regarded as the agent in the resurrection from the fact that Paul uses statements of the pistis-formula, re-cast in participial form, as descriptions of God himself. In Rom. 8.11a he speaks of 'the Spirit of him who raised (τοῦ ἐγείραντος) Jesus from the dead'. In Rom. 8.11b God is 'he who raised (ὁ ἐγείρας) Christ Jesus from the dead'. In Gal. 1.1 God is described as 'the one who raised him (τοῦ ἐγείραντος αὐτόν) from the dead', where the pronoun refers grammatically to *Jesus Christ.*

The recurrence of these three forms, and especially the recurrence of the phrase 'from the dead', show that they are not merely *ad hoc* Pauline formulations but are all based on the pistis-formula.

d. Fragments of the pistis-formula are used not only to describe God as the one who raised Christ from the dead, but also to describe Christ himself. Rom. 7.4 speaks of 'him who has been raised (ἐγερθείς) from the dead'. We cannot directly answer the question of the title here. *Christ* does indeed occur in the same verse, but it is conditioned by the phrase 'the body of Christ'.[20]

e. Finally, the resurrection statement in the pistis-formula occurs variously in I Cor. 15.12–20, an exposition of the formula at vv. 3b–5. Verse 12 has '(*Christ* . . . as) raised from the dead' (ἐκ νεκρῶν ἐγήγερται); v. 20, '*Christ* has been raised from the dead'; and vv. 13, 14, 16, 17, '(if) *Christ* has not been raised'.

The fact that *Christ* appears as the subject of a clause constructed in the passive means that there is direct dependence upon the wording of the formula in vv. 3b–5. The same goes for the perfect tense of the verb, which here replaces throughout the aorist which we observed at Rom. 10.9b etc. But it is interesting that even where he is quoting almost continuously these fragments

---

that Paul departs in this one passage from the wording of the formula than that a copyist who no longer knew or used the formula as such inserted the article himself. I think it more probable that even in this passage Paul follows the wording of the formula, and thus I regard the article as secondary, even though as *lectio difficilior* it would stand. The preceding ἐκ τῶν οὐρανῶν might account for the copyist's error.

[20] There is, of course, an indirect connection, for the 'body of Christ' in Rom. 7.4 is the body given on the cross for mankind. Thus Bornkamm, 'Herrenmahl und Kirche bei Paulus', *Studien zu Antike und Christentum*, 1959, 164 n. 57; cf. Lietzmann, *An die Römer*, 1928, *ad loc.*; Michel, *Der Brief an die Römer*, 1963, *ad loc.* Since this dying 'for' (ὑπέρ) also forms part of the substance of the pistis-formula, there is reason for the occurrence of the title *Christ* in this context.

of the formula from vv. 3b–5, Paul never qualifies the verb 'was raised' by the phrase 'on the third day' which we find there, but by the phrase 'from the dead'.

This leads us to conclude that the traditional pistis-statement about the resurrection of Christ existed in different forms, one type following the pattern of the formula at I Cor. 15.3b–5: '(*Christ*) was raised on the third day (in accordance with the scriptures)'; and the other in the form used at Rom. 10.9, etc., 'God raised him (= *Jesus* or *Christ*) from the dead.' Paul prefers the latter form.

f. The fact that the pistis-statement about the resurrection occurs in the deutero-Pauline and non-Pauline NT writings shows that it is not simply Paul's own creation. The stereotype recurrence of the principal features is striking.

Col. 2.12, in a baptismal context, speaks of 'faith in the working of God, who raised him (πίστις τῆς ἐνεργείας τοῦ θεοῦ τοῦ ἐγείραντος αὐτον) from the dead'. The key word *pistis* is here, but with a typical shift of emphasis by comparison with what we find in the Pauline corpus, for it is trust in God's power to act. The resurrection is no longer as strictly the content of faith as it is for Paul, but rather evidence of God's active power.[21]

In Eph. 1.20 God is the one 'who raised him from the dead'; in II Tim. 2.8 Jesus Christ, 'risen from the dead', is no longer the object of 'believing' but of 'remembering'.

The pistis-statement about the resurrection is frequently found in the kerygma of Acts: 3.15; 4.10, 'whom God raised (ἤγειρεν) from the dead'; 13.30 is similar; 5.30; 13.37 omit 'from the dead'; 10.40, which has 'on the third day' is proof that the statement circulated also in a form akin to the formula in I Cor. 15.3b–5.[22]

Finally we must mention I Peter 1.21, where it is said of Christians, 'You have confidence (πιστοί) in God, who raised him from the dead.' Here, too, the connection has been preserved between the root *pist-* and the resurrection statement.

g. So, with regard to our subject, we conclude that in these

---

[21] If the genitive were to be taken not as objective but subjective, the shift would be even more marked, for although *pistis* and the modified statement of the pistis-formula indeed stand side by side, the link between them is now only an indirect and superficial one.

[22] Wilckens, *Missionsreden* 78, speaks of the 'influence of the formula in I Cor. 15.4 or of similar formulae'.

formulae no single christological title predominates entirely, for except where there is simply a pronoun,[23] both *Jesus*[24] and *Christ* (*Jesus*)[25] are to be found. Certainly we cannot say that in each of these passages the particular christological title used is present because it is 'fixed' in the pistis-formula. In I Thess. 1.10b it is uncertain whether *Jesus* belongs to this formula, and in Gal. 1.1 the title *Jesus Christ* is present on account of its connection with the word 'apostle' and not on account of the pistis-formula. Nevertheless, even if we take into account these differences, we can still say that *Christ* and *Jesus*, or both combined, occur as christological designations in the pistis-formula or in statements which are akin to it. The title *Lord*, on the other hand, is found only in exceptional instances which we shall now explain.

Concerning the fragments of this pistis-formula which are found in the non-Pauline writings we can say with complete certainty that the title *Lord* is never associated with them. This confirms what we found in the Pauline corpus. Of the other titles, *Jesus*[26] (as object), *Christ*,[27] or *Jesus Christ*[28] are all to be found associated with the statement about the resurrection, whilst in other statements, akin to the pistis-formula but less closely connected with it, we find *Jesus* in combinations like those which are common in the kerygmata of Acts.[29]

h. However, three passages containing the title *Lord* seem to contradict our conclusion. They are: I Cor. 6.14a, 'and God raised the Lord . . .'; II Cor. 4.14, 'he who raised the Lord Jesus . . .'; Rom. 4.24b, 'to us who believe in him that raised from the dead our Lord Jesus'.

In all three passages God is the subject, the verb is aorist. The phrase, 'from the dead' is lacking in the first two, but is present in the third. Thus we should regard these three passages as fragments of the pistis-formula. What is unusual is that the title *Lord* should occur in this context.

---

[23] Rom. 10.9b; Gal. 1.1.
[24] Rom. 8.11a; I Thess. 1.10(?).
[25] I Cor. 15.12–20; cf. Rom. 7.4; 8.11b. In Gal. 1.1 the pronoun refers back to a '*dia*'-phrase containing *Jesus Christ*.
[26] Acts 5.30.
[27] Eph. 1.20.
[28] II Tim. 2.8.
[29] Acts 4.10 Jesus Christ the Nazarene; 10.38 Jesus of Nazareth; 13.23 Saviour Jesus.

However, certain observations may lead us further. Immediately before I Cor. 6.14a we find the title *Lord* twice in v. 13. Since other Pauline passages show that Paul's habit is to keep to the use of the same christological title within any one section,[30] we can see that *Lord* in the pistis-statement here is due to the context and does not stem directly from the pistis-formula.

In II Cor. 4.14 the title *Lord* is uncertain on text-critical grounds.[31] It does not appear in the rest of the passage.[32] Since we have seen that Paul's custom is to keep to terms already used, this might presumably be deemed the *lectio difficilior*. Yet the considerations set out in note 19 suggest clearly that a copyist is responsible for the title *Lord* in this instance. But since our concern here is to establish the structure and the wording of the pre-Pauline formula, the title *Lord* in this passage falls outside our scope.

An interesting point is that in v. 13 the key word πιστεύειν appears. Certainly this is not because of any connection with the pistis-formula. But as soon as Paul goes on from the quotation of Ps. 116.10 to talk about 'believing' which finds expression in 'speaking', he mentions its content in terms which are significantly reminiscent of the pistis-formula. This is one more argument for the appropriateness of speaking of a pistis-formula.

In Rom. 4.24 the insertion of the title *Lord* is to be attributed to Paul, for it can be shown that he habitually uses fuller christological titles in closing passages.[33] But this does not mean that the passage in any way contradicts our observation that the pistis-formula was not originally associated with the title *Lord*. We cannot decide for certain whether *Jesus* occurs here because it was originally linked with the formula, or whether it was inserted by Paul together with the title *Lord*. We should add that the key word πιστεύειν appears here also.[34] Thus the passage is yet another indi-

---

[30] Cf. II Cor. 5.14–20: *Christ* 7 times; Gal. 2.16f.: *Christ (Jesus)* 5 times; Gal. 3.22–29: *Christ (Jesus)* 7 times; Gal. 5.1–4: *Christ* 3 times; Rom. 15.16–20: *Christ (Jesus)* 5 times; Phil. 1.20–23: *Christ* 3 times.

[31] The readings of p⁴⁶, Vaticanus and others lack κύριος. Kümmel, in his revision of Lietzmann, *Korinther ad loc.*, considers this reading to be the original.

[32] *Jesus*, on the other hand, occurs frequently: vv. 10a, 10b, 11a, 11b, 14b.

[33] Cf. e.g. Rom. 5.21; 6.23; 7.25; 8.39.

[34] Bultmann, πιστεύειν, *TWNT* VI 211.30–34 (ET, *Faith*, 1961, 74), thinks that here it does not quite carry the specifically NT understanding of the word. But this does not affect the validity of our observation. Indeed we might point out that to describe God in terms of the saving events is in itself a mark of specifically NT thinking.

cation that the root *pist-* is naturally associated with the statement about the resurrection.

i. Our conclusions may be summarized as follows:

1. The widespread distribution of the statement about the resurrection in stereotype form both within the Pauline corpus and outside it proves that the statement, 'God raised him from the dead' is a sentence of fixed structure.

2. The sentence consists of these elements: God is the subject; the verb is aorist; the verb is qualified by the expression 'from the dead'.

3. Because the root *pist-* appears in various forms (πιστεύειν, πίστις, πιστός), we are justified in describing this sentence in the formula as a pistis-statement.

4. Within the fragments of the pistis-formula there is no uniformity in the use of christological titles. As well as a simple pronoun, which is not clearly linked with any one title, we find *Jesus, Christ*, and *Christ Jesus*.

The title *Lord* does not belong originally to this traditional material. Where, despite this, it does occur, its presence is to be ascribed in two cases to Paul himself, and in one case to a copyist.

4. Christ's Death 'for (us)' as a Statement in the Pistis-formula

a. The first part of the pistis-formula in I Cor. 15.3b runs: 'Christ died for (ὑπέρ) our sins in accordance with the scriptures.' Several Pauline passages speak of the death of Christ, e.g. Rom. 5.8: '*Christ* died for us' (Χριστὸς ὑπὲρ ἡμῶν ἀπέθανεν). The similarity with the pistis-statement in I Cor. 15.3b is striking. 1. Christ is the subject of the sentence; 2. The verb is aorist; 3. The death is a death 'for' (ὑπέρ). . . .

But in other respects the two sentences part company, for the phrase 'in accordance with the scriptures' features only in the pistis-formula. They differ, too, in the object to which the preposition 'for' refers. Of the two phrases, 'for us' is the more original, because 'for our sins' represents a more developed interpretation.[35] 'For us' leaves open the question whether substitution or atone-

[35] Cf. the similar development within the synoptic tradition from Mark 14.24b to Matt. 26.28b.

ment is meant; but 'for our sins' clearly interprets the death as an atoning sacrifice.

However that may be, the interpretation of Christ's death as something which happened 'for . . .', i.e. in our favour, is in itself of material importance. For it is an idea which makes it possible to explain Christ's death as bearing upon human existence, and in consequence the death can be understood and proclaimed as a saving event.

b. As with the statement about the resurrection, so now with the statement about the death we find that it recurs several times, and its constituent elements are preserved in stereotype fashion, e.g. Rom. 5.6, '*Christ* died for the ungodly.'

In Rom. 14.15 or I Cor. 8.11 the brother is described as one 'for whom *Christ* died' (in the first case ὑπὲρ οὖ; in the second case δι' ὄν). Gal. 2.21 lacks 'for . . .'; and Gal. 3.13 reads 'having become a curse for us', but here Paul is interpreting the death in terms of the demands and the authority of the law.

c. In the non-Pauline writings the equivalent statement occurs only infrequently and in adapted form.[36] Nevertheless, in I Peter 3.18, in a formula about the saving acts, we find the words, '*Christ* also died for (περί) sins once for all.' John 11.51 reveals a further development which is characteristic: 'that Jesus should die for (ὑπέρ) the nation, and not for the nation only . . . '

d. Our conclusions are:

1. It is evident, from what we have found in Pauline and non-Pauline writings alike, that the statement about the death in the form '*Christ* died for us' is another sentence in the pistis-formula.

2. It is made up of the following elements: *Christ* is the subject of the statement; the verb ἀποθνῄσκειν is in the aorist; the death is described as 'for us'.

3. The christological title used is *Christ* in every instance.[37] There is nowhere any trace of the title *Lord*. In this respect we find that the statement about the death largely coincides with the statement about the resurrection.

4. Finally we have to ask ourselves how far we are right in saying

---

[36] For the references to the passion in the preaching of Acts see the list in Wilckens, *Missionsreden* 109. They are concerned not so much to expound the significance of Christ's death as to show that the guilt for the death lies with the Jews.

[37] Except in John 11.51 (*Jesus*), but this sentence reflects a much more advanced stage of development.

that the sentence about Christ's death is another statement in the *pistis*-formula, for the verb πιστεύειν does not in fact occur in this context.

I Cor. 15.3b–5 shows that the statements about the death and the resurrection of Christ belong together. The latter statement, linked in a variety of ways with the root *pist-*, defines what is believed. Is it not then permissible to describe the sentence about the death, too, as a pistis-statement?

In order to discover whether such a description is appropriate or not, we must examine the complete formula.

5. The Complete Pistis-formula as a Statement about the Death and Resurrection of Christ

a. I Cor. 15.3b–5 is not the only passage within the Pauline corpus which shows how the statement about the death and the statement about the resurrection together make up the one pistis-formula. Behind Rom. 6.3–9 lies a similar formula, certainly fragmented and introduced piecemeal in the course of the argument. Nevertheless its main affirmations can be reconstructed with relative ease. Verse 4, cf. v. 9, reads, '*Christ* was raised from the dead'; in v. 8, '*Christ* died' may be inferred from the statement, 'we have died with Christ'. The reason why the ὑπέρ statement has been omitted here is obvious. In v. 4, '*Christ* was buried' may be inferred from 'we were buried with him'.

So we arrive at the following as the principal statements in the formula:

> *Christ* died
>   was buried
>   was raised from the dead.

The mention of the burial brings us very close to I Cor. 15.3b–5, but in our passage 'he appeared' is lacking, though for the obvious reason that in the setting of a theological exposition of baptism it could serve no useful purpose.

On the other hand, the phrase '(our old self) was crucified with him' goes beyond what we find in I Cor. 15.3b–5. We might infer from it a pistis-statement '(Christ) was crucified', but we have not encountered such a sentence yet in any formula.[38] Within an exposition of the meaning of baptism it could be used naturally alongside the statements about the death and the burial.

Two earlier observations have been confirmed, for here again 'from the dead' is preferred to 'on the third day', and the title *Lord* never appears, though *Christ* appears frequently.

b. We have to admit that the pistis-formula is not found in so complete a form elsewhere in Paul, but here and there we do come across the two statements combined in short form.

In II Cor. 5.15c the Christians' life is defined as a life which is 'for him who for their sake died and was raised'. Just before this in vv. 14, 15 the statement 'he died for all' occurs twice. The formula is reflected, too, in Rom. 8.34a: '*Christ Jesus*, who died, yes, who was raised.'[39] These words appear here simply in order to introduce another formula-fragment which speaks in relative clauses of the exaltation and heavenly intercession. It is typical that the title *Christ (Jesus)*[40] should figure here.

c. The wording of the pistis-formula, as we have established it, is not followed so closely in I Thess. 4.14a: 'For since we believe that Jesus died and rose again', for the verb ἀναστῆναι appears here instead of ἐγείρειν. But a glance at the passion predictions[41] and the sermons in Acts[42] reveals that ἀναστῆναι or ἀνιστάναι figured in a similar formula recounting the saving acts. The presence of the key verb 'we believe that . . . ' in I Thess. 4.14 shows that this formula, too, may be called a pistis-formula, for its content is similar: dying and rising (or being raised) form the substance of what is believed. It is *Jesus* who is named as the subject of these acts.

d. A further variant is given in Rom. 14.9: '(For to this end)

---

[38] Cf. I Cor. 1.13, 23; Gal. 1.1. These passages suggest that Paul uses these words to give extra emphasis to the statement about the death.

[39] The Hesychian group reads ἐκ νεκρῶν. Here again, deciding in favour of one or other reading is a matter of opinion. In any case it is quite conceivable that copyists have restored the phrase which Paul left out when he reduced the formula to verbs only.

[40] In view of Paul's normal usage, the double title in this liturgically styled passage is to be preferred to the simple *Christ*, and we must suppose that Paul himself introduced it. He will not have done so arbitrarily, but because both *Christ* and *Jesus* are associated with the pistis-formula.

[41] Mark 8.31; 9.31; 10.34, each time qualified by the phrase 'after three days'. The subject of the statement is in every instance the *Son of Man*.

[42] Acts 2.24, 32; 13.33, 34; 17.31. The verb here is ἀνιστάναι, but this is related to ἀναστῆναι. Cf. Wilckens, *Missionsreden* 138f.; Braun, 'Zur Terminologie der Acta von der Auferstehung', TLZ 77, 1952, 533f. God is the subject of the action, *Jesus* is the object, and the phrase 'from the dead' appears. Cf. Acts 10.41; 17.3.

Christ died and lived again'. 'Lived again' (ἔζησεν) is to be preferred to the various other readings,[43] for Paul chooses it in order to echo the verb ζῆν which is repeated three times in v. 8. So this is an *ad hoc* adaptation of the wording of the formula. We cannot know whether it is the formula with ἐγείρειν or the formula with ἀνιστάναι which lies behind this variant.[44]

This modified pistis-formula stands in a context in which the title *Lord* occurs frequently.[45] Paul might easily have kept to it and inroduced it into the formula at this point.[46] But since he changes to *Christ*, without keeping to it consistently thereafter, this is a strong indication that in the pre-Pauline tradition which Paul takes up here the pistis-formula was associated with *Christ*.[47]

e. In Rom. 4.25 the same saving events are listed in yet another formula of quite different wording: 'who was put to death (παρεδόθη) for our trespasses and raised for our justification'. In its structure we notice elements which are similar to those of the pistis-formula. 'Put to death for' has precisely the same function as 'died for'. We have already come across the verb 'was raised'. What is new, on the other hand, is that the resurrection is expounded in terms of its saving significance for us. The verb παραδιδόναι is also new. Various scholars consider that these two lines represent pre-Pauline material.[48] It is said that the first line is built on Isa. 53.5, 12 or at least echoes it. Of the whole formula Bultmann and Jeremias[49] say that it has a 'synthetic parallelismus membrorum', which as far as they are concerned fixes it safely.

Against this we must say that it is by no means beyond all doubt that the verse is of pre-Pauline origin. The second line could very well be a Pauline formulation on the analogy of the

---

[43] So Lietzmann, *Römer* 116 *ad loc.*; Michel, *Römer* 303 n. 2 *ad loc.*

[44] Copyists have adopted the latter verb at I Thess. 4.14.

[45] In vv. 6–8 *Kyrios* occurs three times with the article, three times without.

[46] He did this at I Cor. 6.14, when as a result of the context he introduced *Kyrios* into the statement about the resurrection. See 3h.

[47] In the next part of the verse, Rom. 14.9b, it becomes clear how Paul pictures the relationship between the saving acts stated in the pistis-formula and the Lordship of Christ.

[48] Bultmann, *Theology of the New Testament* I, ET 1952, 7.3, 47; 9.4, 82; Schweizer, *Erniedrigung und Erhöhung bei Jesus und seinen Nachfolgern* 2nd ed. 1962, 6c(73) (cf. ET *Lordship and Discipleship*, 1960, 50); Jeremias, *TWNT* V 704.3f. (ET, *The Servant of God*, rev. ed. 1965, 89) and n. 397; Michel, *Römer ad loc.*; cf. Lietzmann, *Römer ad loc.*; Fuchs, *Die Freiheit des Glaubens*, 1949, 116–18. Schrenk, *TWNT* II 228.6–25 (ET, *Righteousness*, 1951, 72), clearly reckons that the verse is Paul's own construction.

[49] See n. 48.

first.[50] If this is admitted, then the verse cannot strictly be regarded as a variation on the pistis-formula. Certainly behind v. 25, which is about the saving acts of the death and resurrection, there lies the pattern of the pistis-formula. But the determinative influence in the formulation of the first line was a formula of a different type, distinguished by the key word παραδιδόναι. Traces of this type can still be found in Rom. 8.32; Gal. 2.20; Eph. 5.2, 25.[51] Characteristic of this type is that it contains only an exposition of the significance of this 'delivering up' of Christ for salvation. We do not find in it any statements which interpret the resurrection. We should notice, too, that παραδιδόναι does not have the same sense in all the passages mentioned above, for although in Rom. 4.25 it clearly applies to the death, in other places, most clearly in John 3.16, it points in a more general way to Jesus, coming into earthly life.[52]

Because the 'delivering up' was taken to refer to the death, it was possible to combine this statement with the phrase which spoke of the resurrection. Rom. 4.25 is the product of such a combination, and it belongs to a later stage in the development of the tradition than the pistis-formula and the formula about the 'giving up' of the Son. This is one more argument for supposing that the verse is of Paul's composition.

Clearly Isa. 53.5, 12 has influenced the formulation of the first line, but it is hardly possible to regard that passage as the source of the key word παραδιδόναι, for at the earlier stage of the tradition, reflected in Rom. 8.32; Gal. 2.20; Eph. 5.2, 25; John 3.16, we find nothing reminiscent of Isa. 53.12.

Finally, we must note, too, that the formula about the 'giving up' was originally associated with the title *Son of God*.[53] It is no

[50] Δικαίωσις is found at Rom. 5.18 as well as in this passage, and there it is a Pauline formulation. The meaning which Paul attaches to the word-group δίκαιος, etc., is obvious.

[51] These parallels are pointed out also by Michel, *ad loc.*

[52] John 3.16 has only the simple form διδόναι. Cf. the wording of the formula about the sending of the Son (Rom. 8.3; Gal. 4.4). We naturally ask here which direction the development has taken. Does the key verb 'to give (deliver) up' belong originally to the statements about the passion (cf. the passion predictions in Mark 9.31; 10.33, where it is certainly not used absolutely but is linked with the term Son of Man), and subsequently become applied in a wider sense to the coming of the pre-existent Son? Or is it in the first place an interpretation of the sending of the Son into the world which was only secondarily narrowed down to refer to the passion? For an answer to this question, see 26a.

[53] Cf. Rom. 8.32; Gal. 2.20; John 3.16; also Bornkamm, 'Herrenmahl', 149. In Eph. 5.2, 25 we find *Christ*, but this is to be regarded as a blurring of original usage. Cf. also the readings of p[46] BD*G it. pc. at Gal. 2.20.

longer possible to discover to which christological title the relative pronoun in Rom. 4.25 originally referred, for other motives caused Paul to use the phrase which precedes v. 25 in the present context.

All this shows how Rom. 4.25 deviates from the original pistis-formula. Certainly it would hardly be conceivable if the pistis-formula had not existed, but equally it would hardly be possible without the influence of other formulae and the developments which they underwent. Thus Rom. 4.25 cannot be used as an argument against what we have established as the shape of the pistis-formula.

6. *The Variants of the Pistis-formula as Stages in the Development of the Tradition*

a. So far, we have been able to discuss three variants of the pistis-formula: 1. The complete formula in I Cor. 15.3b–5; 2. The variant concealed behind II Cor. 5.15: 'Christ died for (us) and was raised (from the dead)'; 3. The brief formula containing ἀναστῆναι at I Thess. 4.14: 'Jesus died and rose again.'

These three formulae represent not only variants but also different stages in the development of the tradition. We cannot say that but one single line of tradition runs through all three stages. It is much more likely that the three variants developed in different ways out of one basic form.

Of the three, the second variant presumably represents the oldest form of the tradition. *Christ* is the subject of both statements, the death is defined as 'for us', and the resurrection as 'from the dead'.

By comparison, I Cor. 15.3b–5 reflects a twofold development, for to each part of the formula there is added a reference to the scriptures and a reference to Christ's burial and his appearing. In this developed form the two parts become, in effect, almost four parts.[54]

[54] Here we may leave out of account that the phrase 'on the third day' replaces 'from the dead', and that the verb 'was raised' is perfect instead of aorist, which means that what is emphasized is no longer the act which happened once for all in the past, but the continuing reality, in the present, of Christ's being raised. This shows that we have real variants here, and not just different stages within the development of the tradition.

But the short formula in I Thess. 4.14 is also secondary, by comparison with the form which underlies II Cor. 5.15. The verbs are no longer qualified, even though the main point of the first line, namely the saving significance of the death, is thereby lost. Moreover, ἀνέστη implies much more markedly than ἠγέρθη an activity of Christ himself.

b. One more question remains to be dealt with here. In all three variants of the full formula the subject of both statements is *Christ* or *Jesus*. In the 'formula-fragment' which speaks only of the resurrection the subject of the sentence is ordinarily 'God'.[55] Its stereotype form indicates that it is pre-Pauline. May we not suppose, then, that the oldest form of the pistis-formula can be inferred from something like a combination of Rom. 5.8 with Rom. 10.9, which would run as follows:

Rom. 5.8: Christ died for us,

Rom. 10.9: (and) God raised him from the dead?

But since a change of subject within so short a formula is highly unlikely,[56] we must assume that this form never existed. But how, then, does it come about that God is named in the statement about the resurrection? It is unlikely that 'God' was inserted only when the full formula suffered a secondary splitting up, because the general development tended in the reverse direction. Originally the resurrection was regarded as God's act, and only gradually did it come to be seen as Jesus' own doing. This consideration points to only one conclusion, namely that the statement about the resurrection was originally formulated for its own sake and it circulated separately. 'God' was its subject.[57] When the statement about the death was added, *Christ* was placed at the head of the entire formula, which meant that the second part was recast in passive form. These reflections bring us directly to the next chapter.

7. *The Origin of the Pistis-formula*

a. Since the formula is pre-Pauline, there are three groups of

---

[55] See 3ai.

[56] In the longer hymn, Phil. 2.6–11, the change of subject is understandable.

[57] Admittedly, in Luke 24.34 God is not the subject, but there the phrase 'the Lord has risen' leads on to the phrase 'and has appeared', and for this reason Christ has to be the subject. The title *Lord* is Lucan

people who fall to be considered as possible authors of it: 1. The Hellenistic Gentile Christian church; 2. The Greek-speaking Jewish Christian church, i.e. the 'Hellenists' of Acts 6.1 (= the 'Stephen circle' in the wider sense); 3. The early Aramaic-speaking church (in Jerusalem).

We begin with I Cor. 15.3b–5, even though this formula does not represent the oldest stage of the tradition. But its relative completeness and also Paul's discussion of it allow us to draw a considerable number of inferences.

Jeremias[58] has referred to the Semitisms in the formula. Certainly the only really compelling points are that ὤφθη occurs instead of ἐφάνη, that the name Cephas stands for Peter, and also that the passive construction is linked with a simple dative rather than with ὑπό and the genitive.

Schweizer[59] states that the formula mentions appearances which do not figure in the synoptic tradition. This at least guarantees that in form and content this statement in the formula is of great antiquity.

Finally, Paul himself emphasizes in v. 11 that the formula is determinative both for his own preaching and also for that of the original apostles.[60]

These three observations mean that we need not consider the Hellenistic Gentile Christian church as a possible author of the pistis-formula. We must now grapple with the difficult question whether the formula is the work of Aramaic-speaking or Greek-speaking Jewish Christians.

b. We pointed out earlier[61] that the statement about the resurrection may be regarded as the oldest piece in the pistis-formula. A further pointer for this is that the formula simply states the fact of the resurrection, without interpreting its saving significance. If we take into account the historical situation of the early Christian Church, we can move a step further.

The appearances to Peter[62] and others gave to the disciples who

---

[58] Jeremias, *Eucharistic Words* 129f.

[59] Schweizer, *Erniedrigung*, 1st ed., 9a (81 n. 343).

[60] Seeberg, *Katechismus* 189, 193, concludes from this that the formula must have arisen in the original circle of the apostles between AD 30 and 35. But he fails to distinguish sufficiently between the time when the formula was known and acknowledged and the time when it originated.

[61] See 6.

[62] Luke 24.34.

had fled to Galilee an awareness by virtue of which they became the Aramaic-speaking Jewish Christian church in Jerusalem. By this Easter experience the church lived, believed and waited. So we may assume that this awareness must have been formulated in some way,[63] possibly in terms like these: 'God' (eventually paraphrased) 'raised Jesus (or the Messiah) (from the dead).'[64]

It is probable that this sentence, or one like it, was used by the early Aramaic-speaking church in its preaching. The statement about the death did not need to be formulated at the same time, for this was known to all and served as the foil against which the resurrection stood out.

This sentence, side by side with the confession of Jesus as Messiah, seems to have played an important part in preaching both to Aramaic-speaking and Greek-speaking Jews.

The further the chain of missionary activity spread beyond the confines of the earliest and smallest circle, the less was Jesus' death generally known or tacitly presupposed. Thus it had to be expressly stated and justified together with the statement about the resurrection. This stage could not possibly have been reached until Greek-speaking Jewish Christians undertook the mission to the Gentiles. So this moment is the *terminus ad quem* for the formulation of the statement about the death.

c. From the texts themselves it is difficult to get clues for putting a date to the statement about the death. All the same, because the death is not merely mentioned, but is interpreted as having happened 'for us' or 'for our sins', we may take it that the formulation does not come from the very earliest period of the Aramaic-speaking church. This is underlined by the observation that in those strata of the synoptic tradition which go back to the early Aramaic-speaking church[65] there is no interpretation of Jesus' death by means of the ὑπέρ phrase or any similar expression. Neither the Q source[66] nor the material peculiar to Luke contain

---

[63] Admittedly the Q source does not speak of the resurrection. All the same, it is presupposed in the sense that only the resurrection makes it possible to await Jesus as the Son of Man.

[64] The passive construction in Luke 24.34 is not likely to be original. Cf. n. 57.

[65] Braun, 'Der Sinn der neutestamentlichen Christologie', *ZTK* 54, 1957, 349, takes no account of this when he concludes from the presence of sacrificial language that this is the theological teaching of the original church.

[66] Admittedly, the passion narrative is altogether absent from Q, and thus many possibilities of interpreting the sufferings and death of Jesus disappear. Yet the absence of the passion narrative seems to be not simply conditioned by the type of

such a conception. Only in Mark 10.45, an ἦλθεν saying,[67] and in Mark 14.24, the saying which interprets the significance of the cup in the account of the Last Supper, does the idea appear. Presumably neither of these sayings goes back to the early Aramaic-speaking church.[68] So it is not possible to show from the texts that the ὑπέρ phrase comes from the early Aramaic-speaking church. But since it is clear that the ideas which lie behind this phrase are Jewish in origin,[69] it must have arisen within a Jewish Christian environment. If we take all these points into account, the most likely supposition is that it was the Greek-speaking Jewish Christians who interpreted Jesus' death in terms of the ὑπέρ phrase and formulated the statement about the death accordingly.[70]

d. If these reflections are correct, then the statement about the resurrection was handed on as a piece of tradition from Aramaic-speaking to Greek-speaking Jewish Christians. The latter then formulated the statement about the death as something which happened 'for us', and then joined the two statements together in one formula of two parts. Because the two statements originated in different places, it is natural that they are not parallel in struc-

---

material in Q (it is, after all, *halakah*—ethical teaching), but part of its theological 'programme'. For it would always have been possible to form sayings which corresponded to the passion. Since this was not done, we may conclude that such an interpretation of Jesus' death does not originate from the Q environment. Cf. also Tödt, *The Son of Man in the Synoptic Tradition*, ET 1965, 251.

[67] Bultmann, *History of the Synoptic Tradition*, ET 1963, 143f. and 155; cullmann, *Christology* 65, takes a different view, seeing in the saying a combination of 'Son of Man' and 'Ebed Yahweh' ideas.

[68] The absence of any interpretation of Jesus' death in the earliest strata of the synoptic tradition fits well with what we can establish as the theology of Q. This source gives evidence of a rigorist attitude towards the Torah (cf. Luke 16.17 and parallels), and also of the expectation of the Son of Man's coming upon Zion (cf. Luke 17.24 and parallels). The Q community's 'christology' certainly sees in Jesus the eschatological teacher of wisdom and preacher of repentance (cf. Luke 11.31f. and parallels), but it does not go so far as to take up and interpret positively the death of Jesus. Of course, the circles responsible for the Q source do not make up the entire early Aramaic-speaking church, but what we have found here is symptomatic. On the theology of Q, see Tödt, *Son of Man*, 232–74, esp. 245–53.

[69] This is so, whether the idea is of an atoning sacrifice (cf. Bultmann, *Theology* I, 7.3, 47; 9.4, 82; II, 33.3a, 295), or of the vicarious sufferings of a righteous man. Cf. Schweizer, *Erniedrigung*, 2nd ed. 6c, 73 (cf. *Lordship* 49–52) and Bultmann, *Theology* I, 7.3, 47.

[70] Schweizer, *Erniedrigung*, 1st ed. 9a, 82 (cf. *Lordship* 50) says only that 'neither Paul nor the Hellenistic church were the first to interpret Jesus' death as atonement'. It is not clear whether this means that he attributes this interpretation to the early Aramaic-speaking church.

ture. The second part affirms the resurrection as a fact, whereas the first part expounds the saving significance of the death. But just because of this the essential unity of the two statements is preserved. For while the resurrection constitutes, or confirms, Jesus' eschatological status, the phrase 'for us' interprets his death as the death of this same eschatological figure.

In the kerygma of Acts this essential unity is broken down into two parts, and the pattern there is, 'You killed him,[71] but God raised him.' Wilckens has shown that this is not an earlier composition than the interpretative statement with 'for us', but is simply Lucan style.[72] Similarly the completely parallel formulation of the two lines in Rom. 4.25 shows features which are clearly secondary by comparison with the formula which we have established above.[73]

Thus we recognize the Greek-speaking Jewish church as the author of the statement about Jesus' death, for Jewish ideas are used to interpret that death; and we recognize the same church as the compiler responsible for combining it with the statement about the resurrection, thus producing the two-part pistis-formula. Moreover, this church appears to have developed the formula and passed it on in several variant forms.[74] In this way the pistis-formula passed into the mainstream of the Jewish Christian mission to the Gentiles and eventually reached Paul. The historical background to Peter's inspection depicted in Acts 8.14 shows that the Aramaic-speaking church kept a watchful eye on the missionary activities of the Hellenists (the 'Stephen circle').[75] On such occasions, we can imagine, the formula would have to meet with the express approval of those who were closest to the original apostles. Such approval would have been the more readily granted

---

[71] Wilckens, *Missionsreden* 109, gives a list. Cf. Acts 2.23; 3.15; 4.10, etc.
[72] Wilckens, *Missionsreden* 120.
[70] See 5e.
[74] Sometimes 'God' remains the subject of the resurrection statement, but at other times the sentence is recast in passive form. This church also extended the two-part formula to include a reference to the scriptures—which we would only expect in a Jewish Christian environment; but it is also extended by adding evidence of particular facts (to some extent using material culled from the early Aramaic-speaking church; see 7a).
This is against Wilckens, *Missionsreden* 76 n. 1, who regards I Cor. 15.3b–5 as a later compilation. In spite of extensions to the formula, it never reached in NT times the scope which Seeberg, *Katechismus* 85, maintains it did. Seeberg overlooks the fact that the individual statements in the tradition have very different origins and come from completely different backgrounds of thought.
[75] Cf. Haenchen, *Apostelgeschichte*, 1956, 258.

if the substance of the formula were in part drawn from their environment, and if the ideas behind the interpretation of Jesus' death were familiar to them.

Thus it is quite conceivable that the pistis-formula represented the point at which the Gentile mission felt most clearly its unity, in faith and preaching, with the original apostolic circle. I Cor. 15.11 expressly testifies to this.

We could discuss here the question of the place which the formula occupied in the life of the Church. We shall defer this, however, to a later stage, for we shall pick up decisive clues on the way.[76]

Now that our examination has given us a clearly defined picture of the pistis-formula's origin and development, we may turn to the question of the christological titles used, in the hope that by combining an examination of texts with an attempt at historical reconstruction an answer will be forthcoming.

8. The Pistis-formula as the Setting of the Christological Designations 'Christ' and 'Jesus'

a. We saw earlier that the statements of the pistis-formula have the following christological designations associated with them:

1. In the statement about the death, the Pauline writings have *Christ*, e.g. Rom. 5.6, 8; and the non-Pauline writings likewise have *Christ*, e.g. I Peter 3.18.

2. In the statement about the resurrection, we find in the Pauline writings: (i) *Jesus* (Rom. 8.11a; I Thess. 1.10?); (ii) *him* (Gal. 1.1; Rom. 10.9); (iii) *Christ* (I Cor. 15.12, 13, 14, 15, 17, 20); (iv) *Christ Jesus* (Rom. 8.11b); (v) *the Lord* (I Cor. 6.14—*Kyrios* here inserted by Paul); *the Lord Jesus* (II Cor. 4.14—*Kyrios* is secondary here); *Jesus our Lord* (Rom. 4.24—*Kyrios* introduced here by Paul). Outside the Pauline writings we find: (i) *him* (I Peter 1.21—referring to *Christ*); also Col. 2.12; Eph. 1.20, referring to *Christ*; Acts 13.30, referring to *the Saviour Jesus*. (ii) *whom* (Acts 3.15; 4.10; 13.37); (iii) *the same* (Acts 10.40); (iv) *Jesus* (Acts 5.30); *Jesus Christ* (II Tim. 2.8).

3. In the two-part formula we find: (i) *Christ* (I Cor. 15.3b–5—

[76] See 14.

in the first line; Rom. 14.9); (ii) *Christ Jesus* (Rom. 8.34); (iii) *Jesus* (I Thess. 4.14); (iv) *Christ* (Rom. 6.4–9—in each separate statement).

b. From these lists we conclude:

1. In the Pauline period the statement about the death is uniformly associated with *Christ.* But since the statement is a pre-Pauline formulation, we may assume that its firm association with the title *Christ* is also pre-Pauline. This is proved (i) by the regularity with which the title appears here; (ii) by the fact that in I Peter 3.18 it appears as a ready-coined phrase; and (iii) by the pre-Pauline association of the title *Christ* with the key words 'believe', 'preach' and 'gospel'. (We have yet to establish this.)[77]

One question, however, must here be left open: When did *Christ* come to be associated with the statement about the death? Does it go back to Greek-speaking Jewish Christians, or was it brought about by the Gentile Christian church?

2. What we find when we come to the statement about the resurrection is less clear-cut. The one certain thing is that for various reasons the title *Lord* was inserted into the text only *ad hoc.* It does not reflect early, pre-Pauline usage.[78] It is also clear that where Paul uses the statement about the resurrection on its own he usually makes *Christ* the subject.[79] But what is the significance of the variants?

(i) *The personal pronoun* αὐτόν. Obviously, once the two-part formula is in use, a simple pronoun appears in the second part, referring back to the christological designation in the first part. In this sense '*him*' in an isolated fragment of the formula is a reproduction of pre-Pauline usage. The origin of this usage is to be sought in the Greek-speaking Jewish Christian church, since this church is presumably responsible for the combination of the two statements.[80] It is not at all likely that a mere pronoun stood in the statement about the resurrection as formulated by the early Aramaic-speaking church.

(ii) *Jesus.* We have to reckon with two possibilities here. Either this name genuinely reflects pre-Pauline usage, in which case it goes back to the early Aramaic-speaking church (or alternatively

[77] See 10–12.
[78] See 3h.
[79] I Cor. 15.12–20; Rom. 6.4–9; cf. Rom. 8.11b.
[80] See 7d.

the Greek-speaking Jewish Christian church) before the two statements were combined; or else *Jesus* is here simply an alternative to *Christ*. If this is the case, then Paul or the Hellenistic Gentile church must be responsible for it, for *Christ* and *Jesus* can only be interchanged when both have become proper names for the one person. Only in the Gentile Christian church is this stage reached.[81]

3. We find a similar picture when we look at the use of the title in the two-part formula. In Paul's day the title normally employed was *Christ*. So to explain *Jesus* in I Thess. 4.14 there are the same two possibilities which were reckoned with above. Either the title has been introduced *ad hoc* into this context as an alternative to *Christ*—in which case it is to be attributed to Paul or to the Gentile Christian church immediately before him; or it reflects earlier pre-Pauline usage and might in the last resort stem from the Aramaic-speaking church's formulation of the resurrection statement. But since we cannot get any sure guide from an examination of the texts, we must turn our attention to the historical situation of the various churches.

c. Examination of the texts has shown that the statement about the death was firmly associated with the title *Christ*, at the very latest in the pre-Pauline Gentile Christian church. But when we looked at the statement about the resurrection (and then at the complete two-part formula) we could not be sure whether *Jesus* reflected the usage of the Aramaic-speaking, or only of the Greek-speaking, Jewish Christians; or whether, in a Gentile Christian environment, it had been introduced *ad hoc* into the text as an alternative to *Christ*.

Thus the two questions which now have to be debated are:

1. With which christological designation was the statement about the death associated in the Greek-speaking Jewish Christian church?

---

[81] I Thess. I.9f. would be helpful to us on this, if we could assume that *Jesus*, together with the words 'whom he raised from the dead', was inserted into a formula which is certainly Jewish Christian (and even originally Jewish in part), for the purposes of the mission to the Gentiles; and also if our opinion were that this insertion is neither Paul's work nor that of the Gentile Christian church immediately before his time. If this were so, the association of *Jesus* with the resurrection statement could be attributed to that part of the Jewish Christian church which concerned itself with the mission to the Gentiles, and it would reflect the usage of the Aramaic-speaking church. Unfortunately, neither of these assumptions can be upheld with any certainty.

2. Which christological designation did the early Aramaic-speaking church add to the statement about the resurrection?

d. The first question is the easier to answer. It was the Greek-speaking Jewish Christians who linked the statement about the death with *Christ.* Two clues point to this. The first is that the stereotype occurrence of *Christ* in this context is most readily comprehensible in Gentile Christianity. Secondly, we have already seen that this statement about the death interprets it as the death of the Jesus whose eschatological status was authenticated by the resurrection. The title *Christ,* translating *meʂīḥā,* presented itself to the Hellenistic Jewish Christians as a term which would clearly indicate the eschatological status of Jesus. Therefore it is by far the most likely that *Christ* was linked with the statement about the death by Greek-speaking Jewish Christians.[82] If this is so, then *Christ,* when first introduced into the statement, must still have had the significance of a (messianic) title.[83] Clearly, the Christian understanding of *Christ* had moved a long way from the Jewish idea of the Messiah already, or it could not have been introduced into this context. To look into the general pattern of contemporary Jewish notions of the Messiah would contribute virtually nothing to an interpretation of *Christ* as it was understood at the stage we are considering. The only thing that the two have in common is the title itself, and the fact that it signifies a personal eschatological entity.

The most we can ask now is this: Why was the title 'Messiah' taken over, rather than the title 'Son of Man'?[84] All that we can say for sure is that the Messiah was thought of entirely as a being in time and space with an earthly destiny, whereas the Son of Man, according to Jewish expectation, was an apocalyptic supramundane figure. Since the Christians' interest was in the death

---

[82] Dahl, 'Der gekreuzigte Messias', *Der historische Jesus und der kerygmatische Christus,* 1960, 160–3 and 166–8, also emphasizes how the death of Jesus and the title 'Messiah' belong together (esp. 161). He sees the basis for this connection in the historical fact that Jesus was crucified on the charge that he set himself up as Messiah. This accusation was shown on the inscription over the cross, and in it the title 'Messiah' figured. From this inscription (according to Dahl) the title made its way into every strand of the Christian tradition, bearing the stamp of the death and the resurrection of Jesus.

[83] It is uncertain whether the article was originally inserted with the title and then dropped when the title was taken over by Gentile Christians. The evidence is insufficient to permit an answer to this question.

[84] Cf. 'Son of Man' in the passion predictions, Mark 8.31; 9.31; 10.33.

and the resurrection of the 'earthly' Jesus, it is possible that 'Messiah' seemed more appropriate than 'Son of Man'. But as we have said, there is no certain answer to this question.

e. The second of the questions we posed earlier is concerned to discover which designation the Aramaic-speaking church linked with the statement about the resurrection. The title 'Messiah' and the name 'Jesus' come up for consideration here, for only these two occur in the context of this statement in the formula. Two points lead us to prefer *Jesus*. The first is that the very presence of the name in this context suggests that it is original, for if the title 'Messiah' had been anchored here, we would expect to find, in the texts which reflect later development, the title *Christ* occurring as regularly as it does in the statement about the death. The second point is that the raising of Jesus from the dead is the basis, or the proof, of his messianic status. The Christian understanding of the title 'Messiah' is perfectly expressed in the sentence, 'God raised Jesus from the dead', and this identity of meaning leads us to suppose that *Jesus* is the name which was used by the Aramaic-speaking church in the statement about the resurrection.[85]

When in Greek-speaking Jewish Christianity the two statements were joined together, the title *Christ* in the first part suddenly came to stand at the beginning of the complete formula, which meant that *Jesus* in the second part was replaced by the personal pronoun. When, on the other hand, only the resurrection was spoken of, it was possible for the name *Jesus* which originally stood in that statement to reappear.

When the formula was taken over by Gentile Christianity, its wording remained unchanged, but *Christ* came more and more to be regarded merely as the name of the person to whom the events stated in the formula had happened. It was at this stage that the formula reached Paul. Although formerly a Jew, nevertheless even he uses *Christ* as though it were essentially a proper name just

---

[85] Passages like Acts 2.36; Rom. 1.4; cf. Acts 13.33 go one step further, for not only do they mention the fact of the resurrection but also they explain its significance for the person who was the bringer of salvation: he is 'made' or 'installed as' *Christ*, as *Lord*, or as *Son of God*, and thus he receives a new dignity and a new function. Cf. Phil. 2.9–11, where the thought is more fully developed. The statement in the pistis-formula, which affirms simply the fact of the resurrection, must be held to be earlier than all these other expressions. This reflection is in itself evidence for the originality of the name *Jesus* in the pistis-formula's statement about the resurrection. The latter says, 'Jesus was raised', whereas the other expressions explain that this resurrection made Jesus the bearer of special honours.

like *Jesus*.[86] For this reason the two names could be combined[87] or used indiscriminately.[88]

f. If, finally, we ask what were the characteristic ideas underlying the term *Christ*, the answer will vary according to the particular environment in which the formula was used.

We may pass over the early Aramaic-speaking church here, as we accepted that it associated the name *Jesus* with the statement about the resurrection.

In the Greek-speaking Jewish Christian church, *Christ*, like the 'Messiah' of later Judaism, represents the title and the eschatological status of an earthly figure. However, we cannot discover any more than this about the general pattern of Jewish ideas about the Messiah. By contrast, we find that *Christ* is fully characterized by the saving events to which the formula bears witness, i.e. by the death 'for us' and the raising by God.[89] *Christ* is seen as connected typologically with scriptural prophecies, as is witnessed by the phrase 'in accordance with the scriptures' and by the quotation of OT passages. All these statements are not merely 'naked' elements given to the Christian Church on which to build its own understanding of *Christ*. It would be truer to say that these statements themselves define the content of preaching and of faith.

We have to say much the same thing when we ask what Gentile Christianity associated with the title *Christ*. It has hardly any longer the significance of a title, and it has virtually lost the power (which it derived from Judaism) to stand on its own, though occasionally in early stages of the tradition we see traces of this independent use, side by side with instances in which it is qualified by the statements of the pistis-formula. *Christ* is merely a proper name, without any lustre of its own, and without any setting in which it may stand alone. Its meaning can be determined only by the content of the pistis-formula. From this stage onwards it is no longer appropriate to speak of ideas constituting an understanding

---

[86] On the remaining traces in Paul's writings of *Christ* understood as a title, see 65.
[87] Cf. Rom. 8.11b.
[88] Cf. Rom. 8.9–11.
[89] So to investigate the Jewish 'Christ' title hardly makes the Christian conception any clearer, for the latter is completely determined by the statements about the death and the resurrection of Jesus. Cullmann, *Christology* 111–36, esp. 122, comes to a similar conclusion, but he thinks that the idea of the 'Servant of the Lord' was used to modify the Jewish doctrine of the Messiah.

of the term *Christ* which is universally held. We must rather put it the other way round, and say that he whom the Church confesses as one who died for them and was raised by God bears the name *Christ*. His eschatological status can no longer be inferred from the designation *Christ*, but depends entirely upon the acts of which the statements in the pistis-formula speak. The name *Christ* is certainly firmly rooted in these contexts, but as evidence of an earlier, more lively relationship between title and statement.

Occasionally *Jesus* can appear in place of *Christ*. This has a double significance, for in the first place it underlines the fact that *Christ* is now only a name; and in the second place it shows clearly that *Jesus* means not merely the 'historical' earthly Jesus but the bearer of salvation.

It was at this stage of its development that Paul came across the formula. What we have established about it so far holds good in general terms for Paul's own use of the formula and of the name *Christ*. All the same, Paul as a former Jew is aware of the original significance of *Christ* as a title, and occasionally he can develop[90] or allude to it.[91]

g. What is important for the purpose of this essay as a whole is that in the pistis-formula we have been able to perceive the measure in which *Christ*, originally a title, was handed down to the Gentile Christian church in the form of a name, defined by the statements about the saving acts. From the pistis-formula run threads of thought which can clarify expressions which in substance and in literary form are connected with the pistis-formula. One possible indication that such expressions exist is the fact that from time to time the christological designation *Christ* appears. Further investigation will show how far this is a reliable pointer.

It remains to us only to notice what an infinitely small role (and demonstrably not original) the title *Lord* plays in connection with the pistis-formula. In terms of form-critical or historical analysis this means that *Lord* was not connected with the formula either originally or in pre-Pauline times. But we should take this as an indication that *Lord* and *Christ* are titles which come from different environments.

[90] Cf. Rom. 9.5.
[91] See n. 86.

B. WORDS RELATED TO THE PISTIS-FORMULA
Faith, Preaching, Gospel, (Apostle)

9. Procedure

Under 'A' our attention was focussed upon a self-contained unit, discernible by its literary form, namely the pistis-formula. We found clear reasons for concluding that the formula was taken over by Paul in the form which we have described.

Now we come to look for other places in which the designation *Christ* is firmly fixed, and the best way of doing this is to concentrate upon certain expressions which are directly related to the pistis-formula in form and in substance.

Of course we cannot simply take for granted that these expressions belong to pre-Pauline missionary terminology and are not of Paul's own creation. So with each of the expressions in question the first thing we have to do is to investigate its origin.

We shall be able to assume pre-Pauline origin if (a) the expression is used in its plain, natural sense; (b) Paul uses the expression in stereotype fashion; (c) the expression is similarly used in non-Pauline writings; (d) there is a recognizable connection with the pistis-formula, or with any of the expressions which have been dealt with already.

In this way we shall hope to build up a little arsenal of the expressions used in pre-Pauline missionary terminology. Should definite tendencies in the use of christological titles reveal themselves, we shall be able to draw conclusions about the range of meaning they contain and about their relations one to another.

10. 'Faith in Christ'

The preceding section 'A' has shown that the pre-Pauline pistis-formula is a unit in which the designations *Christ* and *Jesus* (but not *Lord*) are firmly rooted. But it also pointed beyond this to the fact that there is a connection between the pistis-formula and the key words πίστις and πιστεύειν. If this connection is not purely accidental, we may expect to find these words linked with *Christ* or *Jesus*, even apart from the formula itself.[92]

It is immediately evident that 'faith' is related on the one hand to God,[93] and on the other hand to *Christ* (*Jesus*).[94] Paul finds both these uses ready to hand in current missionary terminology, the formula εἰς θεός going back to Jewish missionary practice. In the earliest stages of the Christian mission the phrase 'faith in *Christ*' belongs primarily to the mission to the Jews, with whom it was taken for granted that 'God is one'. In the Jewish Christian mission to the Gentiles, on the other hand, 'that God is one' formed part of the proclamation, against polytheism.[95]

For our purposes, the passages which interest us particularly are those in which *pistis* is related either explicitly or by implication to *Christ* or *Jesus*. Gal. 2.16bc will serve as a starting point: 'We have believed in Christ Jesus (εἰς Χριστὸν Ἰησοῦν ἐπιστεύσαμεν)[96] in order to be justified by faith in Christ (ἐκ πίστεως Χριστοῦ) and not by works of the law.'

1. This sentence shows that πιστεύειν εἰς Χριστὸν Ἰησοῦν and πίστις Χριστοῦ are identical in sense. Thus the genitive Χριστοῦ is an objective genitive. *Christ* is the 'object' of faith and also describes the content of faith. This is specifically Christian faith.

2. In this passage there is no difference between *Christ Jesus* and *Christ*.

3. Unquestionably it is Paul who formulated this sentence. But the habit of relating πιστεύειν (by εἰς) to *Christ*, or πίστις (by an objective genitive) to *Christ*, is also found outside the Pauline

[92] Clearly we shall not expect this in passages where the OT tradition still colours the understanding of *pistis*. The question is whether we shall find it when *pistis* is used in its specifically Christian sense. On the various component strands of meaning in the word *pistis*, see Bultmann, *TWNT* VI 205.14–215.24 (*Faith* 62–82). Wissmann, *Das Verhältnis von Pistis und Christusfrömmigkeit bei Paulus*, 1926, 34–43, 68–75, weaves these strands into one, thus establishing in its own right the meaning which interests us here.

[93] I Thess. 1.8. In the non-Pauline writings, Heb. 6.1; James 2.19 (qualified by the phrase 'that God is one'); I Peter 1.21. Cf. Wissmann, *Verhältnis* 47–54.

[94] Gal. 2.16 (3 times); 3.22; Rom. 3.22, 26; Phil. 3.9; cf. 1.29. Non-Pauline examples: Col. 2.5; cf. Heb. 12.2.

[95] The NT lacks uniformity in this respect, for 'faith in God' is only occasionally spoken of in the Pauline corpus but more often outside it, especially in Heb., James and I Peter. Presumably this expression belongs particularly to Hellenistic Jewish Christianity, whereas Paul—although a Jewish Christian himself—follows completely the usage of the Gentile Christian church, for whom it is no longer especially necessary to add the preaching of monotheism to the proclamation of Christ.

[96] From a text-critical point of view the word order is uncertain.

writings.[97] So this connection may be reckoned as reflecting pre-Pauline usage.

Within the Pauline corpus we find other similar passages, e.g. Phil. 1.29, το εἰς αὐτὸν (= Χριστὸν) πιστεύειν; Gal. 2.16a, διὰ πίστεως Χριστοῦ 'Ιησοῦ;[98] Gal. 3.22, ἐκ πίστεως 'Ιησοῦ Χριστοῦ.[99]

We need not take account here of Gal. 3.26, for 'in Christ Jesus' is not the object of *pistis*. It is, at bottom, simply an '*en*-formula' used to describe the sons of God.[100]

On the question of the titles used, the important thing is that in all these passages *Christ* or *Christ Jesus* is named as the object of faith. There is only one apparent exception, Philemon v. 5, where the title *Lord* occurs. Here Paul speaks of the ἀγάπη and of the πίστις ἥν ἔχεις πρὸς τὸν κύριον 'Ιησοῦν καὶ εἰς πάντας τοὺς ἁγίους.

On this, several points are to be noticed: 1. *Agape* and *pistis* stand side by side. Textually the sequence is not quite certain, though *agape* placed before *pistis* is better attested and is thus presumably original. The motive for a copyist's reversal of the order might conceivably be the influence of the triad 'faith, love, hope'.[101] It is possible that the phrasing in this passage represents an abbreviation of the triad, in which case it would serve to make clear that there is no sharp distinction between the two expressions.

2. There is a striking parallelism between 'toward (πρός) the Lord Jesus' and 'toward (εἰς) all the saints'. It is impossible to relate the two phrases with precision by saying, for example, that πρὸς τὸν κύριον is to be taken with πίστις and εἰς πάντας τοὺς ἁγίους with ἀγάπη. It is better to take both expressions with both nouns, as Dibelius[102] does when he speaks of 'practising this piety towards God as also towards the Church'. But this means that *pistis* has lost its precise Christian meaning as saving faith, and

---

[97] E.g. Acts 24.24; Col. 2.5; Rev. 14.12 (with *Jesus*). Cf. Bultmann, *TWNT* VI 211 n. 266f. (*Faith* 72 nn. 3f.). The presence of the title *Lord* in this context at several places in the non-Pauline writings is to be regarded as secondary.

[98] The same phrase in Rom. 3.22 with different order of words; and Phil. 3.9 with simply *Christ*.

[99] Likewise Rom. 3.26, but with *Jesus* only.

[100] Thus Schlier, *Galater* 127 n. 1 *ad loc.*, who shows that it is contrary to Paul's custom to make an *en*-phrase the object of 'faith'. Similarly, the progression of thought towards 'putting on Christ' and 'you are all one in Christ Jesus' shows that here we have to do with the *en*-formula.

[101] Cf. I Thess. 1.3; 5.6; Col. 1.4f.; I Cor. 13.13 (where Paul places 'love' at the end because it is love he is emphasizing and because v. 13b follows on from it).

[102] M. Dibelius, *An die Kolosser, Epheser, an Philemon*, 3rd ed. revised by H. Greeven, 1953, 103.

together with *agape* denotes right conduct, right thinking, i.e. piety of the kind which Philemon displays *vis à vis* the Lord and *vis à vis* the Church.

In Philemon v. 5 the *Lord Jesus* is not the object of faith but the one to whom piety is addressed. For this reason the presence of the title *Lord* in this passage does not constitute an exception to the rule that *Christ* or *Jesus* is named in the Pauline writings as the object of faith.

Thus our examination of the *pistis* concept has produced results which are of a piece with those we gained from our examination of the pistis-formula. This suggests that the summary of the saving events which is given in the pistis-formula belongs to the same background of thought as the expression πιστεύειν εἰς Χριστόν or πίστις Χριστοῦ. The probability becomes solid certainty as we turn now to examine the connection between the pistis-formula and the root κήρυγμα/κηρύσσειν on the one hand, and between κήρυγμα/κηρύσσειν and πίστις/πιστεύειν on the other.

11. 'Preaching Christ (Jesus)'

a. We begin with I Cor. 15.11–14. Verse 11 reads, '. . . ., so we preach and so you believed.' Verse 12, 'if Christ is preached as raised from the dead, . . .'; and v. 14, 'if Christ has not been raised, then our preaching is in vain and your faith is in vain.'

1. According to v. 12, to preach *Christ* means to preach the saving events summarized in the pistis-formula. 2. This in itself gives the essence, the sum total, of the preaching. Without the actuality and the truth of the saving events the kerygma is empty and worth nothing (v. 14). 3. Verse 11 harks back to vv. 3b–5.[103] The unity of Paul's preaching and the preaching of the original apostles is founded upon the content of the formula. But by the same token it is also the foundation of the unity of faith, for what is believed is identical with what is preached. 4. The same assumption is repeated in v. 14b in a negative formulation. If the kerygma is without content, then faith is equally so. For Christian *pistis* is

---

[103] Seeberg, *Katechismus* 55f., stresses this connection, albeit to deduce from it that already in the circle of the original apostles the formula was normative for preaching.

identical with acceptance of the *kerygma* of Christ's death and resurrection.[104]

We find this essential unity of preaching and believing also at I Cor. 2.4f.; 1.21, though here without any reference either to the pistis-formula or to the name of *Christ*. The same connection is found, too, at Rom. 10.14–16,[105] although the verb 'to hear' is inserted between 'believing' and 'preaching'.[106] Rom. 10.8 speaks of preaching 'the word of faith' (ῥῆμα τῆς πίστεως), an expression which certainly refers to the content of the kerygma and is thus identical with the pistis-formula.[107]

We frequently find πιστεύειν used absolutely in the sense of accepting the kerygma.[108] Even though none of these passages contains *Christ*, they nevertheless demonstrate the firm connection between 'preaching' and 'believing', and also that the content of the preaching is clearly determined by the content of the pistis-formula. All this shows that the relationship which we have established between πιστεύειν/πίστις and *Christ* or *Jesus* can be precisely stated thus: *Christ (Jesus)* is the object of faith in the sense that his death and resurrection form the substance of the kerygma, and because the kerygma awakens faith, the content of the kerygma is also the content of faith.

b. Another observation confirms this result. The content of preaching is indicated, not only by using a fragment of the pistis-formula, as in the two passages already quoted,[109] but also by means of a christological designation which is used to name the one who is preached.

II Cor. 11.4 is directed against those who preach 'another Jesus', which makes it clear that the Jesus whom Paul preaches is the Jesus who died and was raised. Phil. 1.15–18 shows clearly that what constitutes the value of preaching is not the motives of

---

[104] Bultmann, *TWNT* VI 209.4–6 (*Faith* 68f.).
[105] Verse 17 is a gloss and is therefore to be excluded.
[106] A non-Pauline example of the connection of 'preaching' with 'believing' is I Tim. 3.16, in the context of a formula.
[107] *Pistis* in Gal. 1.23 is to be understood in the same sense. Likewise Gal. 3.2, 5 (ἀκοῆς πίστεως), where the connection with the pistis-statement and *Jesus Christ* in v. 1 becomes very clear. Rom. 12.6 should be included here, too: 'prophecy' is to be tested by reference to the content of the pistis-formula. Cf. Bultmann, *TWNT* VI 214.3–11 (*Faith* 78), 'fides quae creditur'.
[108] I Cor. 3.5; 15.2, 11; II Cor. 4.13; Gal. 2.16b; Rom. 13.11. Cf. Bultmann, *TWNT* VI 215.1–17 (*Faith* 8of.).
[109] I Cor. 15.12; 1.23.

the preachers, whether pure or impure, but simply the substance of what is preached, defined in this instance as *Christ*.

Rom. 16.25 is a non-Pauline example of this connection: 'the preaching of *Jesus Christ*'. This indicates that here, too, we find the same group of christological designations as we found associated with *pistis*, which is a further indication that πιστεύειν and κηρύσσειν[110] are related both in substance and in ideas.

Further examination of the κηρύσσειν passages shows that 'the gospel of God'[111] or 'the gospel'[112] is also given as an object of the verb 'to preach'.

12. 'The Gospel of Christ'

a. In the Pauline writings there are more than 50 passages in which 'gospel' occurs.[113] About half of them have 'the gospel' (without qualification),[114] while 'the gospel of God' occurs six times,[115] and 'the gospel of Christ' nine times.[116] Only in isolated instances does Paul speak of 'my gospel' or 'our gospel',[117] and only once does he use the expression 'the gospel of his (= God's) Son.'[118] The first three expressions are in Paul's day already fixed technical terms in the language of mission.[119]

[110] Two exceptions are to be noted. In II Cor. 4.5, 'what we preach is not ourselves, but Christ Jesus as Lord', preaching means proclaiming Christ Jesus as Lord. But this statement belongs to the range of ideas associated with *Lord*, which means that here we need note only that κηρύσσειν can evidently mean also to proclaim as Lord. Nevertheless, it is not possible to establish so close a connection between κηρύσσειν and this complex of ideas as we have shown to exist between κηρύσσειν and the pistis-formula.
II Cor. 1.19 speaks of 'the Son of God, Jesus Christ, whom we preached among you'. It is probable that in terms of the ideas it contains this passage is linked with the passages we have dealt with above, and therefore ultimately with the pistis-formula. It would appear that Paul has introduced the title *Son* here simply in order to express directly Christ's oneness with the God to whom Paul has appealed in v. 18 ('God is faithful').
[111] I Thess. 2.9.
[112] Gal. 2.2.
[113] Cf. Friedrich, *TWNT* II 724.25.
[114] List in Friedrich, *TWNT* II 726 n. 65.
[115] I Thess. 2.2, 8, 9; II Cor. 11.7; Rom. 15.16; 1.1 (in this last passage without article).
[116] I Thess. 3.2; I Cor. 9.12; II Cor. 2.12; 9.13; 10.14; Gal. 1.7; Rom. 15.19; Phil. 1.27. II Cor. 4.4 speaks of 'the gospel of the glory of Christ', which is evidently Paul's own formulation.
[117] I Thess. 1.5; I Cor. 4.3; Rom. 2.16.
[118] Rom. 1.9.
[119] With Dibelius, *An Die Thessalonicher*, 1925, 5, on I Thess. 1.8. Bultmann, *Theology* I, 9.5, 87 considers only the unqualified εὐαγγέλιον to be a technical term in

Since there are virtually no examples of 'the gospel of Christ' outside the Pauline corpus, we might wonder whether this phrase is not a Pauline formulation. But if Paul was formulating *ad hoc* in each case, we would expect to find from time to time the variant 'the gospel of *Jesus*', or even in isolated instances an association with the title *Lord*. On the other hand, if Paul had consciously invented the association with *Christ* alone, we would have expected to find this phrase more frequently, by comparison with the other variants. It is more than likely that Paul took over 'the gospel of Christ' as one technical term among others.

The passages which interest us here are those which reveal clearly with which particular christological conceptions 'the gospel' is linked. Thus, on the one hand the association of 'gospel' with material from the formula is important, and on the other hand the phrase 'the gospel of *Christ*' is important, too. The expression, 'the gospel of God' denotes that the gospel belongs to God, comes from God.[120] It does not give us any clear christological definition.

b. Again the obvious place to start is at I Cor. 15.1–5, for there Paul describes his quoting of the pistis-formula as 'declaring (γνωρίζειν) the gospel'. This tells us what the content of the term 'gospel' is: it is the message of the saving events, i.e. of the death and resurrection of *Christ*. Or, to put it another way with the question of titles in view, 'gospel' is a term which belongs to the same range of ideas as that in which the designation *Christ* is rooted.

Certainly the connection between vv. 1–3a and vv. 3b–5 is of Paul's making. For this reason, all we may say with confidence is that for Paul 'the gospel' is of a piece with the content of the pistis-formula. We cannot tell from this passage whether this holds good for the pre-Pauline Church as well.

In Rom. 1.1–5 Paul qualifies the expression 'the gospel of God' first of all by the phrase 'concerning his Son', and he links this phrase, not with a formula about the death and resurrection, but with one which speaks of the Son's earthly nature as Messiah, Son of David, and of his heavenly nature as the exalted Son of

---

the strict sense, and thinks that Paul is the first to use it thus. He holds that it is pre-Pauline when qualified by a genitive. Non-Pauline examples are: 'the gospel of God', I Peter 4.17; Mark 1.14; 'the gospel of Christ' (only as 'the gospel of Jesus Christ'), Mark 1.1; 'the gospel' (unqualified), e.g. II Tim. 1.8–10; Mark 1.15.

[120] Subj. gen. Cf. Bl-Debr. para. 163.

God. But the references in this passage are clearly *ad hoc* formulations.[121] This is so, whether the title *Son* in v. 3a was inserted by Paul as a modification of the title *Son of God* in v. 4, where the sense is different,[122] or whether its presence is due to the fact that it expresses as no other title does the unity of the bearer of salvation with God who is its actual author. In the second case, the formula about the Son, for its part, would have been added by association with the title. But either way it is clear that this passage does not reflect any original connection between 'the gospel' and the *Son*-formula.[123]

c. The occurrence of the phrase 'the gospel of Christ' in all the Pauline letters except Philemon is evidence that the ideas behind the pistis-formula and those behind the term 'gospel' belong together. The genitive 'of Christ' serves to define what is the content[124] of the gospel,[125] and is thus to be deemed objective genitive.[126]

If all these observations have brought us close to concluding that the ideas behind the expression 'the gospel of *Christ*' are the same as those which the pistis-formula expresses, then one final piece of evidence will clinch the matter: nowhere is 'the gospel' associated with the title *Lord*.

In view of the great number of passages in which 'the gospel'

[121] On the difference between the christological conceptions which lie behind the title *Son* here and the *Son*-formula, see Schweizer, *Erniedrigung* 8e, nn. 360 and 362, (cf. *Lordship and Discipleship* 58f.); cf. also Michel, *Römer* 30 *ad loc.*

[122] For an analysis of this passage, see 24.

[123] In Rom. 1.9 'the gospel of his Son' is an *ad hoc* formulation based upon the exposition in vv. 1-5. A similar case is Gal. 1.16, where 'that I might preach him' refers to the Son. Cf. Seeberg, *Katechismus* 198 n. 1.

[124] See 10.

[125] Cf. Friedrich, *TWNT* II 728.24f.: 'If we wish to summarize in a single phrase the content of the gospel, then that phrase is, "Jesus (is) the Christ".' We might criticize this sentence on the grounds that its terminology is imprecise, for the gospel is not in the first place the confession that Jesus is Messiah, but rather the proclamation of Christ's death 'for us' and of God's act in raising him. But it is, of course, true that ideas of this sort quickly became part and parcel of the Christian understanding of *Christ*.

[126] See the thorough discussion of this in Schmitz, *Die Christus-Gemeinschaft des Paulus im Lichte seines Genetivgebrauchs*, 1924, 45-88, who comes to the conclusion that it is quite false to see the choice as being between subj. and obj. gen., for here we have a 'neutral genitive'. Although his argument covers the whole field known to him, it is not convincing, because he does not distinguish between the Christian term 'the gospel of Christ' as used in early times in the context of the pistis-formula on the one hand (where it is clearly to be regarded as an obj. gen.—thus Bultmann, *Theology* I, 9.5, 87), and Paul's technical use of the term on the other hand, in which the original associations are often barely recognizable, except in a much weakened form.

occurs, the absence of the title *Lord* cannot be fortuitous, but must be seen as proof that the term 'gospel' belongs to a different range of ideas from the title *Lord*.

d. We shall obtain further information on the question of titles if we examine the other verbs used of preaching and the nouns which describe the message which is preached. 'To preach the gospel' (εὐαγγελίζεσθαι) must have first claim on our attention, on account of its frequent occurrence and its closeness to εὐαγγέλιον. We are immediately struck by the fact that the verb only very occasionally has an object, even though according to its original meaning it is transitive:[127] 'to preach the gospel',[128] 'to preach the faith',[129] 'to preach him (= the Son of God).[130] In this sense the verb in itself means simply 'to preach', and it could be replaced by καταγγέλλειν or κηρύσσειν. We can see that with these passages we are still within the range of ideas to which the pistis-formula belongs, for this is shown not only by the key words πίστις and εὐαγγέλιον but also by the entire theme of I Cor. 15.1–11 and Gal. 1.22–24, for this reflects these ideas completely. The verb εὐαγγελίζεσθαι is more often used without qualification, with the technical sense of preaching the gospel.[131] This is how it is used specifically in missionary terminology. Whoever preaches another gospel (i.e. with a different content) is cursed (Gal. 1.8f.). Thus the verb used in this way without qualification has in fact the same content as is summarized in the pistis-formula. This is confirmed by the phrase in Gal. 1.7 'the gospel of Christ', and in v. 9 by the verb παραλαμβάνειν, which is a technical term for the process of handing on the tradition. Rom. 15.20 points in a similar direction, for the place where the gospel has not yet been preached is a place where Christ has not yet been named. All this goes to show that terminology of this kind lies within the context of thought which is expressed in the pistis-formula, even where there is no christological title to act as a pointer.

[127] Often in Luke and Acts, cf. Friedrich, *TWNT* II 705–18; Schniewind, *Euangelion* I, 1927 and 1931, 81ff.
[128] I Cor. 15.1; II Cor. 11.7; cf. Gal. 1.11.
[129] Gal. 1.23.
[130] Gal. 1.16. But it is clear that the title *Son* has been introduced *ad hoc* into this context for other reasons, for the mention of God brings about the mention of the Son, which is characteristic of Paul (see 54a-d). It is obvious that the pronoun object of εὐαγγελίζεσθαι refers back to the title *Son*. So the passage is not evidence of any original connection between this verb and the title *Son of God*.
[131] E.g. I Cor. 1.17; 9.16, 18; II Cor. 10.16; Gal. 1.8f.; 4.13; Rom. 1.15; 15.20.

The words καταγγέλλειν and ὁ λόγος are associated with certain expressions which we list below:

καταγγέλλειν: with *Christ* as object (Phil. 1.17, 18); with 'gospel' as object (I Cor. 9.14); with 'the testimony of God' as object (I Cor. 2.1, where the content of the testimony is defined in v. 2 as Jesus Christ the crucified); with 'faith' as object (Rom. 1.8). I Cor. 11.26, 'to proclaim the Lord's death', seems to be exceptional. But it is an expression which contains material of formula type and which occurs in the context of the Lord's Supper, in which from a very early time the title *Lord* belongs.[132]

ὁ λόγος: qualified as 'the word of the cross' (I Cor. 1.18); 'the word of reconciliation' (II Cor. 5.19); 'the word . . . which you heard' (I Thess. 2.13). 'The word of God' ([ὁ] λόγος [τοῦ] θεοῦ) makes clear that God is the author of the word (I Thess. 2.13; I Cor. 14.36; Phil. 1.14). Here, too, it is the content of the word that matters, as is shown by II Cor. 2.17; 4.2, where reference is made to those who falsify God's word.

Where ὁ λόγος is used, it does not seem to be connected with any particular background of ideas. The title *Lord* appears twice, in I Thess. 1.8 beside 'gospel' (v. 5) and '*logos*' (v. 6), and also in I Thess. 4.15 in the sense of a private revelation or a word of Jesus.

There is virtually no trace of any direct connection with the pistis-formula. All the same, the genitives which occur in these passages show that the thought here is of the saving acts, rather than of the *Lord* in his exalted state.

e. Thus our observations on the use of the pistis-formula and of the words πίστις/πιστεύειν, κήρυγμα/κηρύσσειν, and finally τὸ εὐαγγέλιον τοῦ Χριστοῦ/εὐαγγελίζεσθαι all combine to produce a unified result which may be summarized as follows:

1. The key words we have just listed are often to be found side by side, or in close association. This we have been able to show by proceeding from the pistis-formula to πιστεύειν, thence to κηρύσσειν and on to τὸ εὐαγγέλιον.[133]

2. This close association is neither accidental nor superficial, but reflects the fact that these expressions belong to a common background of ideas.

---

[132] See 45.
[133] These words are often further linked with each other, e.g. 'gospel/preaching the gospel' with *pistis*, as at Gal. 1.23; Rom. 1.16; Phil. 1.27.

3. In fact we have here a self-contained and unified series of related words, for preaching, faith and gospel all have the one content. This content is summarized in the pistis-formula in two brief sentences. That these three things all have the same content is a sign that the ideas which underlie them are the same as those which are expressed in the pistis-formula, and all speak of the same events.

4. We can now see very plainly that the christological designation which occurs in this context is almost without exception *Christ* (very occasionally *Jesus*), but *Lord*, on the other hand, is absent.

13. 'Apostle' and 'Apostle of Christ'

a. Now the question arises whether there is a term for the person who does the preaching in the series of related words which we have just indicated. If there were such a term for the preacher, we would expect it to be either 'the evangelist' (ὁ εὐαγγελιστής) or 'the preacher' (ὁ κῆρυξ). But the three places in the NT where we find the word 'evangelist'[134] show that this word came into the language of mission only at a late stage. We are still in a position to see what the motive for its introduction was, for, at a time when the term 'apostle' had already come to be applied to a particular and clearly defined circle of pioneers of mission, those outside that circle who had a similar office of preaching were termed 'evangelists'.[135] The difference between 'apostle' and 'evangelist' is not one of function. It is rather that the latter term reflects a later period, say, the second or third generation, by which time the 'apostle' has become either in the Lucan sense a figure in the *Heilsgeschichte* itself or in the deutero-Pauline sense an authoritative first link in the chain of tradition.[136]

Similarly, 'preacher' came into use late,[137] but unlike 'evangelist' it is a term which can also describe Paul, alongside the term 'apostle'. In the Pastoral Epistles the phrase 'for this I was

---

[134] Acts 21.8, of Philip; Eph. 4.11, in a list of functions; II Tim. 4.5, of Timothy.
[135] Similarly Bultmann, *Theology* II, 52.3, 104f.
[136] Cf. Conzelmann in M. Dibelius, *Die Pastoralbriefe*, 3rd ed. rev. H. Conzelmann, 1955, I.
[137] Only 3 times in NT: I Tim. 2.7; II Tim. 1.11 (of Paul); II Peter 2.5 (of Noah).

appointed a preacher and apostle (and teacher)' occurs twice, each time following traditional sentences describing the saving events, and in such a way that the phrase itself is to be regarded as already part of the traditional formulation. This fact in itself goes to show that here we have to do with post-Pauline usage which took shape when Paul's mission to the Gentiles, and indeed his own preaching, had been taken up as eschatological features into the very confession of the Church.[138]

b. Thus neither 'evangelist' nor 'preacher' in the pre-Pauline and Pauline missionary terminology refer to the missionary activity of Paul himself. For this there is another term: 'apostle'. Statistics show that 'apostle' occurs 24 times in the Pauline corpus, 16 times without qualification,[139] twice as 'apostle of Christ',[140] and twice at the very beginning of letters as 'apostle of Christ Jesus',[141] once in the same position as 'apostle through Jesus Christ',[142] and finally as 'apostle to the Gentiles',[143] 'apostle of the churches',[144] and 'your apostle',[145] each appearing only once.

It is beyond the scope of this essay to go into the entire history of the 'apostle' concept, or into the difference between the Pauline, Lucan, and deutero-Pauline understanding of the term. We wish to do only two things, namely to discover through Paul's language what pre-Pauline usage was, and if possible to determine the range of ideas within which the term 'apostle' belongs.

c. It is immediately apparent that 'apostle' is a pre-Pauline technical term. This is shown by the two much discussed passages, Gal. 1.17, 19; I Cor. 15.7.[146] From the second passage it is plain that the circle of the apostles is at this stage not identical with the circle of the twelve.[147] We defer for the present the question

[138] Cf. E. Schweizer, 'Die Kirche als Leib Christi in den paulinischen Antilegomena', *TLZ* 86, 1961, 250f.
[139] I Cor. 4.9; 9.1, 2, 5; 12.28, 29; 15.7, 9 (bis); II Cor. 11.5; 12.11, 12; Gal. 1.17, 19; Rom. 1.1; 16.7.
[140] I Thess. 2.7; II Cor. 11.13.
[141] I Cor. 1.1; II Cor. 1.1.
[142] Gal. 1.1 ('through Jesus Christ and God the Father').
[143] Rom. 11.13.
[144] II Cor. 8.23.
[145] Phil. 2.25.
[146] Klein, *Die zwölf Apostel*, 1961, 38–49 summarizes the 'state of the debate'. It is characteristic that in both passages 'apostle' appears without genitive qualification. Cf. Schmithals, *Das kirchliche Apostelamt*, 1961, 64–77.
[147] Klein, *Apostel*, 44–48 emphasizes this. The expression 'the twelve' is pre-Pauline (cf. I Cor. 15.5), for Paul himself never uses it. Klein leaves this fact out of

whether 'the twelve' (I Cor. 15.5) are included among 'all the apostles' in v. 7, or whether the two groups overlap.[148]

In II Cor. 11.13 Paul invents *ad hoc* the opposite expression 'false apostle',[149] but we cannot tell from this with any certainty whether the opponents were called 'apostles' independently of Paul, having perhaps taken over this description of Paul's status and applied it to themselves.

As far as the function of the apostles goes, they are not officials of any one local church, but they have a status and responsibility which should be defined as 'belonging to all the churches'.[150] They travel around,[151] they preach, they maintain contact with the churches they have founded,[152] and they are regarded by them as in some sense authorities. Apostles in this technical sense are not simply men who are sent round from one church to another.[153]

Apostleship, it is true, is one gift of grace among others, but in any list of these gifts it always takes first place.[154] Thus far, every-

account (46f.) when he uses the absence of this expression in Gal. 1.17 as an argument. Cf. also Neugebauer, *In Christus, Eine Untersuchung zum paulinischen Glaubensverständnis*, 1961, 115 and the literature listed there.

[148] Gal. 1.18 shows that at very least they overlap, for Cephas, i.e. one of the twelve, is counted as one of the apostles. It remains uncertain, from Gal. 1.19, whether the Lord's brother, James, is reckoned as one of the apostles or not. See Schlier, *Galater* 31 *ad loc.*

[149] Cf. with this his pejorative adaptation of the technical term περιτομή in Phil. 3.2. The expression 'the apostle of Christ' in II Cor. 11.13 is certainly a Pauline formulation. On this, see 13a.

[150] Nevertheless, different apostles have different areas of work, e.g. Gal. 2.9. Cf. E. Schweizer, *Church Order in the New Testament*, ET 1961, 24b, 196.

[151] This, at all events, is to be maintained against Klein, *Apostel*, 45f., who on the basis of Gal. 1.17–19 speaks of a 'college located permanently at Jerusalem'. I Cor. 9.5 shows clearly that they travelled, and even Gal. 1.17–19 itself makes this plain. Klein is right to reject as 'fantastic' the supposition (46 n. 191) that Paul, on his first visit to Jerusalem, saw no one but Peter on the grounds that he had to keep himself hidden (thus Lietzmann, *Galater, ad loc.*). But how does he explain the fact that during a fortnight's stay in Jerusalem Paul saw no other member, apart from Peter, of the 'permanent resident college' which did not develop any itinerant ministry? To tell us that 'at the moment no certain answer seems possible' (46) looks very much like an evasion. Surely the truth must be that the apostles mentioned in Gal. 1.17 were resident in Jerusalem and from this base they undertook journeys in the cause of mission (e.g. preaching or inspection tours—cf. the background to Acts 8.14–17). It can hardly be supposed that it was any feeling of independence on Paul's part that caused him not to meet the others 'in Jerusalem', for if Paul had been influenced by any such feeling he would not have gone to Jerusalem at all.

[152] Cf. I Cor. 1.11f.; 9.2, which certainly refer to the relationship between Paul and Corinth.

[153] Thus Phil. 2.25.

[154] I Cor. 12.28f.

thing we have said about the term 'apostle' reflects its use in the pre-Pauline period.

d. But now Paul makes his own claim to be an apostle,[155] applying this designation to himself in the opening sentences of his letters[156] and elsewhere,[157] in a sense which clearly denotes a particular status in the Church.

If we ask how an apostle comes to be an apostle, it is hardly possible to find a pre-Pauline answer, even by the most penetrating examination of Paul's own arguments.[158] But in Paul's case it is clear, for he claims to be an apostle, 'not through (διά) man, but through (διά) Jesus Christ and God the Father'.[159] This *dia*-phrase clearly interprets Paul's understanding of the genitive relationship 'apostle of Christ Jesus' which appears in the opening sentences of the letters to the Corinthians.[160] It is Christ's commission which makes him an apostle. Two passages make it very plain that Paul regards the appearance of the risen Christ as constituting his apostleship: I Cor. 15.6–11 and I Cor. 9.1. Because, for example, Timothy does not fulfil this condition he is never called an apostle. Paul explains the fact that the circle of the apostles is a closed one in terms of his conviction that the appearance outside Damascus was positively the last resurrection appearance.[161]

It is clear how Paul sees his task as an apostle: it is to preach the gospel. In two places Paul uses the verb ἀποστέλλειν in a sense which implies this notion of apostleship.[162] The purpose of this 'sending' is preaching (κηρύσσειν or εὐαγγελίζεσθαι).[163]

In argument with the 'superlative apostles' or the 'false apostles'[164] Paul never uses the polemical argument that they had never wit-

[155] I Cor. 9.1.
[156] I Cor. 1.1; II Cor. 1.1; Rom. 1.1.
[157] I Thess. 2.7.
[158] It is possible that it was only Paul's precise understanding of apostleship which forced the Church towards a clearer conception of the term.
[159] Gal. 1.1.
[160] Cf. I Cor. 1.17, 'Christ sent me'.
[161] I Cor. 15.8, 'Last of all . . . he appeared also to me' is surely to be understood as ending definitively the series of resurrection appearances.
[162] I Cor. 1.17; Rom. 10.15. In II Cor. 12.17, on the other hand, it means simply the sending of an ambassador.
[163] At least in Paul's case it does not consist in baptizing (I Cor. 1.17).
[164] Both these descriptions could refer to the same group. This is against Käsemann, 'Die Legitimität des Apostels', ZNW 41, 1942, 41ff. See Klein, *Apostel* 58 n. 248, who takes issue with Käsemann.

nessed an appearance. Rather he conducts his argument along two lines. On the one hand his appeal is that Christ himself has made him an apostle (or that he, at any rate, has become an apostle on the basis of an appearance of the risen Christ),[165] and on the other hand he binds himself, as well as the other apostles and his opponents, to the content of preaching as it is summarized in the pistis-formula.[166]

Both lines of argument, as is shown by the context in which they occur, spring from Paul's own theological thinking, so if there is a question at all, it can only be about the extent to which 'he appeared' was already in pre-Pauline times the criterion, or a criterion, of apostleship.

e. With all this in mind, we now turn to the question of the christological titles, and we must first recall that 'apostle' is linked with the title *Christ (Jesus)* only five times.[167] In none of the five places is it necessary to regard this usage as pre-Pauline.

Gal. 1.1 clearly reflects Paul's understanding of apostleship, which he expresses by using a *dia*-phrase to qualify 'apostle'.

The expression 'apostles of Christ' in II Cor. 11.13 is evidently a formulation prompted by particular circumstances. Behind it lies the simple title 'apostle', which, contrasted with 'false apostles', is used against his opponents. But now he needs to find another term which will distinguish the true and genuine apostles from the 'false apostles' who claim to be true. It is in this sense that Paul formulates the expression 'apostles of Christ'.[168] If Paul

---

[165] I Cor. 9.1; 15.8–10; Gal. 1.1; cf. I Cor. 1.17.

[166] I Cor. 15.11; II Cor. 11.4.

[167] See notes 140–2 above. The observation that 'apostle' is only in a few places qualified by a genitive tallies with what we find in late Jewish literature, for there the expression 'envoy of God' is not found. Cf. E. Schweizer, *Church Order* 24i, 202.

[168] Klein, *Apostel* 57 n. 244, states (quoting Käsemann, 'Legitimität 37) 'that the term "apostle of Jesus Christ" was commonly used by them (i.e. the apostles agitating in Corinth) to describe themselves and is not of Paul's coining at all'. Against this it must be said, (1) that this is an inexact way of speaking. If it were really a matter of a term used by Paul's opponents to describe themselves, then that term would need to be simply 'apostle of *Christ*', for this is the expression which Paul uses in passages where the style is not particularly distinctive. (2) At this point a lack of clarity in Klein's argument (56–59) becomes apparent. He is concerned to show that in the pre-Pauline period, as well as in Paul's own, 'apostle' is used 'in the full sense' (56), i.e. not as meaning simply someone sent from one congregation to another (e.g. Phil. 2.25), but as a religious technical term. In this respect his concern is legitimate and he comes near to the truth of the matter. But he makes assertions which with regard to terminology are incorrect. What Klein understands as 'apostle in the full sense' is in pre-Pauline terminology simply 'apostle' (distinguished only in practice from someone sent from congregation to congregation, for this sort of

had taken the expression 'apostle of Christ' as his starting point, its opposite would more likely have been 'apostles of Satan' (cf. v. 14) than 'false apostles'. All this suggests that Paul formulated the expression 'apostles of Christ' *ad hoc.*

In I Thess. 2.7 the expression 'Christ's apostles' is not to be regarded as pre-Pauline, for the genitive precedes. This indicates that the expression is formed *ad hoc.*

Of the terms used by Paul to describe himself there now remains the expression, 'apostle of Christ Jesus' (I Cor. 1.1;[169] II Cor. 1.1). It is Paul's custom to add *'Jesus'* in passages where the style is distinctive, and the opening designation in the letters is one such passage.[170] Similarly, the word order in II Cor. 1.1, which is also to be read at I Cor. 1.1, agrees with Paul's habit of placing *Christ* before *Jesus* in genitive constructions.[171] Thus these expressions are to be regarded as of Pauline formulation.

But in all this there has not been the slightest indication that the expression 'apostle of Christ (Jesus)' was already in use as a technical term in the pre-Pauline period. In fact, everything points the other way, suggesting that it is Paul himself who linked the term 'apostle' with the title *Christ.*[172]

---

person is called 'apostle' in Phil. 2.25, and only in II Cor. 8.23 'apostles of the churches'). Paul, too, uses the simple term 'apostle'—only rarely 'apostle of Christ (Jesus)'. 'Apostle of Jesus Christ', the term which Klein is constantly mentioning, is nowhere evidenced in Paul, except as a reading of I Cor. 1.1. Klein would have done better to leave the terminological question alone, for no argument can be got from it for the matter with which he is concerned, without going beyond the evidence of the text, as he has done. (3) Klein says that the expression 'apostle of Christ' (II Cor. 11.13) is used by Paul's opponents to describe themselves. With just as much right, we could say the same about the expression 'servants of righteousness' in v. 15. Klein says nothing about that. He does say, of the 'servants of Christ' in v. 23, that 'it is quite evident' that 'Paul is quoting word for word his opponents' utterances' (n. 244), but here again without taking into consideration the other predicates in v. 22. Thus Klein's method of argument here is unconvincing.

[169] The word order is uncertain. A decision based purely on text-critical considerations is hardly possible here. If the expression is regarded as a Pauline construction, on the analogy of II Cor. 1.1; 11.13; I Thess. 2.7, then the word order 'of Christ Jesus' is to be preferred (cf. n. 19).
[170] See 36g, 59d, and n. 715.
[171] See 61bc.
[172] We have already drawn attention to the fact that the expression 'envoy of God' is not found in Jewish writing. (Cf. n. 167). Indeed genitive constructions of this sort are extremely rare, so that in Judaism the simple *šālîaḥ* in itself is to be regarded as a technical term. Thus from the language point of view, too, there is nothing to contradict what we have found, namely that within early Christianity 'apostle' was originally used without a qualifying genitive.

The other self-descriptive expressions within the Pauline writings present a similar picture. They are linked with *Christ (Jesus)*, not with *Lord*, and in some of the

If we look at the non-Pauline material we find the corresponding expression in the opening designations of the deutero-Paulines,[173] the Pastorals,[174] and the Petrine letters,[175] but with all these passages it is conceivable that they depend either directly or indirectly upon Paul's own usage.[176]

f. This means, with regard to our subject, that we have a negative result, for the association of the term *Christ (Jesus)* and *apostle* is shown to derive from Paul, and is of no value as an indication of any early link between the ideas underlying the term 'apostle' and those of the pistis-formula.

We have a negative result, too, on the question of the origin of the 'apostle' concept and of the way in which it was understood. Since it was Paul who linked the term 'apostle' with the title *Christ*,[177] this link cannot serve as a pointer to the origin of the idea of apostleship. However, to discuss currently prevalent views on this subject lies outside our scope.[178]

---

passages it is quite apparent that the expressions are Paul's own. None of these passages can be ascribed with any degree of certainty to the pre-Pauline church. The expressions are these: 'servant (διάκονος) of Christ'—II Cor. 11.23; 'slave (δοῦλος) of Christ'—Gal. 1.10; 'servant (ὑπηρέτης) of Christ'—I Cor. 4.1; 'under the law (ἔννομος) of Christ'—I Cor. 9.21; 'a minister (λειτουργός) of Christ Jesus'—Rom. 15.16; and in opening designations: 'slave (δοῦλος) of Christ Jesus' (Rom. 1.1; Phil. 1.1); 'prisoner (δέσμιος) of Christ Jesus' (Philemon 1).

[173] Col. 1.1; Eph. 1.1 (II Thess. 1.1 lacks any such expression).

[174] I Tim. 1.1; II Tim. 1.1; Titus 1.1.

[175] I Peter 1.1; II Peter 1.1.

[176] In Titus 1.1; I and II Peter 1.1 the order 'Jesus Christ' instead of 'Christ Jesus' is certainly a deviation from Pauline usage, but it is not sufficient to warrant the postulation that it represents a survival of pre-Pauline tradition or of traditions current in Paul's own period.

[177] We must emphasize expressly that here we are concerned simply with fixing the time at which the terms were linked, and not with disputing that 'apostle' was already, before Paul's time, a religious technical term in the sense of someone who bore office within the Church at large. Klein, *Apostel* 55, is right about this, but he goes astray over the question of terminology. Inexact formulations such as that on p. 55 are regrettable, for there he argues against the view 'that Paul was the first to coin the notion of an "apostle of Jesus Christ"'. But it *was* Paul who coined the *concept*—certainly in the form, 'apostle of Christ (Jesus)' though the idea of the apostle as a special 'official' in the Church was already current in the pre-Pauline church.

[178] Rengstorf, *TWNT* I 414.1–424.33 (ET, *Apostleship*, 1952, 12–31), represents the view that the apostolate is derived from the late Jewish šālîaḥ; similarly, though more cautiously, Neugebauer, *In Christus*, 113–19. Schmithals, *Apostelamt* 87–99, rejects this view, but in *Die Gnosis in Korinth*, 1956, 245–7, puts forward the thesis that the apostolate may be derived from the idea of the envoy in the Gnostic myth. In *Apostelamt* 216, he says, 'there can be no doubt that the early Christian apostolate was taken over from the missionary's office in Jewish or Jewish Christian Gnosis'. There must be considerable doubt about all these possible derivations. Cf. Schweizer, *Church Order* 24i, 200ff., and the literature listed there.

Clearly the idea of apostleship and the term 'apostle', as used in the pre-Pauline language of mission, had already become technical, in the sense that it described a particular though not necessarily closed circle of those who held 'office' within the Church. The actual criterion for judging who belonged to this circle only becomes apparent in Paul, who sees it in terms of appearances of the risen Christ. It is questionable whether this was the main criterion before Paul's time,[179] all the more so since we never hear of women being called apostles. A second criterion at least must needs have been introduced, by which women would have been excluded automatically.[180]

It seems that the expression 'apostle of Christ (Jesus)' comes from Paul. There are two possible reasons why Paul combines 'apostle' with *Christ*, and not with *Lord* or *Son of God*. It was either because Paul saw in the Damascus vision the one whom the Hellenistic church called *Christ*, the one who had died and had been raised; or it was because he understood his vocation as apostle to the Gentiles so much in terms of the content of the message which he was required to proclaim that he inserted the title which expressed that content, i.e. *Christ*, into contexts in which he was describing the character of his apostleship.[181] In either case it would have been the ideas expressed in the pistis-formula which in the last resort determined the wording of the expression 'apostle of Christ'. But even if this is correct, the link between the pistis-formula and the idea of apostleship is not an intrinsic one but is rather the product of theological reflexion on Paul's part.

Luke marks a new stage in the development of the idea, for with him we find a logical narrowing down and an unambiguous definition of the title 'apostle'. But Paul himself, within his own sphere of influence, retains the dominant position as *the* apostle. Evidence for this is the fact that in the Pastorals he alone figures as an apostle,[182] and also that in the deutero-Pauline and Pastoral

---

[179] Even Paul does not apply it clearly to anyone except himself! Certainly in the Lucan conception of apostleship the eye-witness aspect plays an important part, simply because it guarantees the resurrection. Cf. Acts 1.22b; 4.33. To this extent it comes close to Paul's understanding of the term. Cf. Schweizer, *Church Order* 24a, 194f.

[180] Cf. Schweizer, *Church Order* n. 734.

[181] The first possibility is the more likely, because Χριστοῦ is subj. gen. See 13d.

[182] Thus E. Schweizer, *Church Order* 24a, 195.

epistles he himself, together with his work for the mission to the Gentiles, is taken up into the Church's confession of faith.[183] There it is possible to establish a direct connection in terminology between 'Christ', 'message' and 'apostle', but it is the work of the post-Pauline generation.

Thus we have been able to show that before Paul the term 'apostle' did not belong to the series of expressions connected with the pistis-formula ($X\rho\iota\sigma\tau\acute{o}s$—$\pi\acute{\iota}\sigma\tau\iota s/\pi\iota\sigma\tau\epsilon\acute{u}\epsilon\iota\nu$—$\kappa\acute{\eta}\rho\upsilon\gamma\mu\alpha/\kappa\eta\rho\acute{u}\sigma\sigma\epsilon\iota\nu$—$\epsilon\mathring{u}\alpha\gamma\gamma\acute{\epsilon}\lambda\iota o\nu/\epsilon\mathring{u}\alpha\gamma\gamma\epsilon\lambda\acute{\iota}\zeta\epsilon\sigma\theta\alpha\iota$), but was brought into association with them as a result of Paul's theological elaboration of the meaning of apostleship.

14. The Place of the Pistis-formula in the Life of the Church

Having come to the end of our examination of the expressions connected with the pistis-formula, we must now return to the question of the place which the pistis-formula occupied in the life of the Church.

Everything that we have established suggests that it is in preaching that the pistis-formula has its proper place, not in the general sense that practically everything in the life of the Church ultimately has to do with the proclamation of the Gospel, but in the precise sense that the pistis-formula represents the basic text of that proclamation. This is shown, not only by the fact that the formula is associated with the terms $\kappa\eta\rho\acute{u}\sigma\sigma\epsilon\iota\nu$ and $\epsilon\mathring{u}\alpha\gamma\gamma\acute{\epsilon}\lambda\iota o\nu$,[184] but also by the way in which Paul uses the formula in passages of theological discussion and also in ethical instruction.[185] This

[183] E.g. I Tim. 2.7; II Tim. 1.11; cf. n. 138.

[184] No similar connection can be demonstrated between the formula and the word-group $\delta\iota\delta\acute{a}\sigma\kappa\epsilon\iota\nu$. Nevertheless we should not therefore conclude that the formula figured only in 'missionary' preaching but not in local, 'domestic' preaching. The distinction developed by Dodd, *The Apostolic Preaching and its Developments*, 2nd ed. 1944, 7–9, in connection with the words $\kappa\eta\rho\acute{u}\sigma\sigma\epsilon\iota\nu$ and $\delta\iota\delta\acute{a}\sigma\kappa\epsilon\iota\nu$ turns out to be incorrect where the Pauline writings are concerned. 'Preaching', for Paul, means both missionary preaching and also domestic preaching. 'Teaching' is for him of subordinate significance and describes one characteristic activity in the life of the Church among other such activities like 'revelation', 'knowledge', 'prophecy' (cf. I Cor. 14.6, 26). The word-group $\delta\iota\delta\acute{a}\sigma\kappa\epsilon\iota\nu$ becomes more important in the post-Pauline period, as is shown by its frequent appearance in editorial passages in Mark (cf. E. Schweizer, 'Anmerkungen zur Theologie des Markus', *Festschrift für O. Cullmann*, 1962) and Luke. Here the word has taken on a broader meaning, so that it could both be compared with, and distinguished from, the word $\kappa\eta\rho\acute{u}\sigma\sigma\epsilon\iota\nu$ in the Pauline corpus.

[185] Cf. passages like I Cor. 15.1–20 or Rom. 14.16.

reflects the way in which the formula was used in preaching, for preaching also divides into precisely these categories of theological discussion and ethical instruction.[186]

Since the pistis-formula summarizes the content of faith, we must expect to find it also in those places where this faith is expressed or acknowledged. The ceremony of baptism is an instance of this. The candidate declares his faith, the content of which has been explained to him in catechetical instruction. We find evidence of this in the Pauline corpus, for the discussion of the significance of baptism in Rom. 6.2–9 is indeed nothing other than an elaboration of the pistis-formula. We may suppose that at the service of baptism hymns and songs composed at an early stage[187] were recited either together with the pistis-formula or in place of it. But this in no way alters the fact that the actual basic text for baptism is the pistis-formula.

We cannot say the same in the case of the Lord's Supper, for in so far as it is accessible to us in the Paulines it is linked in terminology with the title *Lord*.[188] This points to different formulae, to a different background of ideas, and to a different environment to which the Lord's Supper owes its particular stamp. But our negative findings in this case only serve to show that the connection between the pistis-formula and preaching or baptism is not accidental but essential.

Neither preaching nor baptism are sufficient in themselves but derive their force from the fact that they both point to the saving event of the death and the resurrection of Christ. In preaching and in baptism this saving event which happened *extra nos* in the past becomes capable of arousing faith, and thus of being *pro nobis* in the present.

[186] This, too, is as true of 'missionary' preaching as of 'local' preaching.

[187] Käsemann puts the hymns at Phil. 2.6–11 ('Kritische Analyse von Phil. 2.5–11', *Exegetische Versuche und Besinnungen* I, 1960, 95) and at Col. 1.15–20 ('A Primitive Baptismal Liturgy', *Essays on New Testament Themes*, ET 1964, 149–67) in the setting of the baptismal liturgy.

[188] See 45.

II · LORD

A. THE TRADITIONAL CONFESSION AND THE KEY WORDS
ὁμολογεῖν AND ὄνομα

15. The Confession as Acclamation

a. In the Pauline corpus an early, pre-Pauline setting of the title *Lord* can be distinguished by its literary form. It is the acclamation *ΚΥΡΙΟΣ ΙΗΣΟΥΣ*.[189] In two places the key word ὁμολογεῖν or alternatively ἐξομολογεῖσθαι appears also.[190] For this reason Conzelmann[191] calls the acclamation a 'homologia'. Proof that we really have a pre-Pauline formula here is that in Rom. 10.9a it is mentioned side by side with the pistis-formula as a part of the Church's profession, and that in Phil. 2.11 it occurs within the Christ-hymn which is either pre-Pauline or perhaps contemporary with Paul.

This second passage also shows that the confession really is thought of as an acclamation, for the acclamatory shout is accompanied by a 'bowing of the knee' in adoration.[192] All three passages clearly suggest that the confession belongs to worship. The hymn in Phil. 2.6–11 is recited at worship; in Rom. 10.8f. the pistis-formula and the confession are mentioned as proofs that the 'word of faith' is present in preaching; and finally I Cor. 12.3 uses the acclamation as a criterion for judging whether the many varieties of ecstatic phenomena, both within Christian worship and outside it, are genuine. The fact that the formula is thus rooted in the liturgical worship of the pre-Pauline church tells against the supposition that it was fashioned in later times of persecution on

---

[189] I Cor. 12.3; Rom. 10.9a; Phil. 2.11 (in the extended form, 'Lord Jesus Christ'). On the term 'acclamation' cf. Peterson, *ΕΙΣ ΘΕΟΣ*, 1926, 133f., 141–5.
[190] Rom. 10.9a; Phil. 2.11.
[191] Conzelmann, 'Christenheit' 64.
[192] Foerster, *TWNT* III 1050.14–17 (ET, *Lord*, 1958, 22), draws attention to 'the noticeable frequency of κύριος in the προσκυνήματα' in Egyptian witnesses. Nevertheless he denies any connection with cultic worship.

the analogy of the confession which the state required, namely 'Caesar is Lord'.[193]

Thus the Church acclaims Jesus as Lord. *Jesus* is the name of the person who holds the title and the rank of *Lord*. In grammatical terms, *Jesus* is the subject, *Lord* the predicate of the sentence.[194] But this means that the Church which acclaims Jesus already has a clear idea of what is meant by the title and the rank of *Lord* which it ascribes to him. This immediately raises the question of the ideas which lie behind the title *Lord*. The question would be easy to answer if there were any certainty about the origin of the title. As it happens, however, scholars are anything but unanimous on this particular matter. Our terms of reference here do not allow us to tackle the question of the title's religious and historical background, nor do we propose to assemble all the opinions and hypotheses which have been put forward in connection with this problem, for these are easily accessible elsewhere.[195]

b. But in any case it has already become plain that the pistis-formula and the confession differ both in nature and in function.[196] As we know, the pistis-formula summarizes briefly the saving events of the past, the death and the resurrection of Christ. It is the basic text of preaching, designed to induce acceptance of the kerygma.[197] This acceptance of the kerygma is called faith.

But the *homologia* is different, for it is not concerned with formulating the saving events but with a *direct invocation* in which the Church does obeisance to the Lord by acclaiming his majesty. By 'acclamation' is meant an act of tribute and submission of this sort. In acclamation the Church is not thinking of any particular

[193] Against Cullmann, *The Earliest Christian Confessions*, ET 1949, 28–30, it must be said that nowhere in I Cor. is there any trace of a state of persecution. Cf. Conzelmann, 'Christenheit' 68 n. 6.

[194] Cf. Foerster, *Herr ist Jesus*, 1924, 121–3.

[195] The opinions of scholars between 1913 and 1924 (i.e. from the publication of Bousset, *Kyrios Christos*, 1st ed., 1913 to the publication of Foerster, *Herr ist Jesus*, 1924) have been assembled by Foerster in *Herr ist Jesus* 11–56 (on the question of the title's origin see especially 37–47). Foerster's view is given on pp. 206–208 and in his article, *TWNT* III 1045.14–1056.27; and 1087.19–1094.23 (ET, *Lord*, 13–35 and 97–110). See also Lohmeyer, *Κύριος Ἰησοῦς*, 1927–28; Bultmann, *Theology* I, 7.5, 52f.; 12.2, 123–128; Cerfaux, 'Le titre Kyrios et la dignité royale de Jésus', *Recueil L. Cerfaux* I, 1954, 3–63; Cerfaux, *Christ*, 461–79; V. Taylor, *The Names of Jesus*, 1953, 38–40, 47–51; Fuller, *The Mission and Achievement of Jesus*, 2nd ed. 1955, 111–114; Cullmann, *Christology* 195–237.

[196] For the whole of the section which follows, cf. Conzelmann, 'Christenheit' 67–69.

[197] See 14.

saving event but is putting itself into a relationship which holds good in the present. It is not even thinking of the act by which the *Lord* was installed in his position of honour (that act would have been the resurrection, understood as exaltation), but is acclaiming him as one who has been given the status of Lord, without stopping to consider, at first, how the conferring of such a status came about.

So the acclamation is 'confession' in the strict sense of the word, for the Church confesses its loyalty to this particular *Lord*, and as it makes this confession it is prepared in the last resort to set itself against all other 'lords' to the point of martyrdom.

The *homologia* is not 'preached' but proclaimed with a shout, and thus it is a summons to renewed acclamation and renewed confession.

Of course, the pistis-formula and the *homologia* are brought into relationship with each other at an early stage, and the ideas underlying each become mingled with one another.

The resurrection, interpreted as exaltation, comes to be understood as the enthronement of the *Lord*.[198] Thus Jesus' status as *Lord* comes to be inserted into the series of acts which comprise the saving events in such a way that it can become an additional sentence in the pistis-formula. Conversely the confession, which originally mentioned only the name and the title, comes to be filled out with particular statements which are similar to those of the pistis-formula.[199] But development of this kind only confirms that the pistis-formula and the *homologia* were originally clearly defined entities, different in nature and in function.

c. Using the material in the Pauline texts as our starting point, we must now analyse and interpret such texts as can give us clues to the kind of contexts in which the title *Lord* properly belongs.

We have already established that the acclamation '*Kyrios Jesus*' is rooted in liturgical worship.[200] The variant '*Kyrios Jesus Christos*'[201] makes several further observations possible.

1. Since the *homologia* consists of the title *Lord* and a name, we may regard the combination *Jesus Christ* as being essentially a

[198] This stage has already been reached in the hymn at Phil. 2.6–11.
[199] See I John 4.2 for this development in the acclamation of the Son of God, and also on this 16d below.
[200] See 15a.
[201] Phil. 2.11.

name.[202] This means that *Christ*, originally a translation of the title *Messiah*, had already become merely a second name for *Jesus* at the time when the double term came to be used in the acclamation. But this is conceivable only in the realm of the Greek-speaking Gentile church, for in the Greek-speaking Jewish Christian church (which historically represents the link between the Aramaic-speaking Jewish Christians in Jerusalem and Gentile Christianity) the meaning of the title *Christ* would still live on and be well understood, on the basis of the Jewish Christians' knowledge of the original Aramaic-speaking church and of the Old Testament. No doubt in one respect the original meaning of the title is reflected in Gentile Christian usage, for *Christ* is not linked directly with the title *Lord* but only comes after the simple name *Jesus*.[203] But this does not alter the fact that in the confession 'Jesus Christ (is) Lord' *Jesus Christ* is used as a double name.

2. This has some bearing on the question of the origin of the hymn in Phil. 2.6–11. For if we assume that the acclamation in this extended form (i.e. with double name) was already in use at the time when the hymn was composed, it follows that the hymn must have originated in a Hellenistic setting, for only there was *Jesus Christ* regarded as a double name.[204]

3. The acclamation was already in existence before being taken up into the hymn. So the ideas which underlie the hymn are not to be taken as direct evidence for the ideas which underlie the acclamation. All the same, the hymn is to be taken seriously in this respect, for it gives us one of the earliest settings of the acclamation.

The hymn and the confession are related, to the extent that the hymn is conceived in terms of the confession which forms its climax. But this certainly does not mean that the hymn has simply been 'spun' out of the acclamation, for the christological pattern of humiliation and exaltation[205] which forms the basis

---

[202] Thus Lohmeyer, *Kyrios* 61, though his interpretation of the word order is wrong.

[203] This is the usage which Paul always follows.

[204] This is against Lohmeyer, *Kyrios* 73, who by reading into the hymn a correlation between the terms *Son of Man* and *Kyrios* reaches mistaken conclusions about the origin of the hymn. From this results his remarkable vacillation in dating the hymn historically.

[205] As a result of Colpe's researches and conclusions, in *Die religionsgeschichtliche Schule*, 1961, 62–68, 173–5, 191, 197, it appears that we may no longer say, as

of the hymn is not directly connected with the acclamation.
The hymn certainly regards the 'bowing of the knee' and the
confession as the climax of the events which it describes. Nevertheless the pattern of humilation and exaltation which shapes the
hymn differs in origin from the ideas which lie behind the confession of Jesus as *Lord*.[206] In fact we shall see that the pattern of
the hymn is connected with the title *Son of God* rather than with
any other.

But in one respect the hymn does aid our understanding of
'*Kyrios Jesus Christos*', for its last two verses show that this expression really is a shout of acclamation, and they show also the ideas
with which the acclamation was associated in the Church. The
adoration and acclamation given by the heavenly powers to the
Lord of the cosmos are a reflection in the cosmic realm of what
the Church does in the liturgical realm. This is not to say that the
acclamation of Jesus in the worship of the Church is directed to
him simply as 'Lord of the cult' and not as Lord of the cosmos.
No sharp distinction can be made here between Lord of the cult
and Lord of the cosmos, for the pre-Pauline Gentile church saw
Jesus as both.

If we want to discover, on the basis of this passage, which
particular idea might originally have shaped the understanding of
the title *Lord*, we must bear in mind that adoration and acclamation on the part of powers in heaven and on earth and under the
earth represent an interpretation of the LXX version of Isa. 45.23,
and are thus related to this, and not directly to the acclamation
'Jesus is Lord'. Thus this passage shows that the acclamation was
associated at an early stage with the 'Lord of the cosmos' idea.
It does not necessarily prove that this idea forms an essential
element in the acclamation from the beginning, though of course
it does not disprove it either. Evidence for concluding that the idea
was not originally associated with the acclamation can only be
had from other passages.[207]

It is plain that the hymn, like the acclamation itself, belongs to
the worship of the Gentile Christian church. Lohmeyer supposes

---

Käsemann does, in 'Phil. 2.5-11', without qualification, that this passage represents
a Christian variant of the myth of the heavenly redeemer.

[206] Here we can only hint at what is said in more detail in 27f.
[207] On this question see 67c.

that its setting is in the Lord's Supper,[208] while Käsemann prefers to see it as belonging to baptism.[209] Seeberg's observations on the way in which the Isa. 45.23 quotation is used in the hymn and within Judaism[210] are an argument in favour of baptism as the proper setting, no matter in which direction the question of dependence may run. This suggests that the *homologia* was originally connected with baptism, even though we must admit that its use did not remain confined to baptism but, as I Cor. 12.3 shows, was extended in ever new ways as the Church's acclamation. On this showing it is possible that Phil. 2.6–11 did not remain simply a baptismal hymn in the narrower sense but came to be more generally employed in liturgical worship.

d. Our conclusions are these:

1. The *homologia* 'Kyrios Jesus' was used as an acclamation in which *Jesus* was acknowledged as *Lord*. 'Jesus' is the subject, 'Kyrios' the predicate in the sentence.

2. Congregational worship is the setting of the *homologia*. The neophyte speaks it for the first time at baptism, but in association with adoration it is used as a common acclamation by the whole congregation in worship.

3. The *homologia* is not a Pauline creation but is part of the particular heritage of the Hellenistic church. It is clearly within this church that the extended variant form 'Kyrios Jesus Christos' came into existence, for only here would *Jesus Christ* be understood as a double name. There are no grounds for supposing, on the other hand, that 'Kyrios Jesus' goes back to earlier stages of the tradition. So we are to take it that the acclamation itself originated in the Hellenistic Gentile church.[211]

4. The three passages we have considered do not give any clear information about the ideas underlying the title *Lord*. If it were possible to regard the final verses of the hymn in Philippians as an authentic exposition of the title, then *Lord* would mean the Ruler of the cosmos. But such an assumption is anything but certain. On the other hand, the same verses reveal a 'cultic' element, for it is the congregation which acclaims the Lord in its worship. This seems to suggest rather that the title signifies the

[208] Lohmeyer, *Kyrios Jesus* 65f.
[209] Käsemann, 'Phil. 2.5–11', 95.
[210] Seeberg, *Die Didache des Judentums und der Urchristenheit*, 1908, 74f.
[211] On the cry, 'Maranatha', see 23.

'Lord of the Church'.[212] On account of the pattern of humiliation and exaltation which underlies it, the hymn as a whole appears to have its origin in a background of thought which is different from that in which the title *Lord* originated.[213]

5. On the basis of the three passages examined, all that we can say about the origin of the title *Lord* is that it was used in the Hellenistic Gentile Christian church. The fact that a quotation from the LXX is associated with the *homologia* in Phil. 2.10f. does not help to explain the origin of the title, because the association can only have taken place in a Hellenistic environment, as is shown by the presence of the double name *Jesus Christ*. All that is proved is that in this environment LXX texts were applied to Jesus, the Lord.

16. ὁμολογεῖν and 'Homologia'

a. We have called the acclamation *homologia* because it is twice linked with the key word ὁμολογεῖν or ἐξομολογεῖσθαι.[214] Whether this was appropriate or not will become clear as we now examine these two words.

ἐξομολογεῖσθαι occurs in the NT with four meanings:
1. 'to praise', 'to applaud';[215] 2. 'to confess sins';[216] 3. 'to acclaim';[217] 4. in the active, meaning 'to make a firm agreement or deal'.[218]

Meanings 1 and 2 go closely together and have as their background the OT liturgy of the thank offering, of which we find traces in the psalms of complaint, petition and thanksgiving.[219] Meaning 3 comes from a similar background, but in the NT period it has come to be used technically in the sense of 'to acclaim, i.e. to say the *homologia*'. It is this line of development which interests us most, and we shall pursue it further by examining ὁμολογεῖν.

[212] See n. 207.
[213] See n. 206.
[214] Rom. 10.9a; Phil. 2.11.
[215] Rom. 14.11; 15.9 in OT quotations; Matt. 11.25 = Luke 10.21.
[216] Mark 1.5 = Matt. 3.6; James 5.16.
[217] Phil. 2.11.
[218] Luke 22.6 (of Judas Iscariot).
[219] Cf. Michel, *TWNT* V 202f.

b. This verb, too, means: 1. to confess sins;[220] 2. to make a firm agreement or deal.[221] 3. But in the majority of instances we find it used technically. Michel divides this group, seeing in half the instances a legal sense, 'to make a statement, or to give evidence', and in the other half the meaning 'to make a solemn statement of faith'.[222] But the passages cannot be divided in this way, as is shown by the fact that Michel calls both groups by virtually the same names.[223] It would be truer to say that we are here concerned with two different aspects of 'proclamation', which we could equally well call 'acclamation'. In so far as its statements are ultimately binding before God, the *homologia* possesses a forensic stamp, but it is also a 'cultic' event, since it is uttered in the Church's worship.

c. To examine what this word ὁμολογεῖν contains we must begin with the passage already discussed, Rom. 10.9f., in which Jesus is acknowledged as the *Lord*. In this formula it is not the saving events associated with Christ that are in view, but his status and significance as *Lord*. A similar *homologia* is found in the non-Pauline writings, where Jesus is confessed not as *Lord* but as *Christ*[224] or alternatively as *Son of God*.[225] These confessions doubtless go back to an already existent *homologia*, and this plainly shows that the church which lies behind that *homologia* is neither Pauline nor contemporary with Paul. It is no longer possible to determine the precise historical relationship between the confession of Jesus as *Lord*, of Jesus as *Son of God*, and of Jesus as *Christ*.

Basically two possibilities fall to be considered: 1. The kernel of the whole development is the confession of Jesus as *Messiah*. What that confession expressed came to be formulated afresh in the Gentile Christian sphere, with its different ideas, assumptions and terminology, as the confession of Jesus as *Lord*. By a similar process, in the church which lies behind I John, Jesus is confessed as *Son of God*. 2. The first formula of acclamation on Christian soil was '*Kyrios Jesus*'. The formula which has the title *Son of God* is

[220] I John 1.9.
[221] Matt. 14.7; Acts 7.17.
[222] *TWNT* V 207.22f.; 209.10f.
[223] Cf. e.g. *TWNT* V 208.14 ('proclamatory event') with 210.21f. ('solemn proclamatory statement').
[224] John 9.22; cf. I John 2.22.
[225] I John 4.15; cf. 2.22f.

merely a variation in a church which was more familiar with *Son of God* christology. The confession 'Jesus is the Messiah' would be, on this basis, in the last resort an archaizing retrojection of ideas connected with the title *Lord* into Jewish Christianity, where the concept of the Messiah was still a living one.

But it needs to be said that it is not permissible to arrange these very varied formulae in a tidy pattern in which a single line of development is portrayed. It is much more likely that the formulae arose independently at different times and in different places. The common background of ideas which made this manifold flowering possible was the broad current of general oriental notions of lordship, familiar throughout Hellenism. Adoration and acclamation originally belonged to the oriental enthronement ritual. Naturally, in any given group or area the range of ideas and conceptions which predominated there would influence the choice of the particular title used in acclamation. The best way of explaining the fact that the various kinds of acclamation have a unity of form but a diversity of titles is that in each case the *homologia* acclaims Jesus as one whose status is defined by a title, but each title, as applied to Jesus, reflects the particular thinking of the various churches.

d. It is possible to trace a development of this basic form of the *homologia*, a development which is characteristic. In I John 4.2f. we find a problem raised which is similar to that of I Cor. 12.1–3, namely the problem of knowing how to recognize the Spirit of God amid a welter of spirit-phenomena. In both passages the *homologia* is the objective criterion for distinguishing the spirits. But whereas for Paul the formula in itself is sufficient as a criterion, in I John 4.2 the corresponding acclamation of Jesus as *Christ* does not suffice, for the falsely inspired and the truly inspired alike appeal to the same *homologia*. So the formula itself had to be extended so as to provide a critical standard by which the false prophets would stand exposed. Only the confession that Jesus Christ came 'in the flesh' and not 'without flesh' is sufficient to mark the boundary between Docetists and Christians. This interpretative addition to the *homologia* means that the actual acclamation, in which Jesus is confessed as one who possesses particular honours and majesty, is destroyed by the insertion of a sentence which describes Jesus in terms of his redemptive work. We find exactly the same extension in II John 7, which proves that in the struggle to ward off Docetic tendencies the extended formula had already attained a fixed place.

But this means that the transition from the *homologia* which describes Jesus' exalted status to the pistis-formula which describes the work of salvation has been greatly speeded up. The development from this point onwards is now predetermined. It consists in combining titles and saving acts, 'formulae of the person' and 'formulae of events'. The second article of the Apostles' Creed offers significant evidence of this, for there the three major titles come first and are followed by a recital of the particular saving acts.[226]

e. There are various passages in which ὁμολογεῖν or ὁμολογία stand alone, without any clue to their content, which therefore cannot help us to determine the extent to which this development flourished.[227] But these passages do make the following points clear: first, they presuppose a confession which is of fixed[228] form (though ultimately of various types); second, these formulae were spoken at worship 'before many witnesses';[229] and third, they make very plain the binding character of the confession.[230]

f. At this point we are in a position to understand a third variant, which is a particular formulation of the eschatological significance of 'confession'. The confession by men before other men regarding the exalted status of Jesus is paralleled by Jesus' confession before God regarding men.[231] Such statements are only possible when apocalyptic thinking is combined with the ideas implicit in ὁμολογεῖν. The negative counterpart of this statement is frequently ἀρνεῖσθαι, which is associated with denying Jesus before God or with godlessness.[232] Thus 'to deny' is shown to be the verbal opposite of 'to confess' and is used in just the same summary, technical way.[233]

---

[226] That Pontius Pilate is named in I Tim. 6.13 is very probably indicative of this development. Cf. Conzelmann in Dibelius, *Die Pastoralbriefe* 67 *ad loc.*

[227] Thus I Tim. 6.12f.; Heb. 3.1 (linked with the title 'apostle' and 'high priest'); Heb. 10.23 'the confession of our hope'.

[228] It can be 'held fast', Heb. 4.14; 10.23. Cf. Käsemann, *Das wandernde Gottesvolk*, 1939, 108 n. 8.

[229] I Tim. 6.12. The mention of the calling to eternal life suggests that the primary reference is to a baptismal confession. Cf. II Tim. 1.9.

[230] Käsemann, *Gottesvolk* 106 n. 9, speaks of its 'proclamatory character' and calls ὁμολογεῖν a 'term which has decidedly juridical associations'.

[231] Matt. 10.32f; Luke 12.8f; John 1.20.

[232] II Tim. 2.12.

[233] Cf. Titus 1.16.

Finally, there are two passages which speak of confessing or denying not the *Lord* but his 'name'.[234] This connects with Phil. 2.9f., where the title *Lord* is 'the name above every name'. So this key phrase is the one we must choose as the starting point of our investigation in the following chapter.

g. But first we must summarize the results obtained in the present chapter.

1. The key word ὁμολογεῖν is used in a technical sense in a great number of NT passages. Used thus, it is to be taken to refer to the *homologia*, the acclamation. This justifies us in calling the acclamation *homologia*.

2. In its original sense the *homologia* is seen to be the formula in which Jesus is confessed as having a particular and honoured status, whether it be that of *Lord*, or *Son of God*, or *Messiah*. In the Pauline writings we find Jesus confessed only as *Lord*.

3. So we may say that in the Pauline and immediately pre-Pauline period the *homologia* is one of the early settings in which the title *Lord* belonged.

4. If at this point we ask what ideas were contained in the understanding of the title *Lord*, we must say that the title signifies the status of honour and majesty which Jesus has *vis à vis* the Church and the world—a status which is final and of eschatological import. In the *homologia* the Church acknowledges this status of Jesus and places itself under his rule as the *Lord*.

5. All this is not directly connected in any way either with the saving events of the past or with the parousia and the last judgement. Only in the dispute with Docetism does the phrase 'in the flesh' come to be inserted into the acclamation. The association of ὁμολογειν with apocalyptic ideas takes place along another line of development, but it serves to make explicit an aspect of the *homologia* which was present from the beginning, namely that it is ultimately binding in character.

17. Τὸ ὄνομα and the Homologia

a. Phil. 2.9 speaks of 'the name (ὄνομα) above every name'. This name is the title *Lord* contained in the formula of acclamation

---

[234] Heb. 13.15; Rev. 3.8; cf. 3.5.

which immediately follows.[235] It is the royal name given to Jesus at his heavenly enthronement. The cosmic powers had to acknowledge him, thus enthroned, by bowing the knee in adoration and by acclamation.[236] The Church acknowledges him whenever it says the *homologia* at worship, no doubt with accompanying adoration. So what happens 'at the name' is that worshippers bow the knee while proclaiming the title *Lord* by saying the *homologia*. The expression 'at the name' indicates what is done in the *homologia*. The expression here has exactly the sense which Heitmüller established, on the basis of a thorough comparative analysis: it means doing something 'as the name is named or called out'.[237]

If we bear in mind this precise meaning, we should, strictly speaking, take 'at the name' with the phrase 'that . . . every knee should bow', and only with that phrase, for if we link it with 'and every tongue confess' we get a pleonasm, i.e. to confess, as the name *Lord* is named, that Jesus is *Lord*. But to call out the name *Lord* means simply to say the *homologia*. To bow the knee 'at the name' means nothing more than that adoration accompanies acclamation. This emphasizes that the two actions belong together.

The reason why it is not clear, in this passage, to which of the two actions the phrase 'at the name' refers is that on the one hand the hymn describes what happened at the heavenly enthronement, but on the other hand it not only describes this heavenly acclamation but is itself also an acclamation. Or, to put this in terms of its literary composition, the lack of clarity arises because the acclamation was ready to hand, already formulated, when the hymn, which is based upon different ideas, was composed.

Since the acclamation existed already, before being taken up into the hymn, the title *Lord* in the *homologia* and the key word *onoma* were not originally connected, but in the hymn they were

---

[235] So Heitmüller, *Im Namen Jesu*, 1903, 65 n. 1; Lohmeyer, *Kyrios* 51, 54; Käsemann, 'Phil. 2.5–11' 84; E. Schweizer, *Erniedrigung* 8i, 95 (cf. *Lordship and Discipleship* 61); Bietenhard, *'Onoma'*, *TWNT* V 272.9–14, and others. The opposite view in Foerster, *Herr ist Jesus* 122.

[236] With Käsemann, 'Phil. 2.5–11' 86f. Schweizer, *Erniedrigung* 8i, 98, is inclined to relate adoration and acclamation to the moment of the parousia. This interpretation can be supported on the basis of a variant reading which gives the future tense instead of aorist subjunctive. But this variant could only have been produced when it was no longer understood that the hymn is about the enthronement of Jesus as *Lord* at his exaltation.

[237] Heitmüller, *Im Namen Jesu* 42, 88.

connected *ad hoc*. All the same, it would be wrong to conclude that the connection was therefore entirely fortuitous, because it can be shown that in all the *onoma*-passages within the Pauline corpus which contain a christological title it is the title *Lord* that occurs. If these passages merely reflected Pauline usage we would not need to deal with them here, but since they are demonstrably of pre-Pauline formulation we must have a look at them.

b. I Cor. 5.4 says that the man guilty of incest must be delivered to Satan in the presence of the assembled church. It is not clear from the text whether the phrase 'in the name of the Lord Jesus' is to be taken with συναχθέντων ὑμῶν[238] or with παραδοῦναι.[239] But in any case the sense is that either at the assembly of the congregation or at the handing over of the offender the name of the *Lord* is spoken. In the first case we would imagine an acclamation, and in the second case a formula of cursing—the opposite, as it were, of a formula of exorcism.[240] However that may be, the reference here is to a function of the church at which a formula containing the title *Lord* is spoken.[241]

c. Baptism was another occasion for the naming of the title *Lord*, when the one who administered baptism[242] pronounced it over the candidate. That I Cor. 6.11 refers to this is shown by the three verbs, 'wash', 'sanctify', 'justify'. Parallels in the NT[243] make it clear that the phrase 'in the name' is rooted in the baptismal liturgy. Unfortunately it is no longer possible to recover the exact wording of the baptismal formula. One thing is certain: originally it did not contain the word *onoma*, but pronounced over the

---

[238] Thus Kümmel in Lietzmann, *Korinther* 23 *ad loc*. The arrangement of the clauses favours this interpretation.

[239] Thus Heitmüller, *Im Namen Jesu* 37f. In favour of this view is the fact that both prepositional clauses can hardly be linked with the participial clause, and that σὺν τῇ δυνάμει cannot relate only to πνεῦμα.

[240] Cf. Bultmann, *Theology* I, 12.2, 127.

[241] We might wonder whether, behind this way of speaking, there really is a formula which contains the title *Lord*, and not one which contains some other title. In view of the variety of churches, each in its particular environment, this possibility must be considered. But for the Hellenistic Gentile church, upon which Paul depends directly for his linguistic usage, and for the Pauline churches a formula containing *Lord* is certainly the most probable. A clear indication of this is the fact that wherever *onoma* occurs in the Pauline writings the title *Lord* appears with it.

[242] Cf. Heitmüller, *Im Namen Jesu* 93.

[243] Acts 10.48; 2.38 (with ἐπί and dative). Neither passage contains the title *Lord*; both speak only of the name of Jesus Christ. James 2.7 speaks of 'that honourable name by which you are called' (τὸ ἐπικληθὲν ἐφ' ὑμᾶς), which proves that a christological title was pronounced over the candidate in baptism. Which title it was is regrettably not clear. For evidence from the post-NT period see Heitmüller, *Im Namen Jesu* 91f.

candidate a specific christological title.[244] We may take it as certain
that the title *Lord* was used in this way in the immediately pre-
Pauline and in the Pauline church, to judge from its use in I Cor.
6.11. Of course we must admit that the *onoma*-formulae which
actually only described the event came to be used directly as
baptismal formulae at a very early date. But this is still to be
judged a departure from original usage.

In the context it is appropriate to note that Paul also speaks of
baptism 'into the name', though admittedly only in the negative,
cautionary sense that the Corinthians had not been baptized
'into the name of Paul'.[245] Since this phrase is also found in
Acts,[246] it is obviously well established.[247] For our present
purpose we may defer the question whether there is any difference
between baptism εἰς and baptism ἐν or ἐπί,[248] or whether these are
variants of no consequence which result rather from the impre-
cisions of *Koine* usage than from different backgrounds of thought.
What matters for us is that these phrases show that in the Pauline
sphere the title *Lord* was named at baptism.

d. These observations serve to throw light on the description
of Christians as 'those who call on the name of our Lord Jesus
Christ'.[249] This phrase goes back to the LXX passage, Joel 3.5
(= Hebrew 2.32), which is also quoted verbatim at Rom. 10.13.
The reference in v. 9 to the *homologia* and the entire movement of
thought in vv. 11–13 make it clear that the title *Lord* applies here
to Jesus and not to God.[250] Similar passages in Acts[251] prove that
the phrase is not limited to the personal vocabulary of Paul
himself but represents a technical term common among Christians.

[244] The fact that the baptismal formulae of the Church to this day speak of the
name of Jesus, or of the name of the Father, of the Son, and of the Holy Spirit is due
to their being, at bottom, quotations of Matt. 28.19—the command to baptize—and
so they are not strictly 'baptismal formulae' but a description of them.
[245] I Cor. 1.13, 15.
[246] Acts 8.16; 19.5, in each case with *Lord Jesus*. Cf. Herm. *vis.* III 7.3, also with
the title *Lord.*
[247] The trinitarian command to baptize in Matt. 28.19 also has εἰς. *Did.* 7.1, 3 must
be regarded as a quotation of this passage.
[248] Cf. Heitmüller, *Im Namen Jesu* 127. A different view is taken by Bietenhard,
TWNT V 274.21–275.24, who derives the phrase εἰς ὄνομα from the Heb. *lᵉšēm*, but
this derivation is highly improbable.
[249] I Cor. 1.2.
[250] Michel, *Römer* 228f. *ad loc.*, agrees with this.
[251] Acts 2.21 (literal quotation of Joel); 9.14, 21; 22.16 (description of Christians,
and so the title is replaced by a personal pronoun). Similarly James 2.7; Herm. *sim.*
VIII 6.4; cf. Schweizer, *Erniedrigung* 7b, n. 320.

This observation is reinforced by the pre-Pauline custom of applying to Jesus the title *Kyrios* which replaced the tetragram at public readings of the LXX in the synagogue.[252]

Since in Rom. 10.12, 13, 14 the phrase is related to the acclamation, we shall not go wrong if we regard this as a typical example of 'calling upon the name of the Lord'. From this initial use, the phrase came to be applied to other characteristic activities of the Church such as baptism, expulsion and others of which we can no longer get any clear idea from the texts. All these take place in the worship of the Church, but they are different from the common prayers, for these are addressed to God.[253]

Thus ἐπικαλεῖσθαι means to pronounce the title *Lord* in connection with particular actions within worship. The *onoma*-formula is a way of paraphrasing this.[254]

e. One more instance of the use of *onoma* within the Pauline corpus remains to be examined, i.e. I Cor. 1.10. Here Paul appeals 'by (διά) the name of our Lord Jesus Christ'. The sentence could stand just as well if 'name' were omitted, as corresponding passages in I Thess. 4.2 and Rom. 15.30 show. But this makes it probable that there is a connection with the passages we discussed earlier. To appeal 'by the *Lord*' or 'by his name' means no doubt that the appeal is accompanied by an invocation of this *Lord* which emphasizes one's relationship with him. If this is correct, then it becomes clear that these *dia*-phrases ('by the name . . .') and expressions with ἐν ὀνόματι ('in the name . . .') belong together, for a characteristic activity in the life of the Church, in this instance exhortation, is linked with the naming of the *Lord*. Even with exhortation of this kind we are still in the domain of worship, for it is in worship that such exhortation has its proper setting.[255]

In I Cor. 15.57; Rom. 7.24[256] *thanksgiving to God* is qualified by

---

[252] We found a similar application to Jesus of a LXX reference to God in Phil. 2.10, though there the title *Kyrios* was not used. For a more exact dating of such application of LXX phraseology see 43bc below.

[253] Cf. Bultmann, *Theology* I, 12.2, 125f.

[254] Thus our view of the overall picture accords, too, with Heitmüller's findings. See note 237.

[255] Dahl, 'Formgeschichtliche Beobachtungen zur Christusverkündigung in der Gemeindepredigt', *Ntl Stud*, 1957, 8, regards the genuine *dia*-formula as having its proper setting in preaching which is addressed to the local congregation.

[256] In I Cor. 15.57 it is admittedly not certain which phrase the *dia*-formula actually qualifies. On the analogy of Rom. 7.24 it could qualify the thanksgiving, but its position in the sentence suggests that we must take it with the phrase 'who gives us the victory'.

this same phrase, 'through our Lord Jesus Christ'. It is typical that the key word *onoma* does not appear here, for Paul is not discoursing about thanks which are to be offered in the name of the *Lord*, but is actually giving thanks whilst invoking the *Lord* by means of the *dia*-phrase. So we may conclude: 1. that in the *dia*-phrase we have yet another expression in which the *Lord* was named; and 2. that this phrase, too, suggests a setting in worship. Obviously this is only one way in which the *dia*-phrase was used. We shall turn to other uses directly. But as we do so, we leave behind us the close connection which we have been able to follow between the *dia*-phrase and the key word *onoma*. But first we must summarize our findings so far.

18. Summary

a. We began our investigation with the acclamation, because in the Pauline writings it is one of the clearly defined settings of the title *Lord*, which are distinguishable by their literary form.

b. It appears that to call this acclamation a *homologia*, as we have done, is quite appropriate, because in Pauline and non-Pauline writings alike this key word has repeatedly led us to the acclamation. We have discovered that only in the Pauline sphere, and in the period immediately before him or contemporary with him does the acclamation include the title *Lord*. Elsewhere we find *Son of God* (in the Johannine writings) or *Christ* (in Acts). This means that our result is on the one hand somewhat limited, but that on the other hand it does hold good for the church on which Paul was dependent for his terminology.

c. The key word *onoma*, which though not originally linked with the *homologia* nevertheless came to be associated with it at an early date, as in the hymn at Phil. 2.6–11 (and not as a result of Pauline usage), brought us into contact with certain characteristic activities within the life of the church, some of which were explicitly mentioned, while others could be inferred at least in general terms, but all capable of being included under the general heading, 'calling upon the *Lord*'. This means that in the course of all these activities in the life of the church the *Lord* was named. Among these activities were included baptism, expulsion from the church, exhortation, and thanksgiving to God. We found that in general the phrase 'the name of the Lord' occurs when what has been or is to be done is talked about or referred to indirectly. But when the invocation is made directly, as in the acclamation or in thanksgiving to God, the descriptive and paraphrasing *onoma* is absent. Although this observation holds good for the earliest period, nevertheless the abundance of stereotype *onoma*-phrases shows that even in the NT period they had come to be woven into, or quoted in, many passages in which they replaced direct invocation of the Lord. From that point onwards they rank as a kind of invocation themselves.

Where *onoma* occurs in a christological sense within the Paulines it is accompanied by the title *Lord* (combined with *Jesus* or *Jesus Christ*).[257] This is invariably the case, and it shows how Paul, following earlier church usage, understood the *onoma* to be the title *Lord*. This usage is continued in the deutero-Paulines, i.e. II Thess., Col., Eph.,[258] and in the Pastorals,[259] all of which belong to the Pauline school. In Acts, too, we find from time to time a similar usage,[260] but there the phrase 'the name of *Jesus Christ*'[261] appears alongside others. The Johannine writings, on the other hand, speak of 'the name of the *Son of God*'.[262] These variations help us to evaluate correctly what we find in the Pauline material.

d. All the activities of the Church with which we find the *onoma*-phrase associated in the Paulines point to a setting in worship. So the title *Lord*, no doubt, will originally have signified the 'Lord of the cult', the Lord of the Church. But the hymn Phil. 2.6–11 shows how early the 'Lord of the cult' came to be understood as the Lord of the cosmos. The heavenly powers acclaim the Lord of the cosmos at his enthronement.[263] The Church, too, acclaims the Lord of the cosmos by reciting the

[257] Rom. 1.5 is no exception to this, for we cannot tell for certain which noun the pronoun replaces. At all events it follows a phrase containing *Lord*, though admittedly there is no connection here with *onoma*.
[258] II Thess. 1.12; 3.6; Col. 3.17; Eph. 5.20.
[259] II Tim. 2.22. In 2.19 it must refer also to *Jesus*.
[260] Acts 9.28 speaks of preaching boldly in the name of the *Lord*; in 15.26 and 21.13 the idea of martyrdom appears; 19.13, 17 speak of exorcism and praise. The use of *onoma* in instances like this is one which we have not previously found in the Paulines.
[261] Acts 3.6; 4.10; 16.18 (exorcism); 8.12; 9.27; 26.9 (preaching or persecution).
[262] E.g. John 3.18; I John 5.13 (as the object of faith—cf. I John 3.23).
[263] With Käsemann, 'Phil. 2.5–11' 85.

hymn at its worship. We ought not to pose questions here which demand too clear-cut a choice between the two ideas. Certainly it is the Lord of the cosmos who is acclaimed, but since his status as Lord is not plainly apparent to all, it is acknowledged by the Church *sub specie fidei* as it acclaims him as Lord in its worship.

e. In attempting to summarize the principal features of the ideas which underlie the term *Lord* we run up against the difficulty that the title is nowhere introduced with any explanation or description of what is meant by it. Its meaning is simply pre-supposed. What the Church has in mind when it names the *Lord* can only be inferred from its behaviour and from its expectations.

The first thing to say about this is that the Church acknow-ledges him as the *Lord* by acclaiming him, which means that the Church is aware of his exalted status. This exalted status of the *Lord* is 'confessed' by the Church in a way which suggests that its awareness of his status is not of a merely theoretical kind. The confession is expressed and enacted in acclamation (with adora-tion). The acclamation is in no sense provisional but has absolute validity; that is to say that the *Lord*, in the eyes of the Church, has a standing which is absolute, unconditional. The acclamation takes place in worship—to this extent the *Lord* is certainly 'Lord of the cult'. But his status is not confined to that, for as soon as one thinks of the world, one must stress that he is Lord over that also.

But the Church does not only confess the *Lord's* status as one of honour. He also has, in consequence, a status which is one of power, and the Church lays claim to that power. The power of the *Lord* is claimed in baptism, in expulsion, in exorcism, against negative powers and influences. Appeal is made to this power of the *Lord* when God, too, is addressed in thanksgiving, in baptism and in worship generally. We need not concern ourselves here with the religious and historical background of all this. Heitmüller seems to be on the right lines in this respect.[264]

To what extent this background is 'magical', or to what extent it has been 'sublimated' in the various strata of tradition with which we are dealing, is not a matter of any interest to us here. What matters is simply that the *Lord* has a power of a kind to which appeal can be made.

It is true that in a certain sense the *Lord* thus takes to himself the

[264] Heitmüller, *Im Namen Jesu* 128-222.

absolute status of God, in that he is 'God in his relation to the world'[265] or to the Church. But God is neither displaced nor absorbed by the *Lord*. The clearest expression of this is that thanksgiving is directed to God, not to the *Lord*.[266] The function of the *dia*-phrase is to preserve both the bond and the distinction between God and the *Lord*.

It is in the characteristic activities of the Church which take place in the concrete reality of its life in the present that the *Lord's* status of majesty and power over the cosmos and over the Church is authenticated. Indeed the Church's understanding of the title *Lord* is one which is limited, in temporal terms, to the present. What we mean by this statement will perhaps be clearer if we add that in all the pre-Pauline passages containing the title *Lord* which we have examined so far there has been no mention either of the saving events of the past[267] or of the parousia.

This does not mean that the immediately pre-Pauline church did not know of such events, for they would certainly have formed part of the traditional material known to that church. What it does mean is that there were elements of tradition which originally were not in any way connected with these events, and which do not have to be postulated, for they can be identified by their literary form. Evidence that these elements of tradition have a particular character and content of their own is the fact that in every instance they are associated with the title *Lord*.

f. Naturally, from the passages we have examined it is not possible to reach a plain and unambiguous solution to the problem of the origin of the title *Lord* as applied to Jesus. Certainly we found nothing to suggest that it originated in the early Aramaic-speaking church. Indeed, the absence of ideas about the parousia or about the saving events (including the 'exaltation') makes it highly unlikely that the title *Lord* and the ideas associated with it could have originated in that church.

[265] Käsemann, 'Phil. 2.5–11', 85.

[266] It is appropriate to mention here that the prayers of the Church are always addressed to God and not to the *Lord*. Cf. Bultmann, *Theology* I, 12.2, 126.

[267] This is true even if we include among these the event which was regarded as the exaltation of Jesus. This is not contradicted by the hymn at Phil. 2.6–11, for the exaltation to which the hymn witnesses comes from the pattern of humiliation and exaltation which underlies the hymn, and not from the *Lord*-concept. It is true that the title *Lord* and the acclamation were associated at an early date with the pattern of humiliation and exaltation which we find in the hymn, but nevertheless the association is basically a secondary one. On this, see 27f. below.

Concerning the possibility that the title and the concept of *Lord* might have been derived from the title used at the public reading of the LXX,[268] we must allow that in pre-Pauline times LXX texts had already come to be applied to Jesus as *Kyrios*. We cannot be certain whether Greek-speaking Jewish Christians or Gentile Christians were responsible for this.[269] But in either case this development took place on Hellenistic soil. Certainly this was the environment in which the *Kyrios*-title was current, for it was applied to cult deities of every kind. This situation suggests that it is inherently unlikely that the title derives from the LXX. It would be better to assume that it comes from Hellenism, but that at an early date LXX texts were applied to the *Lord*. This is a sketch of the development suggested by such examples of pre-Pauline usage as are available for examination. We can only judge whether we are on the right lines when we have obtained further material on which to resolve the question.

B. OTHER PRE-PAULINE SETTINGS OF THE TITLE *LORD*

19. Διά-phrases

a. Before we may assume that *dia*-phrases really were a pre-Pauline setting of the title *Lord*, we must be clear on the following points:
1. We must show that *dia*-phrases containing *Lord*, as against those containing simply *Christ (Jesus)* or a pronoun, are primary.
2. We must show that the *dia*-phrases containing *Lord* are clearly used as formulae.
3. Wherever possible, we ought to be able to find a connection between the *dia*-phrases and the passages already examined.

In order to examine the *dia*-phrases from these three points of view it is necessary to make a list of all the material within the Pauline corpus in which *dia* is linked with any of the christological titles. That is the purpose of the following table.

[268] We know that the tetragram still stood in the LXX at that time. Cf. Schulz, *Komposition und Herkunft der Johanneischen Reden*, 1960, 3f.
[269] On this, see 43bc.

In the Paulines we find 26 *dia*-phrases linked with *Christ*,[270] divisible into the following types according to their form:

1. 'through our Lord Jesus Christ' (5 times)[271]
2. 'through Jesus Christ our Lord' (twice)[272]
3. 'through the Lord Jesus' (once)[273]
4. 'through Jesus Christ' (4 times)[274]
5. 'through Christ Jesus' (once)[275]
6. 'through Christ' (3 times)[276]
7. 'through Jesus' (once)[277]
8. 'through him' (3 times)[278]
9. 'through whom' (5 times)[279]
10. 'through him who loved us' (once) [280]

The phase 'through the *Lord*' does not occur.

b. Clearly Paul formulates the expressions containing pronouns in an *ad hoc* fashion as a rule, though even in instances where for rhetorical purposes he rings the changes between various prepositional phrases[281] he is still really drawing on traditional formulations. But these are formulations which have nothing to do with the title *Lord*. Phrase 10 in the above list need not concern us here, either, for it, too, is a particular formulation of Paul's own creation. The same goes for I Thess. 4.14b ('through Jesus'), for *Jesus* is there an insertion echoing v. 14a. On the same grounds the phrase 'through the Lord Jesus' in I Thess. 4.2 can be excluded, for we meet precisely the same combination of christological titles in I Thess. 3.11, 13; 4.1. Finally, the same argument tells against the originality of the expression 'through Christ' in II Cor. 5.18 (cf. vv. 14, 17, 19, 20), and the same, with article, in II Cor. 1.5b (cf. v. 5a). This suggests that the same expression in II Cor. 3.4 cannot be taken to represent the original *dia*-phrase either.

Thus there remain only the two expressions containing *Lord*

[270] For their occurrence in the deutero-Paulines and in other parts of the NT see the list in Schettler, *Die paulinische Formel 'durch Christus'*, 1907, 9.
[271] I Thess. 5.9; I Cor. 15.57; Rom. 5.1, 11; 15.30.
[272] (In the closing sentence of the chapter in question) Rom. 5.21; 7.25. Cf. the closing sentence in Rom. 6.8, 'in Jesus Christ our Lord'.
[273] I Thess. 4.2 (cf. v. 1, 'in the Lord Jesus').
[274] Gal. 1.1; Rom. 1.8; 5.17 ('through the one Jesus Christ'); Phil. 1.11.
[275] Rom. 2.16. [276] II Cor. 1.5; 3.4 (with article); 5.18 (without article).
[277] I Thess. 4.14. [278] I Cor. 8.6; II Cor. 1.20; Rom. 5.9.
[279] I Cor. 8.6; Gal. 6.14; Rom. 1.5; 5.2, 11.
[280] Rom. 8.37.
[281] E.g. I Cor. 8.6 (see 22f. below); II Cor. 1.20.

with the full christological titles, and the phrase 'through Jesus Christ' or 'through Christ Jesus'. We must decide the relative originality of each of these.

It would be practically impossible to reach a decision here, were it not that another observation comes to our aid. In three instances the wording 'through Jesus Christ' is the only reading,[282] and it is also the best attested reading at Rom. 5.17, while at Rom. 2.16 it is difficult to decide which reading is to be preferred.[283] The order 'Jesus Christ' is contrary to Pauline usage, for his custom is to place *Christos* first when the double title occurs in the genitive and in the dative,[284] because only with *Christos* is it possible to distinguish clearly between genitive and dative.[285] Paul uses the same order in prepositional phrases also.[286] But the *dia*-phrases are a marked exception.

This makes it very clear that in *dia*-phrases Paul follows a word order which was already well established. We would be wrong to conclude that this gives us the earliest pre-Pauline form of the *dia*-phrase, for it tells us only what the word order was in cases where the *dia*-phrase contained the double title *Jesus Christ*. But the same word order is found, too, in the phrase which occurs 5 times, 'through our Lord Jesus Christ' (διὰ τοῦ κυρίου ἡμῶν Ἰησοῦ Χριστοῦ), and here the reasons for this word order are obvious. The original word order, going back ultimately to the Aramaic word order *yᵉšūaʿ mᵉšīḥā*, did not need to be reversed, because the initial *Kyrios* made sufficiently clear the particular case intended. A reason for not altering the word order was that if this were done in every instance, *Christos*, which in its original significance as a title conflicted with the title *Kyrios*, would have followed immediately upon κύριος ἡμῶν.

Because this full *dia*-formula containing *Lord* was used relatively frequently, the word order tended to become fixed and was preserved even in formulations in which *Lord* did not appear. Thus it is probable that the phrase 'through Jesus Christ' goes

[282] Gal. 1.12; Rom. 1.8; Phil. 1.11.
[283] The Nestle text gives only διὰ Χριστοῦ Ἰησοῦ here.
[284] Thence also in the accusative.
[285] Cf. Lietzmann, *Römer*, Excursus on Rom. 1.1, p. 23. See 61bc below.
[286] Once ὑπὸ Χριστοῦ Ἰησοῦ (Phil. 3.12); 28 times ἐν Χριστῷ Ἰησοῦ (see n. 503 below); against this, ἐν Ἰησοῦ Χριστῷ occurs once (Gal. 3.14); the phrase, εἰς Χριστὸν Ἰησοῦν occurs twice (Gal. 2.16b; Rom. 6.3); and κατὰ Χριστὸν Ἰησοῦν once (Rom. 15.5). In several passages the word order is not absolutely certain.

back to the older formula 'through our Lord Jesus Christ'. Hence the phrase 'through Jesus Christ our Lord' is to be regarded as a variation of that formula.

c. In view of these conclusions, our primary task now is to examine the way in which the full formula containing *Lord* was used. The texts suggest that the formula 'through our Lord Jesus Christ' was used in two ways. In the first place it is associated with specific activities in the life of the Church such as 'exhorting the brethren',[287] 'rejoicing in God',[288] and 'giving thanks to God'.[289] In the second place the formula is used to qualify the benefits of salvation, such as peace,[290] or salvation,[291] or victory.[292]

The variant form, 'through Jesus Christ our Lord', is used in the same two ways, for it, too, appears on the one hand in connection with thanksgiving to God[293] and on the other hand in connection with the blessings of salvation generally.[294] There is no doubt that the first use reflects the language of worship,[295] but this cannot be said to the same extent of the second. It is quite certain that in the passages we have mentioned the phrase is used in the manner of a formula.

A comparison of Rom. 5.21; 7.25a with Rom. 6.23; 8.39 makes this plain. Each of the four verses is the closing verse in its chapter. In two instances we find the *dia*-phrase, and in the other two an *en*-formula with exactly the same word order. In each case the formula comes at the end, without precise definition, and so is not to be subjected to too rigorous a theological interpretation.

Only in Rom. 7.25a, where the theme is thanksgiving to God, would it be difficult to interchange the *en*-formulae and the *dia*-formulae. In the other three passages which speak of the benefits of salvation the formulae would be easily interchangeable.

[287] Rom. 15.30; cf. I Thess. 4.2, where in similar circumstances the formula is abbreviated to correspond with 'the Lord Jesus' in v. 1.
[288] Rom. 5.11.
[289] I Cor. 15.57 (if the phrase is taken to relate here to thanksgiving, as at Rom. 7.25a, rather than to the gift of victory).
[290] Rom. 5.1.
[291] I Thess. 5.9.
[292] I Cor. 15.57 (see n. 289).
[293] Rom. 7.25a.
[294] Rom. 5.21.
[295] In the case of thanksgiving and exhortation this is evident. But it is also true of 'rejoicing' (καύχησις). In this respect Bousset, *Jesus der Herr*, 1916, 56, and *Kyrios Christos*, ed. 2, 1921, 109, is right, though his reference to Phil. 3.3f. affects nothing. On this, see Lietzmann, *Römer* 60 (on Rom. 5.11), and Michel, 119f. (on the same passage).

But we may not assume from this that the *en*-formula was used side by side with the *dia*-formula from the beginning. The *en*-formula in its various manifestations has all the appearances of being Paul's own creation,[296] whereas the *dia*-formula clearly reproduces pre-Pauline usage. We may defer here the question whether the *en*-formula arose as an alternative to the *dia*-formula.

d. For two reasons it is likely that the *dia*-phrase was originally associated with liturgical activities of the Church and only later appeared in formulations concerned with the blessings of salvation. For in its first use the *dia*-phrase goes hand in hand with the phrase 'through the name of our Lord Jesus Christ'[297] and with *onoma*-expressions generally.[298] The *dia*-phrases actually accomplish what is spoken of in these passages, for where they are used in any particular activity of the assembled church they give to that activity a particular character, for in them the title *Lord* is spoken. This underlines our observation that the *dia*-formula used thus had its original setting in worship.

The second reason is that *dia*-phrases which do not contain the title *Lord* are not used in this way. They all qualify the 'blessings of salvation', though the phrase 'fruits (or blessings) of salvation' is now no longer a sufficiently large category to contain all the passages in which such *dia*-phrases occur. This shows that with time the use of the *dia*-phrase moved further and further away from its original setting. The direction which this development took is an indirect argument in favour of what we have outlined as its original setting.

e. If we ask what were the ideas which lay behind this original *dia*-phrase, we find that the passages of exhortation prove that there is no idea of any 'high priestly activity' on the part of the exalted one, informing God or perhaps another church of one church's particular wishes or concerns. If, at particular liturgical activities, the *Lord* is involved by means of the *dia*-phrase, this means that an appeal is being made to his power. Or to put this in terms of grammar, the *dia*-formula has causal, not instrumental, significance.[299]

[296] See 36 and 50a below.
[297] Cf. especially Rom. 15.30 with I Cor. 1.10, where both times the word παρακαλεῖν appears. See 17e.
[298] See 17 above.
[299] Schettler, *Die Paulinische Formel 'durch Christus'*, 61f., rightly emphasizes this.

Since the regular liturgical activities in the life of the Church take place within the confines of the present, it is natural that the *Lord* is presented primarily in terms of the present. It is now, in the present, that claims can be made upon his position of power and authority. Nowhere are the reasons for this power and authority made clear. Saving acts like resurrection or exaltation do not come within sight.[300] The *Lord's* lordship is simply presupposed.

All the *dia*-phrases which contain *Lord* also contain 'our'. The only exception is I Thess. 4.2, 'through the Lord Jesus'. But since in the Pauline corpus the title *Lord* more often appears without 'our', it seems natural to infer that the two expressions, 'the *Lord*' and 'our *Lord Jesus (Christ)*', either represent two different stages of tradition or else have two different points of origin.[301] It is too early yet to determine the relationship between forms with and forms without 'our', or between those with full titles and those with only *Lord* on its own. We can only do that when we have had an opportunity of reviewing the entire range of the forms and phrases which occur.[302]

f. At this point, however, we may list the following conclusions:

1. The phrase 'through our Lord Jesus Christ' is to be regarded as the earliest pre-Pauline *dia*-formula.

2. It was originally used as a formula in worship. It expressed the particular character of the activities of the Church which were associated with worship, for it served as a particular means of invoking the *Lord*.

3. It is obvious that in essence the *dia*-formula is closely connected with the expressions in which *onoma* occurs.

4. In its subsequent development the *dia*-formula takes another

---

Certainly he is sometimes too systematic and says that the phrase is causal even in places where, as a result of progressive blurring of the original meaning, it is used instrumentally, as at II Cor. 5.18 (cf. v. 19) which is a formulation of the saving events. (This is against Schettler's exposition, 21f.)

[300] This only happens when the title *Lord* comes to be used in formulations which list the fruits of salvation. See n. 299.

[301] The expression 'our Lord . . .' is often regarded as an echo of Jewish or oriental usage, because there the addition of the suffix is normal. Cf. Cerfaux, *Christ* 464 n. 10. *Kyrios* without 'our' would correspond to Greek usage, and thus within Christian terminology would be more recent. See 67.

[302] See 66 and 67.

direction. At quite an early stage it came to be used to qualify the blessings of salvation (i.e. peace, victory, etc.), and it is then used increasingly in this capacity, while the christological titles included in it vary according to the context. Thus in the end the formula can describe God's operation, through Christ, in the saving events.

5. All that we can discover from the *dia*-formula about the actual meaning of the term *Lord* is that his status of power and authority is simply presupposed. The *Lord* is a power in the present, for it is in the present, in the activities of the Church at worship, that his might and authority are appealed to.

This understanding of *Lord* is precisely what we found in the acclamation and in expressions containing the words ὁμολογεῖν and ὄνομα.[303] So we cannot fail to see that in substance the *dia*-phrase is related to these other expressions.

20. The Farewell Formula

a. The farewell formula in the Pauline epistles[304] is largely stereotype and runs as follows: 'The grace of the (our) Lord Jesus Christ be with you (or, with your spirits, or, with you all)'.[305] The mere fact that the form is stereotype does not give us sufficient grounds for deciding definitely whether the farewell formula is traditional pre-Pauline material or a Pauline formulation. But in I Cor. 16.20b it appears that sentences of liturgical type are present, sentences which originally marked the transition from the gathering together of the congregation to the beginning of the Lord's Supper.[306] We may suppose that Paul quoted these words at the end of his letters because he knew that they would be read in the church before the Lord's Supper began. They are of liturgical

---

[303] See 18e.

[304] I Thess. 5.28; I Cor. 16.23; II Cor. 13.13; Gal. 6.18; Rom. 16.20; Philemon 25. Koine, Claramontanus and Itala transfer Rom. 16.20 to a position after v. 23, so that a similarly worded v. 24 has arisen.

[305] Cf. the complete list in Roller, *Das Formular der paulinischen Briefe*, 1933, Appendix, table 4.

[306] This was already indicated by Lietzmann, *Messe und Herrenmahl*, 3rd ed., 1955, 229 (ET: *Mass and Lord's Supper*, 1953, 186ff.). Bornkamm, 'Das Anathema in der urchristlichen Abendmahlsliturgie', *Das Ende des Gesetzes*, 1958, 123, makes it completely clear by specifying the liturgical elements: 1. A summons to the kiss of peace; 2. *anathema*; 3. *Maranatha*; 4. 'the grace of the Lord Jesus . . .'

type and close with 'the grace'. Thus 'the grace' becomes the actual farewell formula at the end of his letters and is regularly used as such.[307]

We are fortunate in being able to verify these observations by referring to Rev. 22.17–21. It is probable that these verses, too, are associated with the Lord's Supper.[308] They also conclude with the phrase 'the grace of the Lord Jesus be with you all', and at the same time they form the conclusion of the whole book. Both in form and in content the similarity with the Pauline conclusion is complete.

This proves that the farewell formula is of pre-Pauline liturgical origin.[309] The fact that we find it in various forms cannot annul this judgment, for liturgical sentences did indeed have a stamp of their own, but their precise wording was not canonically fixed, and so within certain limits could be varied.

b. The relative constancy with variability which we find in these formulae suggests: 1. that obviously in the farewell formula there is no difference in meaning between the variants with or without 'our' and those with or without 'Christ'. 'Our Lord Jesus', 'our Lord Jesus Christ' and 'the Lord Jesus Christ' are used here indiscriminately without any difference in meaning. 2. But all have to do with 'the grace of the *Lord*'. The *Lord* is the author, the dispenser of this grace,[310] and he stands in relation to the Church as the one who disposes the gifts of salvation. The grace of the *Lord* is not just something that was possible in the past or will be possible in the future, but a reality which holds good in the present relationship between the *Lord* and the Church.[311]

Proof that this interpretation is on the right lines is found in the three-part formula at II Cor. 13.14, where the second part runs exactly parallel to the first and speaks of the 'love of God'.

This double formula of exact parallels is extended by means of a third member which is not exactly parallel to the other two in so

[307] The liturgical origin of these words explains why Paul's farewell formula differs both in form and content from ancient practice. Cf. Roller, *Formular* 69f. and nn. 321–4.

[308] Thus Bornkamm, 'Anathema' 126f. Lohmeyer, *Die Offenbarung des Johannes*, 1953, 179.f, *ad loc.*, speaks of a 'situation in worship' and of a 'letter ending' which was originally a 'liturgical ending'.

[309] Philemon 25 provides final confirmation of this, for 'the grace' is addressed to 'you' (plural), although the preceding verses are addressed to Philemon only.

[310] The genitive κυρίου is subjective.

[311] Cf. Rom. 5.21 (which is, of course, Pauline).

far as the 'Holy Spirit' is not the dispenser but is himself a gift of salvation, i.e. the Spirit corresponds, at bottom, to 'grace' and 'love' in the first two parts. Since the expression 'the fellowship (κοινωνία) of the Holy Spirit' means 'participation in the Holy Spirit',[312] thus failing to maintain the congruence of the first two members, we may suppose that this third one was added only after the first two had already been joined. Hence we could say that the two-part formula is pre-Pauline, whereas the extension to three parts is to be attributed to Paul himself,[313] but we cannot be sure about this.

c. 1. If we ask what the farewell formula can tell us about the understanding of the term *Lord*, we may say that the *Lord* here appears as one who in the present moment stands in relation to the Church as the dispenser of the blessings of salvation. Since we have shown that the formula is liturgical, we may add that it is primarily in worship that men are aware of being confronted by the *Lord*. These three features—the setting in worship, confrontation by the dispenser of the benefits of salvation, and the reference to a present state of affairs—all make it plain that here we have an understanding of *Lordship* which historically is directly linked with Hellenistic ideas.

2. Accordingly the sentences in the form in which we found them in I Cor. 16.20–23 belong to the Lord's Supper liturgy of the Hellenistic Christian church, even though particular elements, pre-eminently for example the originally eschatological cry *Maranatha*,[314] go back ultimately to the early Aramaic-speaking church.

3. Thus we may take it that the title *Lord* in the farewell formula of the Pauline letters belongs to the same background of ideas as the *homologia* and the *onoma*-phrases as we find them in the Paulines. The fact that the title *Lord* does not stand simply on its own but is linked with the name *Jesus* (*Christ*) and occasionally with 'our' is due to the tendency in liturgical passages to include weightier phrases and titles for the sake of solemnity.[315]

---

[312] So Lietzmann and Kümmel, *Korinther* 162 *ad loc.*; cf. 214 and the literature listed there. Schweizer, *TWNT* VI 432. 20–33 (ET, *Spirit of God*, 1960, 83f.), takes the genitive as subjective, by analogy with the preceding phrase. According to Schweizer, it makes no essential difference whether the genitive is subjective or objective.
[313] Cf. Phil. 3.10; Philemon 6; I Cor. 1.9.
[314] See 23.
[315] See n. 301 above.

d. It is significant that in the deutero-Paulines and Pastoral epistles the farewell formula differs from that of the genuine Paulines. II Thess. 3.18 conforms, but elsewhere the title *Lord* and the other christological titles are entirely absent, and 'the grace' occurs alone and unqualified. Thus in these writings the farewell formula runs either as 'Grace be with you'[316] or as 'Grace be with you all'.[317] This absolute use of the term indicates a tendency to change earlier usage, a tendency which can be observed also in connection with other key words.[318]

21. God, the Father of the Lord Jesus Christ

a. Three times within the Pauline corpus God is called 'the Father of the (our) Lord Jesus (Christ)',[319] twice in the course of thanksgiving, once in a summons to doxology. Similar passages in the non-Paulines[320] confirm that the phrase does in fact have its fixed place in thanksgiving.

This stereotype use shows that the phrase is really a formula which Paul took over together with its original setting.[321]

Now there is no doubt that 'eulogy', 'eucharist' and 'doxology' all come from Judaism, where they were in use as *berakah* or *hodayah*.[322] These forms, thus taken over, represent a connection with the language of the synagogue or of the pious Jew, and the same is to be said of the use of the title 'Father'. The designation of God as the Father of the Lord Jesus (Christ) is of course a formulation of the Christian, indeed of the Hellenistic Gentile Christian, church. This is clearly true of the complete phrase 'the Father of our Lord Jesus Christ', for it was only in the Hellenistic environment that *Jesus Christ* came to be simply a double name.[323]

[316] Col. 4.18; I Tim. 6.21, II Tim. 4.22.

[317] Titus 3.15. Eph. 6.24 defines 'all' as those who love our Lord Jesus Christ with love undying. Heb. 13.25 has the same phrase as Titus.

[318] E.g. 'love': I Tim. 2.15; 4.12; II Tim. 2.22; Titus 2.2. 'Service': I Tim. 1.12; II Tim. 4.11.

[319] II Cor. 1.3; 11.31; Rom. 15.6. Only II Cor. 11.31 lacks 'our' and 'Christ'.

[320] Eph. 1.3; I Peter 1.3; cf. Col. 1.3, where in a similar context the word εὐχαριστεῖν is added. But *eulogia* and *eucharistia* are closely related and in the NT period are used as alternatives.

[321] Schrenk, *TWNT* V 1009.24–32, evidently considers it to be a Pauline formulation.

[322] Cf. Beyer, *TWNT* II 762.1–31; J. M. Robinson, 'Heilsgeschichte und Lichtungsgeschichte', *EvTh* 22, 1962, section II.

[323] See 60.

Yet the shorter variant, too, at II Cor. 11.31 is not likely to have originated earlier, for the designation of God as 'the Father of the Lord' presupposes a time during which the title *Lord* must have been in common use, and when the question of the relationship between God and the *Lord* was already a live one.

Thus we regard this phrase as the work of the Hellenistic Gentile Christian church, which inserted into originally Jewish forms the title *Lord* to which it was accustomed, in order to define God by this means in christological terms.

b. For our understanding of the term *Lord*, we find that in the phrase 'God, the Father of our Lord Jesus Christ' God and the *Lord* are brought into relation with one another, for the designation 'Father' is a way of expressing this relationship. Certainly we must grant that the phrase came into being, not on the basis of theological reflection, but out of liturgical necessity. The aim was to give clear Christian expression to the designation 'Father' for God, to whom thanksgiving was addressed, and to bring this into relationship with the *Lord*. For when giving thanks to God one could not simply name the *Lord* side by side with God,[324] but had to find for God a designation which would express directly his relationship to the *Lord*. Thus the title 'Father' was chosen for God, and was used to describe his relationship with the *Lord Jesus Christ*. The effect of this was to bring *Lord* very close in meaning to the title *Son*.

Since the phrase speaks of the present relationship between God and the *Lord*, and not of the cause of this relationship, the understanding of the term *Lord* which it expresses is consonant with the understanding which we found in the preceding chapters, despite new features.

22. One Lord

a. But now we must check our findings against two other pre-Pauline formulae which at first sight seem to point beyond the confines of the present. We refer to the phrase *Marana tha* and to

---

[324] This was possible in the salutation at the beginning of the letters, because God and the Lord could be mentioned equally as dispensers of the blessings of salvation.

the formula εἰς κύριος on the other. We shall take the second one first.

In I Cor. 8.6 we read, '. . . one God, the Father,
from whom are all things, and for whom we (exist),
and one Lord Jesus Christ,
through whom are all things and through whom we (exist)'.
The exact parallelism is evidence that the piece is a formula which Paul has taken over. The aim of our investigation is to establish the range of meaning which the title *Lord* has in this formula. The answer appears to be immediately obvious: the *Lord* is the intermediary at creation and as such is pre-existent.[325] But we must be careful here, because on closer examination the formula shows signs of being the product of various elements and influences. Therefore we must make a careful analysis of its form, function and content, in order not to confuse the original content of the title *Lord* with meanings which have come to be added secondarily.

b. We begin our analysis with the expression εἰς Θεός. This is a technical term in the language of the mission to the Gentiles.[326] At this level it is used as a monotheistic formula against heathen polytheism. In this sense it is not specifically Christian, for it was used in exactly the same way as a propaganda formula in Jewish missionary activity.[327] Doubtless in terms of ideas there is a connection with the expression YHWH eḥād in the sheʿma of Deut. 6.4. But in terms of terminology the relationship is certainly not altogether clear. To be sure, the tetragram[328] is kept in the early LXX papyri,[329] but in public reading in the synagogue *Kyrios* was read. We may suppose that 'one God' was chosen as a link with the general designation of God which was customary in Greek. In any case, the formula, like the sheʿma, was used as an acclamation.[330] But acclamation before a forum is at the same time procla-

[325] Cf. Cullmann, *Confessions* 51f.
[326] Cf. I Cor. 8.4; Gal. 3.20; James 2.19; 4.12; cf. I Thess. 1.9; Heb. 6.1.
[327] See 10. Cf. Peterson, ΕΙΣ ΘΕΟΣ 216; Wissmann, *Verhältnis* 50–54. Corresponding texts of Jewish and Christian origin are printed in Seeberg, *Didache* 11 23. Dalbert, *Die Theologie der hellenistisch-jüdischen Missions-Literatur unter Ausschluss von Philo und Josephus*, 1954, 124–30, does indeed emphasize the monotheism of the missionary literature of Hellenistic Judaism, but he passes over the formula 'one God' completely, even though it is to be found in the *Sibylline Oracles* (Prol. 94 [= fr. 1.7f.]; III.11).
[328] Cf. Schulz, *Johanneische Reden*, 3f.; Schulz, 'Maranatha' 128–30.
[329] It is found also on amulets. See Peterson, *Theos* 290.
[330] Bousset, *Die Religion des Judentums im neutestamentlichen Zeitalter*, 1903, 169, calls it 'to some extent a confession'. But the rabbinical quotations given in his note 1

mation. As used in Jewish mission, the formula expresses opposition to or polemic against, polytheism.

In the Christian mission to the Gentiles, too, it keeps this sense. But a parallel formulation, 'one *Lord*' is introduced side by side with it. It is the addition of 'one Lord' which makes a formula which is Christian in character.

The parallelism of the two parts makes it clear that what has been said about the first member holds good also for the second, i.e. 'one Lord', in its original meaning, must be regarded as a formula of acclamation and proclamation. It is asserted in face of a world which knows 'many lords'. This means that the expression 'one Lord' must have originated in a Hellenistic environment.

c. This judgement is confirmed by a development of another kind. The enthronement of various oriental and Greek deities occurred with increasing frequency within Hellenism.[331] One example among many is that of Zeus-Serapis, for which there is plentiful epigraphic and literary evidence.[332] The formula, εἷς Ζεὺς Σέραπις, is encountered frequently. This and similar formulae originally are acclamatory in character, but as Peterson[333] shows they quickly take on apotropaic significance. On the other hand they are not to be understood in a thoroughly monotheistic sense, but rather as cultic expressions of monolatry. As confusion of deities advances there occur mixed formulae containing two or more members.[334] Peterson gives the instructive example of a graffito which gives the title *Lord*:

Εἷς Ζεὺς Σάραπις
μεγάλη Ἶσις ἡ κυρία.[335]

It is against this kind of background that the formula in I Cor. 8.6, 'one God the Father—one Lord Jesus Christ' is to be seen. It is a product of syncretism in the sense that it reveals a combination of 'one God', which goes back to Jewish usage, with the Hellenistic 'one Lord'. In character it is still very close to acclama-

---

about accepting the divine Lordship make it plain that 'acclamation' would be the more appropriate term here. Cf. Peterson, *Theos* 302.

[331] Cf. Kleinknecht, *TWNT* III 75.44–76.23.
[332] In Weinreich, *Neue Urkunden zur Serapis-Religion*, 1919, 24f., and further in Peterson, *Theos* 227–40.
[333] Peterson, *Theos* 158, 304 n. 1.   [334] *Ibid.* 253–56.   [335] *Ibid.* 230.

tion or proclamation, even though theological reflection has contributed to its present form, as we shall soon see.

d. An interesting observation of Peterson's[336] is that within Christianity εἷς κύριος is never found in inscriptions, though it is often found in the oriental liturgies, whereas εἷς θεός is very well attested. This shows how closely the title *Lord* is associated with liturgical functions. Even though clear evidence of this is only found in the period of the early Church, it may also be taken as an indication that in the NT period too the title *Lord* was closely associated with worship.

e. Thus the formula 'one God the Father—one Lord Jesus Christ' is to be seen as the result of a variety of religious and historical influences, having originated in a Hellenistic environment to be used as a formula in Christian mission and modelled on the Jewish formula εἷς θεός. Its liturgical associations and its similarity to the Hellenistic title *Kyrios* are obvious. So far we have not detected any trace of ideas about the *Lord's* mediation at creation or about his pre-existence. But now we must turn our attention to the expressions in I Cor. 8.6 which represent extensions of the formula.

f. God is described as the one 'from whom are all things and for whom we (exist)', and the *Lord* is described as the one 'through whom are all things and through whom we (exist)'. The connection with Rom. 11.36, 'from him and through him and to him (are) all things', is evident. But equally clear is the resemblance of both formulae to the Stoic Marcus Aurelius (IV 23): ὦ φύσις ἐκ σοῦ πάντα, ἐν σοὶ πάντα, εἰς σὲ πάντα.[337] As a Stoic phrase it is presumably of different origin from the phrase 'one God, one Lord'. Perhaps it came to be connected with 'one God' in Hellenistic Judaism,[338] where it would have been taken as a statement about the creation and goal of the world.

When εἷς κύριος was added, as a second part, to the εἷς θεός formula in the Greek-speaking Jewish or Gentile Christian church, the τὰ πάντα formula was inserted into the second part also, and was elaborated. First, ἡμεῖς (which is general in con-

---

[336] *Ibid.* 138.
[337] Cf. Norden, *Agnostos Theos*, 1913, 240–43; Lietzmann, *Römer* 107; Michel, *Römer* 255.
[338] Cf. Philo, *Spec. Leg.* I 208, where a similar formula is used in connection with an admittedly impersonal ἕν, purporting to be the origin and goal of all things.

fessional style) was added to both parts; and second, God is shown as the Creator of all things and the arbiter of men's destiny, while the *Lord* appears as the intermediary in the creation both of the universe and of the Church.

Thus it comes about that the Christians' *Lord* is understood as the intermediary in creation. This understanding has nothing to do with the original understanding of *Lord*. The figure of the intermediary at creation was known in Judaism as the divine *sophia*, though the roots of this idea doubtless lie outside Judaism.[339]

This means that God and the *Lord* are related to one another as the Creator and the intermediary at creation are related in Judaism. By picturing the relationship in this way, both the uniqueness of God, εἷς θεός, and his unity (in function) with the *Lord*, εἷς κύριος, are secured. In this respect Christianity has taken over conceptions which were prefigured in the theological reflection of Judaism. These conceptions were attached to the *Lord* precisely because that title was already in common use in the Christian Church, and because other religious developments at that time had made possible the combination of 'one God' with 'one *Lord*'. But originally *Lord* did not contain the idea of the intermediary at creation. The same is true of the idea which is not directly mentioned in our fomula but is implicit in the idea of the intermediary, namely his pre-existence. Of course the *Lord* is thought of in this passage as 'pre-existent'; but to be precise we should say that this can only happen when the role of intermediary at the creation has been transferred to him. In the present instance this happened as a result of ideas which originated in Stoicism. Neither the notion of pre-existence nor the idea of the intermediary at creation formed any part of the original understanding of the title *Lord*.

g. Paul and the Pauline church will have found ready to hand the formula which is given in I Cor. 8.6. It represents a linking of the title *Lord* with the idea of the pre-existent intermediary at creation. So we may assume that Paul and the Pauline church associated this idea with the title *Lord*, too. But this does not alter the fact that it is the result of a combination of originally separate elements, and therefore, by comparison with the connected series

[339] Wisd. 7.21. Cf. Prov. 8.22–31 (LXX). Further passages in E. Schweizer, *Erniedrigung* n. 414 (cf. *Lordship and Discipleship* 102).

of expressions κύριος 'Ιησοῦς, ὁμολογεῖν, and ὄνομα κυρίου and the meaning of the title *Lord* as we found it there, it is secondary.

So the formula in I Cor. 8.6 gives us only those elements in the original understanding of the term *Lord* which we listed under (e), i.e. that it originated in Hellenism and was used in worship. But these features confirm what we found when we examined the connected series of expressions mentioned above.

23. Maranatha?

a. The second pre-Pauline formula containing *Lord* which seems to point beyond the confines of the present is the prayer *Maranatha*. If it really does this—and it is often said that it does—then we should find that it was originally connected with the range of ideas in which *homologia* and *onoma* are rooted. The mere fact that *Mare* could be translated *Kyrios* in Greek is not in itself enough to prove such a connection.

Three principal passages are to be taken into consideration here:

I Cor. 16.22: 'If any one has no love for the Lord, let him be accursed. *Marana tha.* The grace of the Lord Jesus be with you.'

Didache 10.6: 'Let grace come, and let this world pass away. Hosanna to the son[340] of David. If anyone is holy, let him advance; if anyone is not, let him be converted. *Marana tha.* Amen.'

Rev. 22.20f.: 'He who testifies to these things says, "Surely I am coming soon." Amen. *Come, Lord Jesus!* The grace of the Lord Jesus be with (you) all.'

b. The general problems presented by this formula are well known. We may summarize them as follows:

1. The formula's language is ambiguous, for on the one hand it is not clear where the division comes, and on the other hand, even when the division has been made, the second word can have more than one meaning.[341]

340 With Lietzmann, *Herrenmahl* 237 (*Lord's Supper* 193). Against Dölger, *Sol salutis*, 1925, 208, who regards 'God' as the original, not 'son'.
341 The possibilities are listed and discussed by Kuhn, *TWNT* IV 471.18–473.12; Dölger, *Sol salutis* 200–2; Klein, 'Maranatha', *RGG*, 3rd ed., IV, 732.

We may reckon with the following possibilities:

i) *māranā thā*   = our Lord, come!
ii) *maran atha* 1) as *māran 'ethā* = our Lord, come!
                  2) as *māran 'athā* = our Lord came (perf.);
                          or our Lord is here (pres. perf.).[342]

2. So to decide what the meaning is we must be guided by the style and content of the immediate context. In all three instances this is of liturgical type. *Did.* 10.6 clearly belongs to the liturgy of the Lord's Supper.[343] I Cor. 16.22f. comes from the same setting,[344] as Rev. 22.17–21 must also.[345] Thus all three texts point to the Lord's Supper, which is therefore to be regarded as the original setting of the formula.

3. Since *maranatha* was preserved as an Aramaic formula even in Greek-speaking churches we must assume that it originated in the early Aramaic-speaking church.[346]

c. So now we have to interpret the meaning of this formula which belongs to the celebration of the Lord's Supper in the early Aramaic-speaking church.

1. In that church, as is shown, for example, by the theology of Q, the expectation of the parousia was a live one. Since we do not know of any text relating to the Lord's Supper which is not eschatologically orientated,[347] we must assume that *maranatha* originally had the sense of an appeal for the parousia of Jesus and

---

[342] Klostermann, *Probleme im Aposteltexte*, 1883, 245f., and Hommel, 'Maran atha', *ZNW* 15, 1914, 317–322, suggest that אתא means 'sign', but this solution is to be rejected.

[343] Dölger, *Sol salutis* 199f.; Lietzmann, *Herrenmahl* 236f. (*Lord's Supper* 192f.); Kuhn, *TWNT* IV 474.20–25; Bornkamm, *Das Anathema in der urchristlichen Abendmahlsliturgie* 124. Whether, with Lietzmann, we place 10.6 before 10.1, or with Bornkamm leave it where it is depends on the way in which we imagine that the church of the *Didache* arranged its fellowship meal and the actual eucharist. In any case the dialogue in 10.6 between the president and people belongs to the beginning, not to the end, of the celebration of the eucharist.

[344] Lietzmann, *Herrenmahl* 229 (*Lord's Supper* 186); Bornkamm, 'Anathema' 124; Cullmann, *Christology* 210f.

[345] Bornkamm, 'Anathema' 126f., demonstrates this convincingly.

[346] This is against Bousset's well known theory that *maranatha* originated in the bilingual (Hellenistic) church at Antioch (*Kyrios Christos*, ed. 1, 103 n. 3 [ed. 2, 84]). It is much more natural to suppose that *maranatha* comes from the early Aramaic-speaking church. That 'Bousset's thesis about the origin of maranatha in a bilingual church has not been disproved' (Klein, *RGG* IV, 732) can only be said if one does not allow a much more probable theory to disprove a less probable one.

[347] I Cor. 11.26 ('. . . until he comes'); Mark 14.25 = Matt. 26.29; Luke 22.18, cf. Luke 22.16. On I Cor. 16.22f; Rev. 22.20; *Did.* 10.6 see 23ab.

is therefore to be translated, 'Our Lord, come!' (= *māranā thā* or *māran 'ethā*).[348] *Marana* describes the one whose parousia is expected and prayed for. In this sense it is essentially not far removed from the title *Son of Man*. Or, more precisely, *Marana* describes Jesus, the Jesus whom the early Aramaic-speaking church calls back as the *Son of Man*.[349]

Naturally it would be much easier for NT studies if the early Aramaic-speaking church had used the prayer 'Son of Man, come!' instead of *maranatha*, for this would have made it absolutely clear that the title *Lord* does not have its roots in this prayer by the early Aramaic-speaking church. But Aramaic-speaking Christians did not say 'Son of Man, come!'—though it is now impossible to know why. However, if we examine the NT we find that *Son of Man* is never used in the vocative, indeed we may take it that the title was hardly ever spoken in the church. It is consonant with this fact that in the prayer for the parousia the title *Mara*, not *Son of Man*, is used.

But this still does not explain adequately why the church appealed to the 'coming Son of Man' under the title *Marana*.

2. In the first place we must say that *Mara* was a relatively harmless title, without heavy religious overtones. It is not used in an absolute sense as a title for God.[350] In the language of government it means a high official. To adopt this title was a safe course for the new Christian church, for it avoided an openly competitive relationship with adherents of the Jewish or of any other religion.

3. Against this is the assertion that *Mara* is the Aramaic counterpart of the Hebrew *Adonai*.[351] But for the early Aramaic-speaking church to use *Adonai* as a title for Jesus would have been unthinkable, for in the NT period this was the designation for God which was substituted for the tetragram in liturgical reading of the Scriptures. To apply this title to Jesus would have been

---

[348] This agrees with Rev. 22.20, 'Come, Lord Jesus'! See 23d.

[349] We are not thinking here of passages in which *Son of Man* is used to express the lowliness of the earthly Jesus (Luke 9.58 = Matt. 8.20) or his Passion (e.g. Mark 8.31 and parallels), but of Q Passages like Luke 17.24 = Matt. 24.27; Luke 12.40 = Matt. 24.44, where the reference is to the parousia of the Son of Man.

[350] Dan. 2.47 (*mārē malkīn*) and 5.23 (*mārē šᵉmayyā*) are not evidence to the contrary, for they are not used as titles. They simply outline the position of God vis-à-vis the kings or the gods. Thus Cullmann, *Christology* 201. For what follows, see the recent work of Schulz, 'Maranatha' 134-7.

[351] Cf. Cullmann, *Christology* 199.

equivalent to blasphemy of the crudest kind, and the young church would not have laid itself open to such a charge for as long as it set store by remaining in the synagogue fellowship. For this reason it is impossible to regard *Mara* as the customary Aramaic translation of *Adonai*.

4. But why was the designation *mešīḥā* not used in the prayer for the parousia? The reason must be that this term indicates a person in time and space, whereas in the plea for the parousia an eschatological figure is in mind.

5. Finally we must reject the explanation that Jesus was called *Mara* in connection with his parousia because he had been addressed as *Rabbi*, therefore also *Mari*, during his earthly life. The argument ought rather to run as follows: it is the meaning of *Mara* in secular Aramaic which on the one hand accounted for the polite form of address, *Mari*, and which made it possible to transfer to Jesus the title *Marana*. In early Christian usage this title attained religious significance, for in the eschatological plea *Maranatha* features of late Jewish and early Christian expectation of the *Son of Man* were transferred to Jesus who was called by the title *Marana*. In pre-Christian use, the title possessed neither a religious significance in general nor an eschatological significance in particular. But in Christian use, by contrast, it is the future aspect, the reference to the parousia, which is essential to the understanding of the plea *Maranatha*, and therefore also of the term *Marana*.

d. This is just the kind of thinking which the end of Revelation reflects, for there *Maranatha* is translated 'Come, Lord (Jesus)' (ἔρχου κύριε[352] Ἰησοῦ), which means that *Maranatha* is understood as a plea for the parousia. Now *Marana* is rendered *Kyrios*, hence this title finds its way into parousia material. But this gives rise to further questions.

Why was this title chosen? Is it a simple translation, or were there theological or historical considerations which made this rendering absolutely essential? If it were simply a straight translation, δεσπότης might just as well have been chosen.[353]

The result of this translation is clear, for it led to the title *Lord* being brought into association with ideas of the parousia.[354]

[352] Omission of the suffix is normal in Greek.
[353] But the LXX had already translated *Mare* by *Kyrios* at Dan. 2.47 and 5.23.
[354] In the Paulines *Kyrios* frequently appears in parousia sayings, e.g. I Thess. 2.19; 3.13; 5.23; I Cor. 1.7f., etc.

This would not have led to confusion if the title had not already been in use among Greek-speaking Hellenistic Christians with a different and particular range of meaning. But since this was the case, we have to say that the title *Lord* represents two different complexes of ideas. The first of these is the related series— acclamation, *homologia*, *onoma*—which we pointed out earlier (15—18), and which we may regard as the genuine setting of the title. On account of the many similarities with the idea of *Kyrios* in the Hellenistic *Kyrios*-cults we took it that the title must have come from Hellenism.

But the title is also found connected with ideas of the parousia, and this comes about because the title *Mara*, which in the early Aramaic-speaking church was associated with the expectation of the parousia, was rendered in the Greek-speaking church by *Kyrios*.[355]

e. This raises the crucial question: How are we to understand the relationship between these two complexes of ideas? Do they mark two stages within a single development in the Christian understanding of the title *Kyrios*, or were there originally two entirely different complexes, each containing titles which only accidentally had the same form in Greek?

If the first were true, we would have to regard the parousia expectation, and the title *Mare* associated with it, as the starting point in the development of ideas and terminology alike. In the Greek-speaking church *Mara* would have been reproduced by the term *Kyrios*, with roughly similar sense, which would mean that the latter title would have been primarily associated with the notion of the parousia. This *Mare-Kyrios* concept would have taken over and transformed many of the various elements which were to be found, for example, in the Hellenistic *Kyrios*-cults, so that side by side with the expectation of the parousia there would have appeared a consciousness of the *Kyrios'* status as one of honour and power, acknowledged by the Church as supremely authoritative. Thus the present aspect of the *Kyrios*, whose authority is the ultimate term of reference for everything, both in worship and in the conduct of daily life, would have been

[355] H. Braun, 'Der Sinn der neutestamentlichen Christologie' 352 (n. 5 from previous page), seems to suggest the same thing when he says, 'The bridge between *mār;anā* and κύριος (used without qualification) is a linguistic one, for in terms of theological content there is hardly any connection.'

combined with the future aspect of the *Kyrios* in the expectation of the parousia.

But against this view is an argument of considerable weight. The texts which reflect pre-Pauline stages in the tradition give no basis for it, for nowhere in them do we find any combination of the two complexes of ideas, though separately they occur very frequently. If the development had been such as we have just outlined, we would inevitably find combined or mixed forms. But in the complete absence of such forms we are obliged to assume that the *Mare-Kyrios* idea on the one hand, and the idea of the *Kyrios* as one to whom appeal is made in the present on the other hand, are ideas which are entirely separate in origin.[356]

Therefore it is necessary to make a fundamental distinction between the two complexes of ideas. The only thing they have in common is the word which in each of them is used as a title, namely *Kyrios*, *Lord*. Naturally we may take for granted that this title which they had in common encouraged the fusion of the various ideas contained in them. But this makes it all the more surprising that in the pre-Pauline strata there is no evidence of such fusion, and barely any more in Paul's own writings.

So we have to state as our conclusion that the same title was used by two different churches in connection with two different complexes of ideas and in this double usage entered the stream of tradition. No genetic connection between the two can be discovered. Should anyone find this conclusion at first sight improbable, he might consider the following points:

1. This view of things has been forced upon us simply as a result of examining pre-Pauline fragments discernible by their literary form.

2. We must note that attempts to concentrate upon one complex of ideas at the expense of the other have led to very forced conclusions, for Bousset, in the interests of his (within limits quite justifiable) theory of the *Kyrios* as the 'Lord of the cult', had to deny the formula *Maranatha* to the Aramaic-speaking church,[357] while Cullmann thinks that he disproves Bousset by showing that

---

[356] The theory that the development might have taken place in the reverse direction, from the Hellenistic idea of *Kyrios* to the formulation of the cry *Maranatha* in the bilingual church at Antioch (so Bousset, see n. 346 above), is quite improbable. Schulz, 'Maranatha' 143f., comes to the same conclusion.

[357] Bousset, *Kyrios Christos*, ed. 1, 103 n. 3 (ed. 2, 84). See n. 346 above.

the eschatological cry *Maranatha* 'is cultic in character'.[358] Of course *Maranatha* is set in the context of worship, being part of the Lord's Supper 'liturgy' of the early Aramaic-speaking church, but that church's worship was quite differently orientated from that of the Hellenistic Christian churches. If one takes certain specific acts associated with these services, such as the acclamation and the formula *Maranatha* (for these can be discerned by literary examination), one realizes how different they are in character. But then at the same time it becomes very clear that they come from quite different backgrounds of thought which account for the fact that the one title *Kyrios* can have quite different meanings.

3. The same can be shown in the case of the title *Son of God*. It represents two complexes of ideas which are of different origin and character. On the one hand we find it connected with the idea that Jesus was installed as *Son of God* at the resurrection (Rom. 1.4), and on the other hand it is connected with the idea of pre-existence, from which God sent his *Son* into earthly life (e.g. Gal. 4.4). We find these two complexes of ideas combined (at least superficially) at Rom. 1.3f.[359]

These three considerations ought to show that the clear differentiation we have made between the two complexes of ideas with which the *Mare-Kyrios* and the 'acclamation-*Kyrios*' are associated is a distinction which is appropriate and necessary.

f. Which of these *Kyrios*-titles, and therefore which complex of ideas, is to be regarded as primary is a question which, in view of what we have said, is to be handled with caution. For each title, within the church which uses it, is as 'original' as the other. It would be quite improper to allow apologetic concerns to influence this question, for it is not a matter of deciding whether the development of terminology and thought in the Hellenistic Gentile-Christian church was less 'correct' or less 'Christian' than in the Aramaic-speaking Jewish-Christian church. Both churches were formulating what in their own particular circumstances they hoped for, or 'confessed', with regard to Jesus.

[358] Cullmann, *Christology*, 211–15. Under this heading distinctive features of Gentile-Christian worship are read back by Cullmann into the worship of the early Aramaic church, and this then gives such a broad basis that even the *homologia* 'Kyrios Christos' (*sic*—not 'Kyrios Jesus') can be described as having its origin in 'ancient tradition' (by which he clearly means tradition which goes back to the early Aramaic-speaking church) (p. 215).
[359] See 24.

If the question of primacy is simply a question about the moment at which each of these complexes of ideas crystallized as a formula, it is easy to answer. Naturally the cry *Maranatha*, and the combination of the *Mare*-title and the expectation of the parousia which went with it, is older than the acclamation in the Gentile-Christian church, but it represents neither the foundation nor the cause of the latter's origin.

We cannot determine with any certainty whether the rendering of *Mare* by *Kyrios* is conditioned by purely technical considerations of translation, or whether it results from the fact that *Kyrios* at the time of translation was in current use as a religious title in the Hellenistic cults or even in the Gentile-Christian church. Whatever the answer may be, it tells us nothing about the way in which the particular ideas behind *Kyrios* came to be formed, but only about the considerations which influenced the choice of this particular term.

The question whether *Mare-Kyrios* ideas are earlier than 'acclamation-*Kyrios*' ideas or not might lead us on to ask which of these two complexes of ideas predominates in the course of later development. But to such a question no general answer seems possible, because for almost every NT writer we would have to define differently the relationship between the two.[360]

g. So side by side with the pistis-formula about the death and the resurrection of Jesus, in which from pre-Pauline times the title *Christ* is set, and the *homologia* which acclaims Jesus as *Kyrios*, a third formula has come to light—a formula which originally was about the parousia, and with which the title *Mare* (= *Kyrios*) is associated. The peculiarity of this third formula is clearly shown, not only by its content but also by its use. For whereas the pistis-

---

[360] A twofold illustration must suffice here:

1. The words 'The Lord is at hand' (Phil. 4.5) refer primarily to the parousia (cf. 3.20f.). This sentence has rightly been regarded as closely related to the *Maranatha* formula (e.g. Dölger, *Sol salutis* 199; cf. Kuhn, *TWNT* IV 472.7). What Paul draws from these words is, in terms of content, a summons to prayer and a blessing, but in terms of form he echoes liturgical language.

2. Peterson, *Theos* 130f., shows that *Maranatha* was used as an anathema. This is so in the case of the inscription *CIG* 9303 which Peterson cites, but it does not apply in the case of *Didache* 10.6, which is earlier. This then shows the course of development, and the relative correctness of regarding *Maranatha* as a 'curse-formula', as Bousset does (*Jesus der Herr* 22f). But he, too, confuses the usage of the original Aramaic-speaking church with later usage. Thus the parousia idea has receded into the background or disappeared altogether. The *Mare-Kyrios* of the original *Maranatha* has been modified in favour of an understanding of *Kyrios* which derives from Hellenism.

formula names the saving acts which form the substance of faith, and the *homologia*, by means of the act of acclamation in worship, acknowledges the enthronement of Jesus as *Kyrios*, the *Maranatha* is a prayer for the parousia, and its proper setting is in the Lord's Supper.

So, with regard to our investigation of christological ideas, we have shown that the parousia had no original connection either with the pistis-formula or with the *homologia*, but found expression in a third, independent, formula. This picture, which is basically very clear, is marred only by the fact that *Mara* is rendered by *Kyrios*, i.e. by a term already employed in the *homologia* with quite different meaning. From that point onwards we may expect to find in subsequent times many kinds of confusion, cross-influence and blurring.[361]

[361] In order to avoid confusion we shall indicate the two *Kyrios* titles more precisely as *Mare-Kyrios* and 'acclamation-*Kyrios*'. Schulz, 'Maranatha', has recently adopted this terminology, but introduces a third term, 'tetragram-*Kyrios*'.

III · SON OF GOD

The Traditional 'Son' Formulae

24. 'Designated Son . . .'

a. A pre-Pauline formula which represents an early setting of the title *Son* is found at Rom. 1.3b–4: '. . . who was made of the seed of David according to the flesh, and designated Son of God in power according to the Spirit of holiness by his resurrection from the dead.' It is generally recognized that we have here a pre-Pauline formula.[362] This is suggested by Semitic abstractions, not typical of Paul,[363] participial construction,[364] and parallelism in the sentence structure.[365] The grammatical subject to which the formula must have referred originally is most likely to have been simply 'Jesus'.[366]

The pattern of the formula is clear. Two christological statements stand side by side, in such a way that each one says something about the nature of the person who is the subject. The first speaks of his earthly nature 'according to the flesh', and the second speaks of his 'heavenly' nature 'according to the Spirit'. The two titles 'Son of David' ('of the seed of David') and 'Son of God' correspond to these two modes of existence. Since 'Son of David'

---

[362] Cf. Bultmann, *Theology* I, 7.5, 49; Schweizer, *Erniedrigung* 8e, 91 (cf. ET *Lordship and Discipleship* 37); Cullmann, *Christology* 292.

[363] E.g. 'Spirit of holiness' as in Test. Levi 18.11 from *ruaḥ haqqôdheš* (Isa. 63.10f.; Ps. 51.13); cf. Schweizer, *Erniedrigung* n. 360; Jesus as 'of the seed of David'; 'flesh' (σάρξ), related to *bāśār* of OT and late Judaism; cf. Schweizer, *TWNT* VII 125.36–126.5. This term marks the earthiness of human existence. The two expressions κατὰ σάρκα and κατὰ πνεῦμα do not have here their specifically Pauline significance. For 'to designate' (ὁρίζειν) cf. Acts 10.42.

[364] This will have been a feature of the original formula. Paul has simply put the whole formula into the genitive, in order to make it fit his own sentence structure.

[365] Participle + 'according to the flesh', participle + 'according to the spirit': cf. I Tim. 3.16; I Peter 3.18.

[366] Bultmann, *Theology* I, 7.5, 49, puts the title *Son* here, no doubt influenced by v. 3a. But this is too narrow and hasty a procedure, the more so since the title *Son* in v. 3a reflects Paul's interpretation and not that of the formula.

is to be understood in a messianic sense, it is clear that the expression 'according to the flesh' in the first clause is not strictly a saying about the lowliness of the Son. All the same we must recognize that the qualifying phrases 'according to the flesh' and 'according to the Spirit' are not entirely on a level with one another. Regarded as evaluations, the second clearly indicates the greater worth. It is even clearer that these two concepts are not to be understood in the Pauline sense as descriptions of the domain of sin and the domain of life.[367]

Certainly the second clause describes a more exalted state than the first, but not its complete antithesis. Strictly, it is not a pattern of humiliation and exaltation we should speak of here,[368] but rather one of adoption: a person who is already of high rank is 'adopted' and receives a status which is supreme. The fact that the Son of David's 'this-worldly origin'[369] is mentioned does not detract in any way from the exalted status described in this saying, because it is an essential element in the idea of the Messiah that he will be born as a man.

The second clause speaks of Jesus' installation as *Son of God*, and this mode of being is described as 'according to the spirit of holiness'. The ideas which lie behind this statement are those which originally were associated with the enthronement of the king, for in Israel the enthronement of the king is interpreted as his adoption as son of God.[370]

[367] Bultmann, *Theology* I, 7.5, 49, does not consider these two expressions to be part of the original formula, but this is only because he understands them in the Pauline sense, which is in fact to misunderstand them.

[368] This is against J. M. Robinson, *A New Quest of the Historical Jesus*, 1959, 53 n. 2, who speaks of 'a dialectic within the humiliation line itself'. Against this we must state that in the first clause it is not a question of any 'dialectic' but of asserting Jesus' messiahship, and therefore also of ascribing to him a particular worth. Robinson is quite right to draw illustrations of what he has in mind from Ignatius and Justin (53 n. 3). But it is precisely in their writings that the difference between them and Rom. 1.3b becomes clear. There is a 'dialectic' in Ignatius and Justin, but it results from the fact that Jesus' 'sonship', whether of Mary or of David (in either case implying an exalted status), is there employed in the struggle against Docetism as proof of the genuine bodily humanity of Jesus. But this reflects a stage in the development of the early Church's confession which at the very point we are discussing differs characteristically from Rom. 1.3b.

[369] Robinson, *New Quest* 53.

[370] Cf. Ps. 2.7 *beˈnī ˈattā ˈᵃnī hayyōm yᵉlidtīkā* — υἱός μου εἶ σύ, ἐγὼ σήμερον γεγέννηκα σε. Since we lack evidence that this saying was applied in pre-Christian Judaism to the Messiah (cf. Dalman, *The Words of Jesus*, ET 1902, 268–73, esp. 270f.), we must reckon that it was the Jewish Christian church which did this. Lövestam, 'Die Frage des Hohenpriesters', *Svensk Exegetisk Årsbok* 26, 1961, 95f., nevertheless considers that the passage was interpreted messianically in pre-Christian Judaism. Similar

The formula gives the resurrection as the moment at which Jesus is 'adopted', though the expression ἐξ ἀναστάσεως νεκρῶν is somewhat ambiguous.[371] Thus the idea of the installation of Jesus as *Son of God* is an interpretation of the resurrection. This makes it plain that the events which in the later Church were described as resurrection and ascension are at this stage not separated. The death does not come within sight, or if it does it is interpreted positively.

Thus the formula combines two christological conceptions, though neither is placed in a competitive or polemical relation to the other.[372] Only the phrase 'in power' comes near to suggesting anything competitive. Yet it is precisely this expression which, in view of the structure of the first clause, is seen to be superfluous and would not have formed part of the original formula. Since it was introduced only later (by Paul himself?), it must refer to 'Son of God'. But this puts all the emphasis on the second clause and brings about a new interpretation, or at least a change of emphasis in favour of the pattern of humiliation and exaltation. This is to be regarded as a shift away from the ideas stated in the original formula.

b. The particular ideas and range of meaning belonging to the term *Son of God* may be summarized as follows:

1. Jesus was installed, adopted, by God as *Son of God*. Underlying this view is the idea of a legal act. Nothing in this statement suggests any idea that God and the Son of God are 'consubstantial'.

2. The act of adoption was accomplished at Jesus' resurrection. This means that the idea of pre-existence lies outside this formula's range of vision. On the other hand we ought not to press the adoption statement so far as to speculate whether Jesus was not Son of God *before* the resurrection, for the formula says that before the resurrection he was Son of David.

---

enthronement formulae occur in the pericope of the baptism (Mark 1.11 and parallels) and the transfiguration of Jesus (Mark 9.7 and parallels). Cf. Luke 1.35. Michel und Betz, 'Von Gott gezeugt', *Festschrift für J. Jeremias*, 1960, 11, consider that 1 QSa 2.11 is certainly a messianic interpretation of Ps. 2.7; also Lövestam, *op. cit.* 96. M. Smith, ' "God's Begetting the Messiah" in 1 QSa', in *NTS* 5, 1958/59, 218–224, esp. 222, takes the passage to apply to the 'High Priest', not to the Messiah.

[371] ἐξ ἀνασταστάσεως ἐκ νεκρῶν would make it clearer that it is the resurrection of Jesus rather than the resurrection of the dead which is meant here, but the sense suggests taking it this way.
[372] Contrast Mark 12.35–37a and parallels.

3. Obviously the formula is one which looks back, the second part looking back to the resurrection. It is, therefore, an interpretation of the saving event, but in such a way that it expresses the meaning of the resurrection for Jesus, rather than its saving significance for mankind.[373]

4. It is obvious that the background of the formula, both in language and ideas, is Jewish.

5. This means that the formula must have originated in the Jewish-Christian church.[374] Because the formula reflects a very early stage in the formation of the confession, in which the first concern was to express the importance of Jesus rather than to explain his saving significance for mankind,[375] we may take it that the early Aramaic-speaking church is the author of this formula. Greek-speaking Jewish Christians will have passed it on, in Greek, to Gentile Christianity.

6. Whereas attention had been focussed upon the resurrection (interpreted as exaltation) as the moment at which Jesus was 'adopted' as *Son of God*, it was subsequently focussed upon his continuing status as *Son of God* for ever. At this point the idea of the *Son of God* approaches the idea of the *Kyrios*, for in both cases it is the present, sovereign status of Jesus that is emphasized. Evidence of this is the fact that the Jesus who is named in the formula is described by Paul as 'Jesus Christ, our Lord'.

But this observation has already taken us beyond the pre-Pauline stage before we have examined all the early settings in which the title *Son of God* is to be found. So we shall turn back and look at another 'Son' formula.

25. The 'Sending' of the Son

a. Before we examine other formulae in which the title *Son of God* is rooted, we must say briefly what we mean here by the term 'formula'.

[373] This does not mean that the Church did not also ascribe to this adoption a significance which concerned itself. The connection with ideas of kingship suggests that Christians saw in the Son of God their king. Nevertheless it is significant that the formula does not explain this, but speaks of what has happened to Jesus.

[374] Thus Braun, 'Der Sinn der neutestamentliche Christologie' 345.

[375] We recognized the corresponding stage as the earliest in the development of the pistis-formula too. See 7b.

We cited I Cor. 15.3b–5 as a fixed formula on account of the key words contained in it. The acclamation, too, was described as a formula on account of its brevity. It is also correct to describe the formula of adoption which we have just examined as a 'formula' on account of the stylistic features it contains.

In what follows we shall again and again come across sentences which are not fixed to the same extent. But they are similar, and not accidentally so. For not only do the same key words recur in them in stereotype fashion, but also it is possible to detect in them a particular pattern. Where these two conditions are fulfilled—fixed key words and a clear formal pattern—we shall speak of 'formulae', even though sometimes, in particular instances, the wording may within limits be subject to variation.

One such formula speaks not of the installation of the Son but of the *sending* of the Son. This type appears in many different forms which may be identified by the verb which is used.

b. The formula about 'sending' with the verb (ἐξ) ἀποστέλλειν.[376]

The fundamentals of Gal. 4.4f. are derived from a pre-Pauline formula.[377]

'. . . God sent forth (ἐξαπέστειλεν) his Son,
born of a woman,
born under the law,
to redeem those who were under the law,
so that we might receive adoption as sons.'

It is well known that there are difficulties in the way of discovering how much of this passage belongs to the original content of the formula, or in what order the very obvious insertions should be arranged, and what is conditioned, in the last resort, by the Pauline text.[378] We shall begin our investigation with the first line of the formula, for it includes the 'sending' of the Son in

---

[376] In the language of the *Koine* there is often no difference between the simple and compound forms.

[377] Cf. e.g. Robinson, *New Quest* 53 n. 3, though the emphasis there is not on the sending of the Son but on the earthly birth of Jesus. For a different view see E. Schweizer, 'Zur Herkunft der Präexistenzvorstellung bei Paulus', *EvTh* 19, 1959, 68, who considers that Gal. 4.4 is a Pauline formulation.

[378] Dibelius, 'Jungfrauensohn und Krippenkind', *Botschaft und Geschichte* I, 1953, 29 n. 47, and J. M. Robinson, *Kerygma und historischer Jesus*, 1960, 69 n. 2, take 'so that we might receive . . . sons' to relate to the first participial clause 'born of a woman', though they do not say that the intervening clauses, similarly constructed, are secondary.

which we are particularly interested here. The closest parallels to this are found in the Johannine writings: John 3.17; I John 4.9, 10, 14.[379] They show a definite pattern, for the first clause speaks of the 'sending', the next unfolds its saving significance, sometimes by means of a ἵνα-clause,[380] sometimes by a phrase in apposition.[381] Of course, these Johannine passages do not reproduce the exact wording of the original formula,[382] but their form is sufficiently definite to permit a reconstruction of the pattern which underlies them. The pattern is this: coupled with the statement about the 'sending' of the Son is a second clause which explains the saving significance of the 'sending'. If we now look back at Gal. 4.4f., it seems obvious that the final clause, which is an exposition of the saving significance of the 'sending', should be related to the first clause, i.e. 'God sent forth his Son, so that we might receive adoption as sons.' Thus we have arrived at a sentence which not only satisfies the formal pattern which we have discovered but also corresponds to the 'teleological pattern'[383] which Dahl has established in another connection. Moreover parallel terminology in the two parts of the sentence has now come to light.[384] For these reasons we may take it that these two clauses represent the original structure of the formula. The inserted clauses, 'born under the law to redeem those who were under the law', are most probably by Paul himself, for they reflect Paul's view of the law.[385] In the case of the words 'born of a woman' it is more difficult to decide. One's inclination is to say that Paul found this expression ready to hand,[386] but it is impossible to decide whether it was linked with the first line by Paul himself or before Paul.

As far as the *content* of this formula is concerned, what is important for our present context is that the agent in the 'sending' is God. We are not told exactly what kind of 'sending' is thought of

[379] With ἀποστέλλειν throughout.
[380] John 3.17; I John 4.9; cf. John 3.16.
[381] I John 4.10, 14.
[382] The various extensions or abbreviations show this.
[383] See Dahl, 'Formgeschichtliche Beobachtungen' 7.
[384] 'Son'—'adoption as sons'. Cf. in the same verse the similar position of the phrase 'under the law'. Cf. also II Cor. 8.9: '. . . though he was rich, yet for your sake he became poor, so that by his poverty you might become rich.'
[385] It is no doubt because of this that Schweizer, 'Zur Herkunft der Präexistenz-vorstellung bei Paulus', *EvTh* 19, 1959, 68, concludes that v. 4f. is a Pauline formulation.
[386] Cf. 'born of . . .' in Rom. 1.3b.

here. The inserted clauses interpret the 'sending' in terms of the birth and earthly existence of Jesus, but originally, no doubt, the thought will have been not of a single act but of Jesus' entry into earthly circumstances and relationships, i.e. of his 'becoming man', in general terms.

But the idea of the sending of the *Son of God* into earthly life assumes his pre-existence, so that we might say that the formula is about the sending of the pre-existent 'Son' into the life of the world. This brings out clearly the difference between the *Son of God* concept in this formula and that which Rom. 1.3b–4 contains. There it is an earthly figure (the Messiah) who is installed, 'adopted', as *Son of God*, whereas here it is the pre-existent one who is sent into the life of earth. So the one formula is about an earthly figure who is 'adopted', the other about a pre-existent figure who is 'sent'.

The second formula, however, is designed to show the purpose of the 'sending', and this is formulated in the final clause. Thus the second part of the formula explains the first, for it gives the saving significance of the 'sending'. This is a further difference between this formula and the 'adoption' formula of Rom. 1.3b–4 which contains no such interpretative clause. So we are to understand the sending of the pre-existent *Son* as the saving event. What is envisaged here is neither the death nor the resurrection, nor even simply the birth, but the 'coming' of Jesus, his life viewed as a whole. This man, whose particular earthly career is put on record, is understood to be the pre-existent *Son of God* who was sent into the world. So this formula, too, looks back.[387] The saving event consists in the fact that there was one who came, and this is interpreted as meaning that there was one who was 'sent'. But the formula is concerned to show the saving significance of the sending of the *Son* 'for us men', and this gives the formula a present reference. Thus in explaining the significance of the sending of the Son 'for us' the formula achieves what it set out to achieve. It says nothing about what happened afterwards to the one who was sent. There is no mention of any 'post-existence' of the pre-existent one.

We now turn to another formula about the sending of the Son, a variant of the one we have just examined.

[387] The verb is aorist in every instance except I John 4.14.

c. The formula about 'sending' with the verb πέμπειν.

In Rom. 8.3 we find the statement, 'God, sending (πέμψας) his own Son in the likeness of sinful flesh . . .' Here again it is clear that the statement about the sending of the Son is given 'in the form of an old tradition',[388] but it is not at all certain where the formula ends and where Paul's own words begin again. We shall not attempt to analyse the whole passage, but will turn our attention to the statement about the 'sending' which is our particular interest here.

We might wonder whether this passage ought not to have been taken in conjunction with the first variant of the formula. But we have only to look at the Johannine literature, where the phrase 'the Father, who sent (ὁ πέμψας)' occurs 26 times[389] in stereotype fashion, to see that a variant of the formula with this wording existed in its own right and had considerable influence. This justifies us in giving separate treatment to Rom. 8.3, where this wording occurs, and in regarding it as a fragment of this variant. As in the first variant which we examined above, God is the agent in the sending. The formula speaks emphatically of 'his *own* Son'. This kind of language suggests that here again we have the idea of the pre-existent Son of God. But in the present instance we cannot be so sure about the clause which interprets the saving significance of the sending, for although this is indeed spoken of, the language seems to be Paul's own. For this reason we regard the statement in Rom. 8.3 about the sending of the Son as containing simply a fragment of the original πέμπειν formula. Its similarity in substance and ideas with the variant discussed above is evident, in spite of the differences we have noted.

26. *The 'Giving up' of the Son*

a. The key word παραδιδόναι brings us to a third type of *Son* formula in addition to the formulae about the 'adoption' and the 'sending' of the Son.

---

[388] Michel, 160 *ad loc.* This assertion is reinforced by the fact that the material from the formula does not fit very easily into Paul's sentence.

[389] Rengstorf, *TWNT* I 404.15f. Rengstorf's own comparison of the way in which ἀποστέλλειν and πέμπειν are used (403.40–404.19) would justify the conclusion that two variants of the formula, each with its own wording, existed. Rengstorf, indeed, does not draw this conclusion, which is why he has to resort to very forced distinctions between the two terms (404.20–28).

We shall take Rom. 8.32 as our starting point: 'who did not spare his own Son but gave him up (παρέδωκεν) for us all.' We can be fairly sure that this portion of the sentence represents pre-Pauline traditional material,[390] but even so the word 'all', at least, seems questionable. A similar formula is found also at John 3.16. It is of no significance that the verb there is given in the simple form διδόναι.[391] The points common to both these formulae are important: 1. The agent in both cases is God. 2. Both speak of God's 'giving' or 'giving up'. 3. The one who is 'given up' is the *Son*, whose close relationship with God is emphasized by the words 'own' or 'only-begotten'. 4. Both formulae state clearly the saving significance of God's 'giving up' the Son. Certainly, in John 3.16 Johannine terminology is apparent in the words 'whoever believes in him'. The conjunction 'so that' (ἴνα) which introduces the saving significance of the act must have formed part of the original formula. In this case we might indeed have expected the first person plural, the 'we' representing the speaker in such formulae, but this was suppressed by the Johannine addition 'that whoever . . .'

The first person plural is found at Rom. 8.32, where the words 'for us' express the saving significance of the 'giving up' of the Son. But whether there was originally a further ἴνα clause explaining this in more detail is a matter of uncertainty, because we cannot be sure whether Paul has given us the formula completely intact here.

A glance at points 1, 3 and 4 reveals a striking similarity of structure between this formula and the formula about 'sending'. This prompts us to ask what exactly were the ideas which underlie the use of the verb 'to give up'. Basically there are two possibilities, for either the verb may be taken in the sense which it has in the context of the passion, or, because this formula is so like the formula about 'sending', it may be understood in a broader sense as a commentary on the sending of the Son of God.

For several reasons it is difficult to reach a clear decision on this. All the same, the connections with the context of the passion are by no means as clear as might at first sight appear. For in that

[390] Thus Fuchs, *Die Freiheit des Glaubens*, 1949, 116, and Michel, *Römer* 184 *ad loc*. Verse 32b is regarded as a Pauline conclusion drawn from v. 32a.
[391] See n. 376.

context the verb παραδιδόναι is in the first place used technically for the betrayal by Judas,[392] and in the second place it is found, together with the title *Son of Man*, in the so-called passion predictions,[393] always (and this is characteristic) with an indication of the persons to whom the Son of Man was 'delivered up'.[394] There is nowhere in these contexts any statement that God gave up his Son or that the Son gave himself up.

But this is regularly stated in the formula about the 'giving up' of the Son. Here, though, there is no indirect object indicating to whom the Son of God was 'given up'. It is a 'giving' in the widest possible sense. Moreover its saving significance is explained, and this is never done in the passion sayings. Since in all these points the formula about 'giving' agrees with the formula about 'sending', it must be related to the latter rather than to the statements about the passion.[395]

If these reflections are correct, the verb 'to give up' is used in a comprehensive sense. Originally it was not limited to the death of Jesus but spoke of the coming of the *Son of God* into the life of the world. Of course, all the implications of this coming are present, including the death, but they are not individually stressed.

Naturally in the course of development—and finally under the influence of terminology relating to the passion—the idea of this 'giving up' was narrowed down, so that it came to refer to the sufferings and the death of Jesus, but the various parallels with the formula about the 'sending' of the Son reveal that in the beginning it was otherwise.[396]

---

[392] E.g. Mark 3.19; 14.10, 11, 18 etc. and parallels; John 6.64, 71; 12.4 etc. Cf. I Cor. 11.23.

[393] Mark 9.31 = Matt. 17.22 = Luke 9.47; Mark 10.33f. = Matt. 20.18f. = Luke 18.32. Also used in several passages to describe the handing over of Jesus to be crucified (Mark 14.41 and parallels), to Pilate (Mark 15.1 and par.), and to the governor (Luke 20.20). In a similar sense, but without indirect object, Acts 3.13. Cf. Büchsel, *TWNT* II 172.1 12.

[394] Indicated either by an indirect object or by means of the phrase 'into the hands of men'.

[395] The observation that in the formula the verb 'to give up' is aorist, thus signifying a single act in the past, is not a compelling argument for relating the statements of the formula to the statements about the passion, for in the formula about the 'sending' of the Son the verb is also aorist.

[396] The fact that it is the more recent parts of the tradition which relate the 'giving up' to the death makes it plain that the development took place in the direction we have indicated, and not conversely from the statements about the passion to a more developed interpretation as in the formula about 'sending'. Cf. Rom. 4.25. More is to be said about this in what follows.

b. Gal. 2.20 adds little that is new. The formula about the giving up of the Son is used here to describe faith as 'faith in the Son of God, who loved me and gave himself for me'. Clearly it is Paul who has put the first person singular in place of the plural, because from v. 18 he is formulating in terms of the singular (i.e. the confessing 'I'). The verb 'to love' appears beside the verb 'to give up'.[397] But it is noteworthy that here the Son of God himself has become the agent as well as the object of the 'giving', for he gives 'himself'.

From the wording of the sentence it is not completely clear whether the 'giving' refers to his entry into human life or in a more restricted sense to his death. Since Paul is using the formula as a definition of *pistis*, it is likely that by analogy with the pistis-formula he is thinking primarily of the death of Jesus. The explanatory phrase in v. 20, 'I have been crucified with Christ', would confirm this.

Here, too, the saving significance of the Son's 'giving' of himself is formulated, though only briefly: He gave himself 'for me'. Because the formula is used here to define faith, it comes very close to the pistis-formula. Perhaps it is under the influence of the pistis-formula that the words 'for me' appear here.

c. The same formula is found at Eph. 5.2, 25: 'Christ loved you[398] and gave himself up for us . . .'[399]

The similarity is striking, for here, too, the verbs 'to love' and 'to give up' appear side by side; God, originally the agent, is not mentioned at all; and the saving significance of the 'giving' is expressed by the phrase 'for us'. But the differences are no less instructive. No longer is it the *Son of God* who is named in the formula but *Christ*. So the formula is a striking illustration of the fact that there is no longer any awareness that a particular title has its proper setting in a particular complex of traditional material.[400] Furthermore, in the two Ephesians passages the formula is used in a new way, for it has been inserted into a 'rule of conformity'[401]

[397] Cf. also John 3.16.

[398] The change from second to first person plural is revealing. 'You' in the first clause appears because the context is one of exhortation, while 'us' in the second clause follows the wording of the formula.

[399] In Eph. 5.25 the formula is adapted *ad hoc* to apply not to 'us' or 'you' but to 'the church'.

[400] A sign of the same development is that p[46] BD*G it. at Gal. 2.20 speak of 'faith in God and in *Christ*' instead of faith in the *Son of God* who was 'given'.

[401] Thus Dahl, 'Formgeschichtliche Beobachtungen' 6. His term is *Konformitäts-Schema*.

which forms the basis of exhortation and determines its content.[402]

In both these passages it can hardly be questioned that the verbs 'to give up' and 'to love' no longer refer to Jesus' coming into the world but to his passion and death. This is further evidence of the shift from the original meaning of the formula.

d. This brings us to a passage (Rom. 4.25) in which the 'giving up' is clearly understood to refer to the death: '. . . who was given up (παρεδόθη) for our trespasses and raised for our justification.' Here 'given up' refers only to the death of Jesus, which is why it became possible to combine it with the statement about the resurrection. As a formulation of the two statements about the death and the resurrection it is reminiscent of the pistis-formula. Indeed the passage can only have come into being as a result of the pistis-formula and the formula about the 'giving' of the Son, both of which were already current and must have contributed to the formulation of Rom. 4.25, which was further influenced by Isa. 53.12. The title *Son of God* is no longer included.

All this suggests that Rom. 4.25 represents a late stage in the tradition of the formula about the 'giving' of the Son. It is conceivable that Paul himself formulated it, using material from the other formulae.[403]

In every respect Rom. 4.25 has moved a long way from the form and content of the original formula about the 'giving up' of the Son. But precisely for this reason it has great value, for it shows how the effects of one formula upon another, and of external influences also, could bring about combinations of christological ideas and titles in which scarcely anything of the original forms is recognizable.

27. A Comparison

The many similarities between the formulae containing the verb 'to give up' and those containing the verb 'to send' justify a more detailed comparison and evaluation of the two types.

a. The basic idea common to both types is the idea of the

[402] In Eph. 5.2 OT phraseology is used to interpret the formula in sacrificial terms. This makes it clear that the formula has been combined with material from other christological traditions.
[403] On all this see 5e.

coming of the *Son of God* into the life of the world. It is pre-supposed that the *Son of God* is pre-existent. Thus the formulae mark two places at which the idea of pre-existence found its way into christological reflection. In this sense they are of the greatest significance for early Christian christology.

The ideas contained in these two types differ in that the formula about 'sending' emphasizes that it is *God* who sent the *Son*, whereas the formula about the 'giving up' of the Son is concerned to define the manner of the Son's coming: he came as one who was 'given'.

From that point a twofold development took place, for on the one hand all mention of God in the formula was suppressed, the Son himself becoming the agent in the 'giving'; and on the other hand the idea of pre-existence receded into the background, so that the 'giving' came to refer simply to the sufferings and death of the Son of God, and no longer in general terms to his entry into earthly life. This development led ultimately to the creation of various mixed types of formula.

b. Both formulae have a common underlying pattern, for not only is the 'fact' of the coming of the Son of God mentioned, but its saving significance for mankind is also explained. In this respect the pattern differs markedly from that of the 'adoption' formula.

The development seems to have taken place in such a way that the saving significance of the Son's coming, which originally was expressed in a complete clause, came increasingly to be expressed by means of the phrase 'for us' (no doubt under the influence of the pistis-formula).

c. Since both types are linked so consistently with the title *Son of God*, there can be no doubt that at a very early stage this title had a fixed place in this particular complex of traditional statements. The structure of these formulae can help us to discover what elements were contained in the pre-Pauline understanding of the title. Jesus is *Son of God* because he was sent by God from his pre-existent state into the life of the world, or because he 'gave' himself by entering earthly life (with all that this implied), with the object of achieving the salvation of mankind.

Particularly in the case of the formula about the 'giving' of the Son we might be tempted to think that the idea of 'humiliation' is present. But in the case of the formula about 'sending' we must be quite clear that there is nothing which could remotely suggest such an idea. It is important to bear in mind that there is no trace of exaltation, either, in our formula. A 'post-existence' of the pre-existent Son is simply not considered. The *Son of God* is he who came from his pre-existent state and by his coming brought salvation.

d. At this point we must pose the historical question: From what environment does the idea of the sending of the *Son of God* originate, and from what context of religious thought? Only in Rom. 4.25, in a quotation of Isa. 53.5f., 12,[404] did we find any echo of the Old Testament. But this happened at a very late stage in the tradition of the formula and was a secondary development, so that the only real argument for the derivation of our formula from OT ideas thus drops away.

On the other hand it is equally impossible to regard the 'gnostic myth of the ransomed redeemer' as the background of our two formulae. For quite apart from the unsolved problem of chronology, and even if we admit that the gnostic myth, though chronologically post-Christian, may have had pre-Christian manifestations, we still cannot shut our eyes to the fact that the myth's 'pattern' appears in our formulae at most in so stunted a form that the best we could say is that the formulae contain a theme which is also to be found in the gnostic myth. If the idea of the sending of the Son of God really had come from such a myth, it would be impossible to explain why there is not a syllable in our formula which speaks of his ascent.

If we are to reckon with a connection between the *Son of God* formulae and what is described as the 'gnostic myth', then such a connection cannot be more than a common dependence upon a common background of thought.

Late Jewish speculation on 'Wisdom' (*sophia*) must rank as a crucial element in this background of thought, for it, too, contains similar statements about 'sending'.[405] Many passages assert the pre-existence of God's *sophia*.[406] These similarities suggest that

---

[404] Schulz, *Untersuchungen zur Menschensohnchristologie im Johannesevangelium*, 1957, 90, relates Rom. 8.32a and Gen. 22.16, but this rests solely on the word φείδεσθαι which they have in common.

[405] Cf. Wisd. 9.10 which includes the verbs ἐξαποστέλλειν and πέμπειν. Here, too, the purpose of the 'sending' is given in a final clause introduced by ἵνα.

[406] E.g. Wisd. 9.9, the verse which immediately precedes the statement about the 'sending'. On the connection between Wisdom speculation and the idea of

the particular *Son of God* formulae which interest us here must have originated in the Hellenistic Jewish-Christian church.

e. If we ask what function the *Son of God* formulae fulfilled in the early Christian church, without losing sight of their relation to Wisdom speculation, we may suppose that they were instrumental in the more strictly theological working out of the significance of Jesus.

But since they were understood as formulations of the saving events (at first in a comprehensive sense as the total 'coming' of Jesus, and subsequently in a more limited sense as the passion and death of Jesus), they came to have a meaning similar to that of the pistis-formula, and like the pistis-formula they were used in worship. That is why the *Son of God* formula can be used quite naturally in Gal. 2.20 to define the content of *pistis*. All this shows that the pistis-formula clearly influenced these two types of the *Son of God* formula.

f. One final line needs to be added to our picture. If the idea of 'sending' or 'giving' is what constitutes these two types of *Son of God* christology, then Phil. 2.6–8—the first half of the 'Christ-psalm'—must belong to the same range of ideas. For here the theme is none other than the coming of the pre-existent one into the life of the world, and his coming results in his death.[407] True, it is not God who 'sends' him, for the one who comes is himself the agent. But that was the case in the formula about the 'giving up' of the Son, too. True, the psalm is expansive where the formula is brief, but it is precisely in this respect that the different character of the two literary forms comes to expression. True, the psalm presents new phrases and new words, but it is largely characteristic of them that they connect with the ideas of the formulae, as expressions like 'he emptied himself' or 'he humbled himself' show.

So the first half of the psalm must reflect the kind of thinking

---

pre-existence in the Pauline corpus see Schweizer, 'Zur Herkunft der Präexistenz-vorstellung bei Paulus' 65–70, esp. 69. Since Schweizer regards statements about the 'sending', like those at Gal. 4.4 and Rom. 8.3, as Pauline formulations, he concludes that 'it was through Wisdom speculation that Paul came by the idea of Jesus' pre-existence.' We regard these formulae as pre-Pauline, but the influence of Wisdom speculation on their formulation is not to be doubted.

[407] 'The death of the cross' is a Pauline addition. Thus Lohmeyer, *Philipper* 96 *ad loc.*; Käsemann, 'Phil. 2.5–11', 82.

which is fundamental to one type of *Son of God* christology, even though the title *Son of God* is lacking.[408] But where do the ideas come from which underlie the second part of the hymn? It will not do to point vaguely to the 'gnostic myth of the redeemer' as the source, for Colpe's work has made it impossible to do this any longer.[409] Nor can we explain the second part of the hymn as simply an exposition of the clause in the formula about the 'sending' which explains the saving significance of the 'sending', for this second part introduces the key expression 'highly exalted' and goes on to describe the bestowal of the 'name above every name'. So here the theme is the exaltation of Jesus and his elevation to new dignity. But do not these ideas come very close to the formula of 'adoption' in Rom. 1.4 which represents another type of *Son of God* christology? If we are on the right track in making such a supposition, the title *Son of God*, which had a fixed place in both groups of ideas, would be the bracket within which the two parts of the hymn were brought together. In this case the hymn would be in its own way the product of a combination of various traditional christological ideas, and therefore an illustration of the way in which the pattern of 'humiliation and exaltation' was arrived at.[410]

However that may be, the hymn turns out to be the product of combination in another sense, for at least in its first part it is governed by the idea of the 'sending' of the *Son*, but it reaches its climax in the acclamation of Jesus as *Lord*. Ideas of Sonship and Lordship are combined with one another. This shows to what extent cross-influencing had already taken place between different christological formulae and ideas, even before and during the Pauline period. So it cannot be surprising that similar tendencies are to be observed in Paul's own usage.

28. The Parousia of the Son

a. The only passage which concerns us here is I Thess. 1.9b, 10:

[408] Unfortunately there is no way of telling whether the title never featured in the hymn or whether Paul omitted it when he inserted the hymn into his own context.

[409] Colpe, *Die religionsgeschichtliche Schule*, esp. 62–68, 173–5, 191, 197.

[410] If this is so, then the 'humiliation—exaltation' pattern must represent a relatively late stage in the development of the tradition and therefore cannot be regarded as the only or even the primary source of NT christology.

'. . . (how) you turned to God from idols, to serve a living and
true God,
and to wait for his Son from heaven,
whom he raised from the dead,
Jesus who delivers us from the wrath to come.'

Paul introduces this passage in such a way that it will fit into his context. Two observations show that we really have pre-Pauline material here: 1. 'Idols' ($\epsilon\check{\iota}\delta\omega\lambda\alpha$) is here used in the sense which it has in Jewish polemics (cf. Isa. 44.9–20) and not in the Pauline sense. For Paul, the term describes powers whose existence is not disputed, but who, even as 'powers', are still creatures and therefore subject to God and ultimately powerless.[411] 2. Jesus' function as Redeemer is understood purely eschatologically as rescuing the believer from before the judgement. This is not in keeping with the general trend of Paul's theology.[412]

It is quite apparent that the formula in its present compass is the product of combination. A fragment from the pistis-formula ('whom he raised from the dead') has been inserted, and this no doubt caused the name *Jesus* to be added. It is impossible to decide with any certainty whether it was Paul or someone before him who inserted this fragment into the original formula, but at any rate it is possible to make out broadly what has happened. A formula which spoke only of the parousia and judgement (or rescue from judgement) has been brought into association with a statement which names the resurrection of Jesus (implying, no doubt, his death also)[413] as the saving event.

b. This means that the original formula contained two kinds of statement, the first theological, the second christological, which must be taken to interpret the 'turning'. The summons to 'serve the living God' is monotheistic preaching of a kind already familiar in Jewish missionary practice. The christology is related solely to the parousia and thus points back to the early Aramaic-speaking church.[414] Rescue 'from the wrath to come' ($\epsilon\kappa$ $\tau\hat{\eta}s$ $\dot{o}\rho\gamma\hat{\eta}s$ $\tau\hat{\eta}s$ $\dot{\epsilon}\rho\chi o\mu\dot{\epsilon}\nu\eta s$) has its verbal parallel in Q ($\phi\upsilon\gamma\epsilon\hat{\iota}\nu$ $\dot{a}\pi\dot{o}$ $\tau\hat{\eta}s$

---

[411] E.g. I Cor. 10.19; 12.2; cf. 8.4, 7.
[412] Cf. e.g. the transition from Rom. 4.25 to 5.1, where Jesus' redemptive function is interpreted in terms of the present.
[413] This would at least be implied by whoever added the fragment from the formula about the death and resurrection.
[414] Cf. the *Son of Man* christology in Q, e.g. Luke 17.24 = Matt. 24.27.

μελλούσης ὀργῆς).[415] This does not necessarily mean that there is any relationship of direct dependence between the two expressions, but it does indicate that Judaism or Jewish Christianity must be the environment from which such language comes. It is clear that the whole formula originated in Jewish Christianity. Its two-part structure suggests that it was used in the Jewish-Christian mission to the Gentiles, for in preaching to Jews the first part of the formula would have been superfluous, since among Jews monotheism would have been taken for granted. But the mission to Gentiles was only conducted on a large scale by Hellenistic, i.e. Greek-speaking Jewish Christians, so the formula must be attributed to them. We naturally assume that they used material drawn from the Aramaic-speaking church.

c. In the portion of the formula which interests us most, the statement about the parousia includes the title *Son of God.* The crucial question now is: Why is it this title which is linked with the statement about the parousia? Four possible answers are to be considered.

1. It was in connection with ideas about the parousia that the title *Son of God* first entered the Christian tradition.

2. There is no original connection between the title *Son of God* and the statement about the parousia. The title was chosen in this passage simply on account of its affinity with 'God'. Thus its connection with the statement about the parousia is 'fortuitous'.

3. The title was not introduced into Christian terminology because it formed an integral part of the parousia concept. *Son of God,* being a Jewish-Christian title, is more likely to have come from the idea of adoption.[416] Because the 'one who is to come' is thought of as the one who was 'adopted', the title *Son* was transferred to the person who was to appear at the parousia. This means that we have here a secondary, albeit very early, combination of the title *Son of God* with the statement about the parousia.

4. It is purely accidental that the title *Son of God* and the statement about the parousia are combined in this formula, for both title and statement belonged to the traditional terminology of Greek-speaking Jewish Christianity, even though each had an

[415] Luke 3.7b = Matt. 3.7b.
[416] Cf. Rom. 1.4.

entirely separate origin. They were combined for the first time in this formula and quite by chance.

Which of these answers is the right one? Answer 1 is to be rejected, because if the title *Son of God* had been integral to the statement about the parousia from the beginning we would have expected to find more evidence of such an association persisting later.[417] And if it really had played any significant role within early Christianity, we would have expected, too, to find some anticipation of it within Judaism or elsewhere.

Answer 2 would be convincing if the title *Son of God* had been inserted into the formula by Paul, for it is his custom to use the terms *God* and *Son of God* together.[418] But since I Thess. 1.9b is pre-Pauline and there is nothing to indicate that the title is a secondary insertion, this answer must likewise be rejected.

Which of the two remaining answers is the right one must be in the last resort a matter of opinion. It is important to recognize that the connection of the title *Son of God* with the statement about the parousia is a secondary one, but nevertheless very early, i.e. pre-Pauline. In the Pauline period no further traces of it remain.

So I Thess. 1.9b, 10 turns out to be not a fourth original type of *Son of God* christology but the product of a combination of various ideas. The title *Son of God* did not originally belong to the idea of the parousia but came to be associated with it as a result of processes of combination or merging which can no longer be demonstrated in detail.

29. Review of Part One

a. Our examination of the christological titles has led to the happy discovery that within the pre-Pauline material each of the principal titles is set in a formula which is distinguishable by its literary form. The statements contained in these formulae mark the contours of the early Christian understanding of the terms *Christ*, *Lord*, and *Son of God*. They show how these titles were conceived and they give expression to the ideas with which the titles were

---

[417] To point to the early disappearance of the title *Son of Man* is not to contradict this conclusion, because the title *Son of God*, unlike *Son of Man*, has been preserved in the Christian tradition.

[418] See 54a.

first associated, before passing into the stream of Christian tradition.

b. Christ belongs properly to the pistis-formula, in which the saving events of the past are recorded. *Christ* is the one who died 'for us' and whom God raised. He is the content both of faith and of preaching. This title, both in use and in meaning, comes from Jewish Christianity. *Christ* is understood as the one who died and was raised, the one to whom faith and preaching relate.

c. The title *Lord* belongs to the *homologia*, in which the Church confesses its allegiance to the heavenly *Lord*. The *homologia* makes no mention of any historical acts. When the Church says the *homologia* it is effectively submitting to the dominion of the *Lord* Jesus, a dominion which holds sway in the here and now. The function of the *homologia* is to effect a legally binding relationship. Its thought is not so much in historical as in spatial terms. The title *Lord*, understood in such terms, constitutes a claim upon the Church and a summons to acclamation. Both in use and in meaning it has its origin in the Hellenistic Gentile-Christian church. It is employed primarily in numerous activities associated with worship.

d. We find the title *Son of God* first of all in the formula about 'adoption', which interprets the resurrection as the installation of Jesus as *Son of God*. Although the formula's primary reference is to this initial act in the past, nevertheless this very fact means that it has something to say about the present status of the Son, for the *Son of God* is the risen and exalted one. Both in use and in meaning this title, thus understood, comes from Jewish Christianity. The distinctive mark of this understanding of 'Sonship' is that it includes the basic features of the understanding of *Christ* and *Lord*.

Son of God is also found in the formula about 'giving' or 'sending', in which the entry of the pre-existent one into the life of the world is regarded as a saving event. The *Son of God* is the pre-existent one who was sent or given 'for us'. Both in use and meaning the title, thus understood, has its origin within Hellenistic Jewish Christianity. This understanding of 'Sonship' is distinctive in that its interest is not in any particular historical act but rather in describing Jesus' significance in terms of metaphysical and cosmological speculation, by introducing the notion of his pre-existence.

e. Thus far, in our summary of the ideas underlying the titles *Christ, Lord* and *Son of God*, we have not had occasion to mention either the birth of Jesus or his parousia. Our examination of the pre-Pauline material has shown no trace of any title being associated particularly with the birth of Jesus. On the other hand, when we examined the '*Mare-Kyrios*' title we found that it was associated with the idea of the parousia.

This title has its setting in the cry *Maranatha*, which is a prayer for the parousia. The *Mare-Kyrios* is the *Lord* whose parousia the Church awaits. In use and in meaning the title originated in the Aramaic-speaking church. Its function is to sum up the Church's expectation of the parousia.

f. In this way the christological titles entered the stream of Christian tradition, each with its own particular content and each with a distinct range of application. Paul is to take these titles over, and in the second part of this essay we must show to what extent he adopts pre-Pauline usage and to what extent he reshapes it.

PART TWO

The Pauline Material

30. Procedure

As we now turn our attention to Paul's own usage we must bear in mind that it was largely from the Pauline corpus that we drew even the pre-Pauline material. This shows at the outset the very considerable extent to which Paul took over traditional formulations and habits of language from the pre-Pauline church, and it shows too how faithfully he preserved them. We shall not need to refer to this fact again, for the first part of this essay is sufficient evidence of it.

Our concern here must be to examine and to describe how Paul himself uses the christological titles, and here, too, we shall take the three titles *Christ (Jesus), Lord, Son of God*. This will reveal immediately how Paul's use of the titles both resembles and differs from that of the pre-Pauline church.

I · CHRIST (JESUS)

31. 'Christ' in Statements Related in Content to the Pistis-formula

a. Passages which speak of the crucifixion are closely related in substance to the statement in the pistis-formula about the death of Christ. So it is natural that Paul uses the christological title *Christ (Jesus)* in conjunction with the words 'cross' and 'crucify'.[419] In I Cor. 1.23; Gal. 3.1 the expression 'Christ crucified' denotes the content of preaching. This illustrates the essential connection with the pistis-formula which is, after all, a short summary of the content of preaching.

But the two passages might seem to be out of place here because they contain the title *Lord*. But in each case the reason for the insertion of this title is very obvious. In Gal. 6.14 the phrase runs: 'to glory . . . in the cross of our Lord Jesus Christ'. The word 'cross' is here taken up from v. 12. 'To glory' is also found at Rom. 5.11, with a *dia*-phrase and the full christological designation 'our Lord Jesus Christ'.[420] If, as we assumed earlier, 'glorying' (using the *dia*-formula) really was one of the activities associated with the Church's worship, we can immediately understand how in Gal. 6.14, where he takes up the word 'glory', Paul involuntarily uses the full christological titles which go with the *dia*-phrase, even though he is composing *ad hoc* in a passage about the 'cross'. The result is that 'cross' and the title *Lord* are brought into association, even though they belonged originally to two separate spheres.

A similar case is I Cor. 2.8, which speaks of 'the rulers of this age' who have crucified the *Lord*. The entire passage (I Cor. 2.6–16) takes up terminology, gnostic in tendency, of a kind which we find in the Wisdom theology of Hellenistic Judaism on the one hand and in the Hellenistic mystery religions on the other. In such a setting it was natural to put the title *Kyrios* and thus intro-

---

[419] I Cor. 1.17 (the cross of *Christ*); Gal. 6.12 (. . . of *Christ Jesus*); Phil. 3.18. Also I Cor. 1.23; 2.2; Gal. 3.1 (*Christ* crucified). The last two have *Jesus Christ*.
[420] See 19c and note 295.

duce it *ad hoc* into statements about the 'cross'. Thus the association of 'cross' with the title *Lord* again turns out to be secondary.

b. Similarly the connection between the pistis-formula and the expressions 'the body of *Christ*'[421] and 'the blood of *Christ*'[422] is plain. Of course Paul is not solely responsible for these expressions, for the transition from v. 16 to v. 17 in I Cor. 10 shows that v. 16 reproduces the phraseology of a pre-Pauline liturgy of the Lord's Supper.[423] But Rom. 7.4, on the other hand, alludes not to the Lord's Supper but very clearly to the saving significance of the death of Christ,[424] so it is beyond question that these passages are Pauline and have a common background of ideas.

c. We know that the pistis-formula, besides stating the fact of Christ's death, also indicates its meaning 'for us'. Many Pauline passages are to be regarded as extended commentaries on this. Thus it is *Christ* who has redeemed us,[425] who has set us free,[426] who is himself the end ($\tau\acute{\epsilon}\lambda os$) of the law,[427] through whom God has reconciled us to himself,[428] or, echoing OT sacrificial ideas, is described as 'our passover'.[429] The verbs in the aorist underline the fact that these expressions have the saving events of the past in view.

Two further statements must be mentioned here which are quite a long way from the background of thinking which we have considered here. They are: *Jesus Christ*, the foundation which is laid,[430] and *Christ*, the rock (understood typologically).[431] These passages bring us to a new series of expressions with which Paul frequently associates the title *Christ*.

32. 'Christ' and the Blessings of Salvation

a. Christ is found linked with the following expressions: The love

[421] I Cor. 10.16; Rom. 7.4.
[422] I Cor. 10.16.
[423] With Käsemann, 'The Pauline Doctrine of the Lord's Supper', *Essays on New Testament Themes*, ET 1964, 109–12.
[424] With Bornkamm, 'Herrenmahl' 164 n. 57.
[425] Gal. 3.13.
[426] Gal. 5.1.
[427] Rom. 10.4.
[428] II Cor. 5.18.
[429] I Cor. 5.7.
[430] I Cor. 3.11.
[431] I Cor. 10.4.

of Christ,[432] the Spirit of Christ,[433] the affection (σπλάγχνα) of Christ Jesus,[434] the blessing of Christ,[435] the power of Christ,[436] the truth of Christ,[437] the sufferings of Christ,[438] the glory of God in the face of Christ,[439] the law of Christ,[440] the sharing abundantly in comfort through Christ,[441] the fruits of righteousness (which come) through Jesus Christ.[442]

To try to connect these expressions directly with the pistis-formula would be artificial and forced. Of course it is possible that individual words like *stigmata* and 'sufferings' are linked with *Christ* on the grounds of their association with the passion and death of Christ. But this connection is not sufficient to explain the frequent association of these words which describe the blessings of salvation with the title *Christ*. We must note, too, that these same words are also linked with *God*,[443] or with *Lord*,[444] or sometimes stand alone.[445] Thus we shall guard against asserting invariable rules instead of being governed by the statistics. All the same, we can understand why the title *Christ* occurs in this context, for *Christ* is the person in whom the saving events took place, and therefore the blessings of salvation are also to be described in terms of him. But the association is a very general one.

So we must admit that here there is a certain indiscriminate use of *Christ* and *Lord*, though the *Christ* passages are in the majority. The reasons for this will be investigated later on.[446]

---

[432] II Cor. 5.14. In Rom. 8.35 the expression is joined to a fragment of the pistis-formula, so it is impossible to decide with any certainty whether *Christ* is simply taken up from the pistis-formula or whether it is the title which appropriately qualifies 'love'.

[433] In Rom. 8.9 'the Spirit of Christ' and 'the Spirit of God' both occur. Phil. 1.19 has 'the Spirit of Jesus Christ'.

[434] Phil. 1.8. On text-critical grounds the title is to be deleted from 'in the grace of Christ' (Gal. 1.6). Thus Lietzmann, *Galater* 5 *ad loc.*, and Schlier, *Galater* 12 n. 2 *ad loc.*

[435] Rom. 15.29.

[436] II Cor. 12.9; in I Cor. 1.24 Christ himself is the 'power of God'.

[437] II Cor. 11.10.

[438] II Cor. 1.5. Cf. Gal. 6.17 'the *stigmata* of Jesus'.

[439] II Cor. 4.6; cf. 4.4 'the gospel of the glory of Christ'.

[440] I Cor. 2.16.

[441] II Cor. 1.5.

[442] Phil. 1.11.

[443] E.g. 'the Spirit of God' (I Cor. 2.11; 3.16 etc.).

[444] E.g. 'the Spirit of the Lord' (II Cor. 3.17; cf. Gal. 4.6 'the Spirit of his Son', where the title Son of God must have been inserted to echo the formula in Gal. 4.4).

[445] E.g. 'the Spirit' (Rom. 8.23, 26 etc.).

[446] See 57b.

33. 'Christ' in Descriptions of Individual Christians or of the Church

a. As well as the term 'apostle', by which Paul describes his own office and which he links with the title *Christ*,[447] we find other terms in the Paulines which we shall list here: the servant (διάκονος) of Christ,[448] the slave (δοῦλος) of Christ,[449] the servant (ὑπηρέτης) of Christ,[450] under the law (ἔννομος) of Christ,[451] a minister (λειτουργός) of Christ Jesus;[452] and in the opening sentences of letters, on the analogy of 'apostle of Christ Jesus', we find: the slave (δοῦλος) of Christ Jesus,[453] a prisoner (δέσμιος) of (= for ?) Christ Jesus.[454]

Here too it is impossible to trace a direct connection between these terms and the *pistis*-statements, even though Paul regularly links them with the title *Christ*. It is noteworthy that even designations like 'slave' and 'servant' which seem to cry out for *Lord* as their counterpart, are nevertheless linked with *Christ* throughout. Expressions like 'the slave of the Lord' and 'the slave of the Lord Jesus Christ' are found only (and typically) in the deutero-Pauline[455] and late non-Pauline writings,[456] and they represent a stage at which there was greater imprecision in the use of the christological titles.

The genitive in these phrases is a genitive of belonging and thus indicates that the Christian belongs to him who brought salvation. It is more difficult to say precisely what ideas are implied in this notion of belonging. In the case of the terms which Paul uses to describe himself we would have to think of the Damascus experience or of his office as preacher and missionary to the Gentiles. We would then have to say that because it was *Christ* who had appeared to Paul outside Damascus, Paul inserted into the expression which referred to himself the title of him who had died and had been raised. Alternatively we could say that because Paul in his preaching knew that he was bound by the kerygma as summarized in the pistis-formula, he therefore linked

[447] See 13b.   [448] II Cor. 11.23.
[449] Gal. 1.10.   [450] I Cor. 4.1.
[451] I Cor. 9.21.   [452] Rom. 15.16.
[453] Rom. 1.1; Phil. 1.1.   [454] Philemon 1, 9.
[455] II Tim. 2.24.   [456] James 1.1.

the expressions which referred to himself with the same christo-logical title as is set in the pistis-formula.

We cannot go beyond reflections such as these. Conclusive answers cannot be given. But this uncertainty in our explanation cannot bring into question the unequivocal nature of the evidence, for this is reinforced by the passages in which Paul speaks more freely of missionary activity.[457]

b. We find the following expressions used to describe the Church: You are (or: I am) Christ's,[458] those who belong to Christ,[459] to be Christ's,[460] called to belong to Jesus Christ,[461] the churches of Christ.[462] In these expressions too we must reckon the genitives to be genitives of belonging.[463] This again prompts us to ask what ideas underlie such expressions. There is no trace of any connection with the pistis-formula. But in Gal. 3.28b, 29 similar phrases ('you are all one in Christ Jesus' and 'you are Christ's') are used to describe the effects of baptism. Again, the words 'I am Christ's' (I Cor. 1.12f.) lead Paul immediately to recall both baptism and the saving events. Evidently Paul regards baptism as the basis of belonging to Christ. If we couple with this Paul's presentation of baptism in Rom. 6.3–11 (which is in fact an exposition of the pistis-formula), then we can no longer overlook the fact that there is a clear progression of thought which may be summarized like this: the Church belongs to Christ; this is based upon the act of baptism; baptism is something which is done 'with' Christ, i.e. it is genuinely connected with the saving events of the death and the resurrection of Christ. It is in fact to this kind of thinking that we must attribute the statements which affirm that the Church belongs to *Christ*.

c. It goes without saying that the title *Christ*, which thus found

---

[457] *Christ* sent him to preach the gospel (I Cor. 1.17); it is he who speaks in him (II Cor. 13.3); Paul will say only what *Christ* has done through him, and he evangelizes only in places where *Christ* has not yet been named (Rom. 15.18, 20); as an ambassador for *Christ* he pleads for him (II Cor. 5.20); he wishes to 'take every thought captive to obey *Christ*' (II Cor. 10.5); for the sake of *Christ* he endures persecution and hardships (II Cor. 12.10) and in the world's eyes he is accounted a fool for *Christ*'s sake (I Cor. 4.10). See 13f.

[458] I Cor. 3.23; Gal. 3.29; I Cor. 1.12.

[459] I Cor. 15.23 (οἱ τοῦ Χριστοῦ).

[460] II Cor. 10.7.

[461] Rom. 1.6 (κλητοὶ Ἰησοῦ Χριστοῦ).

[462] Rom. 16.16.

[463] This must apply also in the case of Rom. 1.6 (cf. n. 461), for according to Paul it is always God, not Christ, who calls. Cf. Schlier, *Galater*, p. 12 n. 1, on 1.6.

its way into statements about the Church, is also found in ecclesiological discussions and expressions, even when the connection with baptism or with the saving events is barely (if at all) discernible. In this category we must put the baptismal statement about 'putting on Christ',[464] but also expressions like 'Christ Jesus has made me his own',[465] and '(Jesus) Christ in you'[466] belong here.

Other passages speak of the Church. *Christ* is called 'the body' (σῶμα),[467] or individuals are called 'members of Christ'[468] or 'fellow heirs with Christ'.[469] There are also more fanciful designations, such as 'the aroma of Christ',[470] 'the glory of Christ',[471] 'a letter of Christ'.[472] God establishes the Church 'in (εἰς) Christ',[473] Paul fears that the Church's thoughts will be led astray from a sincere and pure devotion 'to (εἰς) Christ'.[474] Epaenetus is called 'the first (convert) in Asia for (εἰς) Christ'.[475] To those who would submit to circumcision 'Christ will be of no advantage', for they are 'severed from Christ'.[476]

In terms of their substance, those of the Pauline *en*-formulae which speak of the nature of the Church[477] also belong here. But since they have a stamp of their own they demand separate treatment, which is why we merely mention them here in passing.[478]

34. 'Christ' in Passages of Exhortation

a. Christ is found frequently in passages of exhortation. In two places the connection with the pistis-formula is apparent.[479] The fact that *Christ* died for the brethren determines the conduct of every Christian towards the brethren. If in one's dealings with

[464] Gal. 3.27.
[465] Phil. 3.12.
[466] II Cor. 13.5; Rom. 8.10; cf. Gal. 2.19f.
[467] I Cor. 12.12.
[468] I Cor. 6.15.
[469] Rom. 8.17.
[470] II Cor. 2.15.
[471] II Cor. 8.23.
[472] II Cor. 3.3.
[473] II Cor. 1.21.
[474] II Cor. 11.2, 3.
[475] Rom. 16.5.
[476] Gal. 5.2, 4.
[477] See notes 510, 523.
[478] See 36 below.
[479] I Cor. 8.12; Rom. 14.15 (though here *Christ* is admittedly not repeated).

the brethren one does not conform to Christ's own conduct one is sinning not only against the brother but also 'against Christ'.

A similar thought is expressed in the 'conformity-rule',[480] though here it is no longer a fragment of the pistis-formula which is used to mention the saving events. The formulation is here in freer terms, adapted to whatever ethical instruction is to be associated with it. The clearest examples of this pattern are found at Rom. 15.7 ('Welcome one another as *Christ* has welcomed you') and Rom. 15.2f. ('let each of us please his neighbour for his good, to edify him. For Christ did not please himself'). These expressions show how ethical instruction in preaching had a christological basis, i.e. it was based upon the saving work of Christ. It would be a mistake to read into these passages the ideas of the later Church about the *imitatio Christi*, for the acts which form the basis of our salvation cannot be 'imitated'.[481] But the practical instructions derive their obligatory character from the fact that they conform to the conduct of Christ—the very conduct which made our salvation possible. There is also another reason why the 'conformity-rule' is worthy of attention, for it shows how the actual situation in which a church finds itself can become the source of new christological formulations and statements. Finally this 'conformity-rule', because it encourages in every situation a new formulation of the saving events, demonstrates that the title *Christ* in exhortation of this kind is by no means accidental, for *Christ* is the title used in the formula which is the traditional summary of the saving events.

It is in the light of this 'rule' that we are to understand Paul's admonition of the Corinthians 'by the meekness and gentleness of Christ',[482] for here the idea of conformity, though not explicitly stated, is brought in by means of this appeal to Christ's qualities. The same is intended when Paul speaks of the 'law of Christ'[483] which is fulfilled by those who bear the transgressions of others.

The expression 'in accord with (κατά) Christ Jesus'[484] contains the same idea, as the much discussed sentence 'Have this mind

[480] See n. 401.
[481] Similarly Dahl, 'Formgeschichtliche Beobachtungen' 7.
[482] II Cor. 10.1.
[483] Gal. 6.2.
[484] Rom. 15.5.

among yourselves which you have (ὁ καὶ ἐν) Christ Jesus'[485] does also.[486] Finally the same pattern underlies the summary sentence 'Be imitators of me, as I am of Christ',[487] except that it has been adapted to express the relationship between the church and the apostle, rather than that between the church and Christ.

b. Clearly the idea of the 'conformity-rule' is left behind when *Christ* is regarded as one who confronts the Church as the final arbiter of its ethical conduct. Thinking in these terms, Paul speaks of forgiveness 'in the presence of Christ',[488] of being 'in the service of Christ'.[489] We must seek 'the (good) things of Christ Jesus'.[490] Paul prays that the sharing of Philemon's faith 'may promote the knowledge of all the good that is ours in (εἰς) Christ',[491] but εἰς Χριστόν eventually becomes a vague statement, no longer clear in its reference. We should also include here Paul's remark that the Galatians received him 'as Christ Jesus'.[492]

It is highly significant that the same expressions as we find in this second group of passages are combined elsewhere with the title *Lord*, and not with *Christ*.[493] But this shows that these expressions are not to be understood solely in terms of the ideas associated with the title *Christ*. We shall show later on to what extent they may also be explained in terms of the ideas associated with the title *Lord*.[494]

35. 'Christ' in Statements about the Parousia

In only three passages is *Christ* associated with a statement about the parousia. All three are in Philippians and in all three the phrase used is 'the day of Christ'[495] or 'the day of Christ Jesus'.[496]

---

[485] Phil. 2.5.
[486] This can be said, no matter how we understand the sentence in other respects. This has already been pointed out by Dahl, 'Formgeschichtliche Beobachtungen' 7.
[487] I Cor. 11.1.
[488] II Cor. 2.10 (ἐν προσώπῳ Χριστοῦ).
[489] Rom. 14.18.
[490] Phil. 2.21 (τὰ Χριστοῦ 'Ιησοῦ).
[491] Philemon 6.
[492] Gal. 4.14.
[493] Cf. Rom. 14.18 ('serving *Christ*') with the reading at Rom. 12.11 ('serving the *Lord*'); or Phil. 2.21 ('seeking the things of *Christ Jesus*') with I Cor. 7.32, 34 ('being anxious about the things of the *Lord*').
[494] See 47a and 57b.
[495] Phil. 1.10; 2.16.
[496] Phil. 1.6.

If we also take into account that in Philippians *Christ* is used far more frequently than *Lord*,[497] then obviously we must reckon with the fact that *Christ* occurs in contexts which originally were associated with other christological titles. This is exactly what has happened in the statements about the parousia. For except in Philippians Paul always links with these statements the title *Lord*,[498] which makes it clear that there is an essential connection with the prayer *Maranatha*.[499]

This means that we must regard the presence of the title *Christ* in these statements about the parousia as the result of a fading of the original meaning of christological titles.[500]

36. The Formulae ἐν Χριστῷ 'Ιησοῦ and ἐν Χριστῷ

a. Here we cannot take up a position on the entire range of the problems presented by the *en*-formulae,[501] but must concentrate on the question whether the various types of *en*-formula each have a particular range of application or are used indiscriminately.[502]

If we examine the 28 passages in which the formula 'in Christ Jesus' occurs,[503] giving particular attention to their formal structure, we discover that in 11 instances the formula occupies a position at the end of the sentence, and in 17 instances positions elsewhere in the sentence. This shows that at the end of sentences

[497] The ratio of *Christ (Jesus)* to *Lord (Jesus Christ)* is 21:5, excluding the *en*-formulae. *Lord* stands on its own in Phil. 4.5, a sentence which in origin is connected with *Maranatha*. In the hymn at 2.11 the acclamation is traditional, and in 1.2 the title *Lord* is included in the full christological designation which Paul habitually uses in the introductory greeting. There remain only two verses (3.8, 20) in which Paul has used *ad hoc* the full designation containing *Lord*.

[498] See 48ad.   [499] See 23c–e.

[500] This is an argument (against Michaelis, *Einleitung in das NT*, 1946, 207f.) in favour of the view that Philippians is late, i.e. written during imprisonment in Rome. In the non-Paulines we find the expression 'the day of the Lord' only at II Thess. 2.2 and II Peter 3.10, in the second instance in the well known statement that the day of the Lord will come as a thief in the night (cf. I Thess. 5.2). Otherwise, 'day' occurs on its own, or qualified by OT expressions.

[501] The recent monograph by Neugebauer, *In Christus, Eine Untersuchung zum Paulinischen Glaubensverständnis*, 1961, deals with the problems relating to the *en*-formulae. His essay 'In Christo', *NTS* 4, 1957/58, 124–138, which is really a shorter version of the monograph, is in many respects even clearer by virtue of its brevity and precision.

[502] This is evidently the opinion of Oepke, *TWNT* II 537.20–538.38.

[503] I Thess. 2.14; 5.18; I Cor. 1.2, 4, 30; 4.15, 17b; 16.24; Gal. 2.4; 3.14, 26; 3.28; 5.6; Rom. 3.24; 6.11; 8.1, 2; 15.17; 16.3; Phil. 1.1, 26; 2.5; 3.3, 14; 4.7, 19, 21; Philemon 23.

it is this type of *en*-formula which is preferred.[504] The following list shows how these 28 passages are distributed:

1. 6 occur in the opening designation, the preamble, and the farewell prayer[505]
2. 4 occur in personal messages[506]
3. 2 occur in exhortation[507]
4. 16 occur in theological argument[508]

b. What this distribution might have led us to suspect is confirmed when we examine the content of these 28 passages, for the formula is used 11 times to qualify the blessings of salvation,[509] nine times to define the Church,[510] and eight times in a variety of contexts which include such things as Paul's missionary activity, the right kind of pride, or the description of fellow-workers.[511] As far as the first two groups are concerned, Neugebauer's observations hold good;[512] but when he describes the third group as 'relating to the apostle', this collective heading gives the impression of a unity which in reality is not there. For in this third group, in

[504] See 36d.
[505] Phil. 1.1; I Cor. 1.2, 4; 16.24; Phil. 4.7, 19.
[506] I Cor. 4.15, 17b; Philemon 23; Rom. 16.3.
[507] I Thess. 5.18; Phil. 2.5 (each time giving a brief factual basis for exhortation).
[508] I Thess. 2.14; I Cor. 1.30; Gal. 2.4; 3.14, 26, 28; 5.6; Rom. 3.24; 6.11; 8.1, 2; 15.17; Phil. 1.26; 3.3, 14; 4.21.
[509] Thus 'redemption' (Rom. 3.24. Even if Paul has borrowed the word, together with v. 25, from elsewhere, it is still he who has linked it with the phrase 'in Christ Jesus'); 'sons of God . . .' (Gal. 3.26. The following vv. show that the expression is not to be taken with the word 'faith', cf. Schlier, *Galater* 127 *ad loc.*); 'the Spirit of life . . .' (Rom. 8.2); 'the upward call . . .' (Phil. 3.14); 'God's riches in glory . . .' (Phil. 4.19); 'the will of God . . .' (I Thess. 5.18). In a few instances the formula is rather to be taken with the accompanying verb, e.g. God 'gives grace . . .' (I Cor. 1.4); Christians 'have freedom . . .' (Gal. 2.4); the 'blessing of Abraham' is to 'come upon the Gentiles . . .' (Gal. 3.14); 'the peace of God will keep' hearts and minds . . . (Phil. 4.7); faith 'avails . . .' (Gal. 5.6).
[510] Thus 'the churches of God in Christ Jesus which are in Judea' (I Thess. 2.14); Christians are 'in Christ Jesus' (I Cor. 1.30; Rom. 8.1); though racially and sociologically diverse, the Church is 'one in Christ Jesus' (Gal. 3.28); thanks to the gift of salvation, the Church 'lives to God in Christ Jesus' (Rom. 6.11); life 'in Christ Jesus' demands a particular way of thinking and acting (Phil. 2.5); in Paul's opening designations and farewell prayers the Church and its members are described as holy or sanctified 'in Christ Jesus' (I Cor. 1.2; Phil. 1.1; 4.21).
[511] Paul became the father of the Corinthians 'in Christ Jesus through the gospel' (Rom. 4.15); he describes his evangelistic activity as his 'ways in Christ Jesus' (I Cor. 4.17b); he speaks of 'being proud' or of 'glorying' 'in Christ Jesus' (Rom. 15.17; Phil. 1.26; 3.3). In the greetings we find the expressions 'my fellow workers' or 'my fellow prisoner' 'in Christ Jesus' (Rom. 16.3; Philemon 23). Such phrases are associated elsewhere with 'in the Lord' (cf. Rom. 16), so that it is now impossible to know what particular ideas lie behind these phrases. The same goes for the farewell greeting 'My love be with you all in Christ Jesus' (I Cor. 16.24).
[512] Neugebauer, 'In Christo' (*NTS*) 131; cf. also his *In Christus* 119–130.

contrast to the other two, we find no principle to account for the formula's occurrence in each particular instance. So we shall not be surprised if, in the passages which contain this third use of the formula, there is indiscriminate use of the christological titles.

c. If we ask what significance the designation *Christ Jesus* has in the formula, we are bound to notice that it is God who is often explicitly named as the agent. This is particularly true of the group in which the formula serves to qualify the blessings of salvation, for in 7 out of the 11 instances in this group the theme is the relationship between God and mankind. In these instances the formula 'in Christ Jesus' describes the character of the divine gift of salvation, or the act by which that salvation was wrought, or the manner in which it was wrought. So there is a kinship between this formula and the pistis-formula, at least in structure, for the pistis-formula in its earliest form not only has the title *Christ (Jesus)* but also represents God as the agent in the saving events. We find nothing like this in the case of the formula 'in the *Lord*' (ἐν κυρίῳ).[513] This indicates that the kinship we have referred to between the pistis-formula and the expression 'in Christ Jesus' is not accidental. If we try, with this in mind, to define the sense which the expression 'in Christ Jesus' has, we come close to the paraphrase proposed by Neugebauer: '. . . determined by the fact that Jesus Christ died and rose'.[514]

d. When we come to examine the formal structure of the 25 passages in which the expression 'in Christ' occurs, we notice immediately that in 23 instances it is used as a formula,[515] and only in one instance (I Cor. 15.19—'hope in Christ') is it used differently, but this is due to the syntax. In II Cor. 5.19 it is uncertain whether ἐν ought not to be taken with the participle. But since we cannot be sure about this we shall consider the passage here. The formula occurs 18 times within the body of sentences and 6 times at the end of sentences. Its occurrence at the end of sentences is thus only half as frequent as was the case with the fuller formula 'in Christ Jesus'.[516]

The distribution of these passages is as follows: 1. 7 occur in

---

[513] See 50b.
[514] Neugebauer, 'In Christo' (*NTS*), 131.
[515] I Thess. 4.16; I Cor. 3.1; 4.10, 15; 15.18, 22; II Cor. 2.14, 17; 3.14; 5.17; 12.2, 19; Gal. 1.22; 2.17; Rom. 9.1; 12.5; 16.7, 9, 10; Phil. 1.13; 2.1; Philemon 8, 20b.
[516] See 36a.

personal messages;[517] 2. 2 occur in exhortation;[518] 3. 14 occur in theological argument.[519] This corresponds to what we found in the case of the formula 'in Christ Jesus', except that 'in Christ' is never found in the opening designation, the preamble, or in the farewell prayer. This is natural, for the short formula is less suited to the more formal style in these portions of the letters.

In two instances we find the article inserted into the formula.[520] In the first instance this is due to a desire to make the two expressions 'in Adam' (ἐν τῷ Ἀδάμ) and 'in Christ' (ἐν τῷ Χριστῷ) exactly parallel. The article is not an indication that *Christ* is here used as a messianic title. In the second passage it is not clear why the article was inserted.[521] But the context gives just as little ground for asserting that *Christ* is used here as a messianic title.

e. If we now examine the content of these passages, we get a result which characteristically resembles what we found in the case of the formula 'in Christ Jesus', and yet just as characteristically differs from it. For the expression 'in Christ' is also used to qualify the blessings of salvation, the Church, and the apostle and his fellow workers, etc. But the frequency of its occurrence in these contexts is exactly the reverse of what we observed in the case of the fuller formula.

Only five times does the short formula qualify soteriological terms.[522] It is used eight times to define the Church or groups within the Church,[523] and it serves eleven times to describe particular persons, circumstances or acts.[524] This third group is

[517] I Cor. 3.1; II Cor. 12.2, 19; Gal. 1.22; Rom. 16.7, 9, 10.

[518] Phil. 2.1; Philemon 20b.

[519] I Thess. 4.16; I Cor. 4.10, 15; 15.18, 22; II Cor. 2.14, 17; 3.14; 5.17; Gal. 2.17; Rom. 9.1; 12.5; Phil. 1.13; Philemon 8. Also, perhaps, II Cor. 5.19.

[520] I Cor. 15.22; II Cor. 2.14.

[521] It is just possible that the article was inserted in order to echo the rather formal τῷ δὲ θεῷ . . . τῷ . . .

[522] In the first place there is the phrase which paraphrases the saving event, 'God was in Christ' (II Cor. 5.19)—if this really is to be counted among the *en*-formulae. Paul has much 'boldness in Christ' (Philemon 8); Christians seek to be 'justified in Christ' (Gal. 2.17); they are 'made alive in Christ' (I Cor. 15.22); only 'in Christ' is the veil at the reading of the OT taken away (II Cor. 3.14).

[523] Thus 'the churches of Judea . . . in Christ' (Gal. 1.22); the members of the Church are 'one body in Christ' (Rom. 12.5); 'in Christ' is itself a designation of the Church (II Cor. 5.17); Paul describes himself as 'a man in Christ' (II Cor. 12.2); Christians are 'wise in Christ' (I Cor. 4.10), but they can also be 'babes in Christ' (I Cor. 3.1); and finally Christians who have died are described as 'the dead in Christ' (I Thess. 4.16) or as 'those who have fallen asleep in Christ' (I Cor. 15.18).

[524] Thus the Church might conceivably have 10,000 'guides in Christ' (I Cor. 4.15); those to whom greetings are addressed are 'those who were in Christ before

even more difficult to summarize under a single heading than was its counterpart in the case of the formula 'in Christ Jesus'. When Neugebauer subsumes these passages too under the heading 'relating to the apostle',[525] the unity implied by such a heading is a pure fiction. If the term 'apostle' appears here and there, it does so for the simple reason that Paul, the author of the letters, is an apostle. But to use this term as a means of classification is to sacrifice all precision. It cannot be denied that in a number of the passages belonging to this 'group' the expression 'in the *Lord*' could just have well have been used.[526]

f. If we ask what the connection is between the expression 'in Christ' and the ideas which underlie the pistis-formula, the first thing we must say is that only in four passages is God explicitly named, and in two of these it is man who is the agent.[527] In II Cor. 5.19 there is a direct connection with the saving death of Christ, for the sentence 'God was in Christ reconciling the world to himself' is really a paraphrase of the statements in the pistis-formula. But it is not certain whether ἐν in this passage ought not to be taken with the participle, in which case it could not count as evidence of the *en*-formula 'in Christ'. All the same there are associations here which make it natural that the formula with *Christ* and not with *Lord* should appear in this context. We can hardly say more than that.

g. Finally, if we compare the ways in which the formulae 'in Christ Jesus' and 'in Christ' are used, we must say that the fuller formula, having greater rhetorical weight, is preferred at the end of sentences and in sections within the letters where a more formal style is used. But if we group the formulae according to the content of the passages in which they occur, their respective

---

me' (Rom. 16.7); Urbanus is a 'fellow worker in Christ' (Rom. 16.9), and Apelles is 'approved in Christ' (Rom. 16.10); Paul uses the formula in protestations: 'in the sight of God we speak in Christ' (II Cor. 2.17; 12.19), or 'I am speaking the truth in Christ' (Rom. 9.1); the difficult phrase about God 'who in Christ leads us in triumph' (θριαμβεύων ἡμᾶς ἐν τῷ Χριστῷ, II Cor. 2.14) no doubt emphasizes, as does the context, the effect upon onlookers, which brings it close to another passage which speaks of imprisonment which everyone can see to be 'in Christ', i.e. in Christ's cause (Phil. 1.13). Finally the formula occurs in specific exhortation, 'refresh my heart in Christ' (Philemon 20b) and in the expression 'encouragement in Christ' (Phil. 2.1).

[525] Neugebauer, 'In Christo' (*NTS*) 131.
[526] This is true particularly of those in Rom. 16, but it applies also to those in passages of exhortation. See 50, 56.
[527] II Cor. 2.17; 12.19.

frequency-curves run in opposite directions. This indicates that the shorter formula has already moved further away from the ideas which originally constituted it, and this has facilitated its insertion into the most varied contexts. But in spite of these differences of emphasis in the use of the two formulae we should not overlook their basic unity. Both alike are placed in soteriological and ecclesiological statements, but they both have a wider range of application, too, in which their use and their meaning become increasingly indefinite. Because of these similarities we are justified in bringing together these two formulae, thus forming a large group of *en*-phrases which may be compared and contrasted with the other group, namely that in which the title *Lord* occurs.

37. The Expressions διὰ 'Ιησοῦ Χριστοῦ *and* διὰ Χριστοῦ 'Ιησοῦ

Here we need only return briefly to the *dia*-phrases which do not include the title *Lord*.[528] The two phrases διὰ (τοῦ) Χριστοῦ[529] and διὰ τοῦ 'Ιησοῦ[530] were prompted by reasons which we discovered earlier.[531] In all these passages the title used is the one which for various reasons occurs in the preceding verses. So the occurrence of these particular types of the *dis*-phrase is determined by considerations of form, and not of content.

But this cannot be said of the other two types, 'through Jesus Christ'[532] and 'through Christ Jesus'[533]. To be sure, the reason why the double title was chosen in these five passages is clear, for in every instance the phrase occurs either in the opening designation or in the preamble or at the end of a sentence. But it is difficult to say why the full formula including *Lord* was not chosen. In the case of Gal. 1.1 it could be pointed out that the phrase is a substitute for the designation of the apostle as 'apostle of Christ Jesus', and that in Phil. 1.11 the title used in vv. 6 and 8 was determinative. But in the case of the other three passages the full designation containing *Lord* could just as well have been used, for all three

---

[528] On the problems connected with the *dia*-phrase and on the version of it which contains the title *Lord* see 19ab.
[529] II Cor. 1.5; 3.4; 5.18.
[530] I Thess. 4.14.
[531] See 19b.
[532] Gal. 1.1; Rom. 1.8; 5.17; Phil. 1.11.
[533] Rom. 2.16.

qualify either an activity associated with worship or the blessings of salvation. It is precisely in such contexts that elsewhere the full designation containing *Lord* is used.

Since we saw earlier that this full form of the *dia*-phrase is in fact the earliest form, and one which was used in worship, we must regard the two versions 'through Jesus Christ' and 'through Christ Jesus' as secondary, i.e. the result of a fading of the christological titles' original significance.

38. The σύν Phrases

In the Paulines there are only a few instances in which σύν is associated with any of the christological titles. Nevertheless we do find the expressions 'with the Lord',[534] 'with Jesus',[535] and 'with Christ'.[536] Even these few instances show that Paul uses σύν in two senses, the first sacramental (in connection with baptism),[537] and the second eschatological (in connection with the parousia or the resurrection).[538] The two senses are not isolated from one another, for the sacramental presupposes the eschatological. It is consonant with the origin of the title *Christ* in the pistis-formula that the sacramental σύν is associated with *Christ*, for baptism is interpreted as a sharing in the saving event of the death and resurrection of Christ. The eschatological σύν relating to the parousia is linked in I Thess. 4.17 with the title *Lord*. This is not surprising when one remembers that Paul's statements about the parousia are based upon ideas connected with the *Maranatha* with which the title *Lord* was originally associated.[539]

We may take it that in the reference at II Cor. 4.14 to resurrection 'with Jesus' the proper name is simply a repetition of the 'Jesus' in vv. 10, 11, 14a.

Phil. 1.23 is interesting. Here it is not the sacramental σύν that is meant, so it must be eschatological. The passage does indeed have eschatological significance, for it is about life after death. But this

---

[534] I Thess. 4.17.
[535] II Cor. 4.14.
[536] Rom. 6.8; Phil. 1.23.
[537] Rom. 6.8.
[538] I Thess. 4.17; II Cor. 4.14; cf. Phil. 1.23.
[539] See 23cd.

'eschatology' does not have in view the parousia of the *Mare-Kyrios* but the moment following immediately upon death. The parousia does not come within sight.[540] We might be tempted to think that this explains why the eschatological σύν is linked in this particular instance with *Christ* and not with *Lord*. But a closer look at Philippians reveals that the title *Christ* appears there even in statements about the parousia. Indeed Philippians represents a stage at which *Christ* is increasingly inserted into contexts in which originally the title *Lord* belonged. For this reason we must not take the change in christological terminology as an indication that in matters relating to eschatology or to resurrection the range of ideas connected with the title *Lord* gave place to those connected with the title *Christ*.

39. 'Christ' in References to the Old Testament

Paul also puts the title *Christ* in places where he takes up OT material and relates it, usually typologically, to Christ. Thus 'the seed of Abraham' is interpreted as referring to Christ, and the law is called a 'tutor to conduct us to Christ'.[541]

Of the passages which we have already discussed we should mention here I Cor. 5.7; 10.4, in which *Christ* is described respectively as 'our passover' and as 'the rock'. The very fact that it was possible to discuss these passages when we were dealing with the blessings of salvation shows clearly how here and there one can be in doubt about the actual motive which prompted the choice of whatever title was used. But what is significant, in our present context, is that any such motives governing the choice of christological titles can be picked out at all.

40. Other Reasons for Using the Title 'Christ'

a. In view of what we have just said, it would be a mistake to regard any of our detailed arguments as anything more than an attempt to show (by referring to the content of various passages)

---

[540] Unless the parousia is implicit in Paul's thinking here because for him the interval between death and parousia is practically of no account.

[541] Gal. 3.16, 24.

what were the motives underlying the choice of the title *Christ*. But there are formal considerations, too, which immediately become apparent if we take into account Paul's custom of sticking to one title within any given section. Passages which illustrate this and which we have not classified so far are: II Cor. 5.16, within the section 5.14–21; Gal. 2.17, within the section 2.15–21; and Phil. 1.20f., within the section 1.12–26.[542]

The same principle is at work where Paul repeats within a sentence or a sequence of sentences the title he has just used.[543]

b. Finally there remain a few passages in which it is impossible to explain why *Christ* occurs.[544] But such passages are rare and do not affect our general conclusions.

41. Summary

The grouping we have just made of the passages containing the title *Christ* is not a merely superficial list of statistics. As the passages were grouped according to the matter they contain, so the motives came to light which caused Paul to choose this particular title. These we must now summarize.

1. It is clear that even in passages which are of his own formulation Paul follows the traditional use of the title, as represented most concisely in the pistis-formula. We can see how Paul follows the tradition in passages in which he is speaking of the saving significance of *Christ*, and also in places where he discusses the blessings of salvation in general. But in the latter case it is true that we also find formulations which include the title *Lord*.

2. As a result of Paul's interpretation of the significance of *Christ* for salvation, we can understand how *Christ* comes to be employed in ecclesiological statements also. The ἐν-phrases and the sacramental σύν-phrase belong to this category.

---

[542] Further examples are: I Cor. 15.12–24 (where admittedly the theme is a limited one); Gal. 3.22–29 (*Christ* or *Christ Jesus* 7 times); Gal. 5.1–4 (*Christ* 3 times); Rom. 15.16–20 (*Christ* or *Christ Jesus* 5 times).

[543] Thus I Cor. 3.23, 'you are Christ's, and Christ is God's'. I Cor. 11.3, 'the head of every man is Christ . . . and the head of Christ is God'. *Christ* in the first part of this sentence no doubt has been determined by 11.1. Cf. also I Cor. 1.12f.

[544] Thus Phil. 3.7. We must expect this here and there in Philippians as a whole, where *Christ* has almost completely ousted *Lord*. II Cor. 6.15 should also be noted here, unless 6.14–7.1 is a post-Pauline interpolation.

3. In passages of exhortation the implications of the saving event in *Christ* are drawn out in such a way that concrete propositions governing practical ethics can be based upon it. It is to this end that the 'conformity-rule' is used. The *content* of such admonitions (and not any claim they may make to command obedience) springs directly from the saving event in *Christ*. Where *Christ* is mentioned in a general sense as one who has authority over the Christian's life we also find similar statements which contain the title *Lord*.

4. When OT material is drawn upon it is again the title *Christ* that is used. This is evidence of the fact that the title originally came from Judaism, and that *Christ* was a person in time and space, who could therefore naturally be linked with data drawn from the Old Covenant.

5. The fact that *Christ* features in statements about the parousia bears no relationship to the original meaning of the title but must be taken as evidence that in the course of their development the titles lost their original precise sense and came to be used in an increasingly random fashion.

Basically the same thing is to be said with regard to the variants of the *dia*-phrase which we discussed earlier.

So two things are to be said about Paul's use of the title *Christ*, namely that on the one hand he evidently continues pre-Pauline uses, but that on the other hand there is already a tendency to allow a particular title to penetrate contexts to which originally it would not have been suited.

II · LORD

A. LORD JESUS CHRIST

42. 'Lord Jesus Christ' in the Salutation

a. It has been argued for some time[545] that the opening designation in Paul's letters follows a pattern common in the Near East. Its arrangement in two parts, the naming of sender and addressee in the third person, and then a change to the direct form of address —all these are clear pointers to this.[546] But Friedrich, in criticizing Lohmeyer's thesis, has shown that Paul is also influenced in his opening designations by the Greek pattern,[547] for it is consistent with this pattern that 'the sender is given in the nominative in a phrase which is without predicate'. This means that the formal structure of the opening designation in Paul's letters is derived from Near Eastern models, modified by the Greek pattern. In its present form (with due allowance made for its dual derivation) we must regard it as Paul's own work.

b. According to Friedrich the same is also true of the salutation, which is our particular concern here. In the Pauline letters the salutation runs as follows: I Thess. 1.1 '(Paul, Silvanus and Timothy, To the church of the Thessalonians in God the Father[548] and the Lord Jesus Christ): Grace to you and peace.'[549] I Cor. 1.3;

---

[545] Most hotly (and one-sidedly) by Lohmeyer, 'Probleme paulinischer Theologie I', *ZNW* 26, 1927, 158–61; cf. Lietzmann, *Römer* 22; Michel, *Römer* 25; Kuss, *Der Römerbrief*, 1957, 2, calls it 'the pattern familiar in early Judaism'.

[546] Lietzmann, *Römer* 22, gives examples.

[547] Friedrich, 'Lohmeyers These über "Das paulinische Briefpräskript" kritisch beleuchtet', *ZNW* 46, 1955, 273f.

[548] The variant 'in God our Father' is not so well attested, but is readily understood as a later attempt to bring this into line with the opening greeting in the other Pauline letters, or with passages in which God is described as 'our Father', e.g. I Thess. 1.3; 3.11–13; Phil. 4.20.

[549] ℵAℜ continue: 'from God our Father and the Lord Jesus Christ', which gives the same wording as is found in the other Pauline letters and in II Thess. But this addition is proved secondary by the fact that the same group of texts also at other places tends to expand short forms for the sake of harmonizing, e.g. II Thess. 1.2.

II Cor. 1.2; Gal. 1.3; Rom. 1.7b; Phil. 1.2; Philemon 3: 'Grace to you and peace from God our[550] Father and the Lord Jesus Christ.'

Lohmeyer[551] claims that the language used here is liturgical and not Pauline and so he concludes that the salutation is a liturgical formula which was used at the beginning of worship. But Friedrich has examined Lohmeyer's arguments and has shown that they do not hold. In particular he has produced examples of letter-designations in which 'grace' and 'peace' occur together,[552] so that presumably Paul's phraseology is drawn from this source. There is nothing to indicate that the salutation was used in worship during the pre-Pauline period.

c. It is only when the expressions 'God our Father' and 'the Lord Jesus Christ' are added to the salutation that it becomes specifically Christian. We must assume that it was Paul who added them, for on the one hand there are nowhere any pre-Pauline examples of it, and on the other hand we find the change from the one form of the salutation to the other form (which must be regarded as different stages in its development) within the Pauline corpus itself.

In I Thess. 1.1 the salutation consists simply of the words 'Grace to you and peace'. The givers of these blessings are not named, but

[550] The variant reading at Gal. 1.3 (witnessed by p[46],[51] BℵDG and others) puts 'our' with 'Lord Jesus Christ' and not with 'God'. This reading, rather than the form which tallies with salutations as found in the other Paulines, is to be regarded as the original text, for thus the Nestle text is readily explicable as a harmonization with the other Paulines. To take it the other way round would mean that the disharmony is deliberate, but this is quite incomprehensible. A third possibility, namely that 'our', qualifying 'Father', was inadvertently omitted, would leave unexplained how 'our', qualifying 'Lord Jesus Christ', was 'inadvertently' inserted. So this reading is to be considered the original form of the text. From this there is a conclusion to be drawn. In the case of the form 'from God the Father and our Lord Jesus Christ' it is clear that 'God the Father' and 'our Lord Jesus Christ' are parallel to one another, both dependent upon the preposition 'from'. Since the salutations in the rest of Paul's letters stand in a similar position and in a similar context, they must have the same meaning. Thus we must say that in the other Paulines, too, 'God our Father' and 'the Lord Jesus Christ' are parallel (similar parallelism is found at I Thess. 1.1; 3.11; cf. also I Thess. 1.3; 3.13; Gal. 1.4), and therefore we must reject the possibility that the sense might be 'from God our Father and the Father of the Lord Jesus Christ', even though Paul can describe God in other places as 'the Father of Jesus Christ' (e.g. II Cor. 1.3; Rom. 15.6). For there is no passage in which God is clearly referred to as simultaneously 'the Father of the Lord' and 'our Father'. Since then there is no difference in sense between Gal. 1.3 and the rest of Paul's salutations, it is possible to include these passages under the same heading.

[551] Lohmeyer, 'Probleme' 161–64. Bultmann, *Theology* I, 12.2, 126 n. 1, agrees with Lohmeyer.

[552] Friedrich, 'Lohmeyers These' 273, quotes Syr. Baruch 78.2 and mentions letters from the late Assyrian and late Babylonian times, as well as the Elephantine papyri.

only the gifts. Instead the addressees are described as those who are 'in God the (our) Father and the Lord Jesus Christ'. Even if the reading with 'our' is secondary, it is still striking that it is by these titles that in the other Pauline letters the givers of these blessings are described. Since the Church which receives these blessings is never again described in this way (except in I Thessalonians) with 'God' and 'Christ' mentioned together,[553] and since elsewhere in this context the epithets 'Father' for God and 'Lord' for Christ are absent, our conclusion must be that Paul himself, having employed these two fuller titles *ad hoc* in I Thessalonians, transferred them in the other letters to the salutation,[554] which thus came to have its characteristically Pauline form.

Thus we regard the salutation as Paul's creation, for though it is based on pre-Christian models it is he who added particular designations of God and of Christ.

d. It is immediately apparent that these fuller designations come from the language of worship, for in worship God was appealed to as 'Father',[555] and it was in worship, too, that expressions containing the full christological designation 'our Lord Jesus Christ' were used.[556] In this sense the salutation also represents the adoption of pre-Pauline *Christian* material. But this is limited to the christological titles themselves. Nevertheless the fact that it is these full christological titles that Paul adopts is consistent with his custom of combining the various titles in passages in which the style is somewhat formal. The particular combination here of the title *Lord* with the double name *Jesus Christ* shows that the language used is that of the Hellenistic Gentile-Christian church, for only there was *Jesus Christ* understood as a double name, thus making possible its combination with the title *Lord*.

e. Finally it remains to us to interpret the noteworthy fact that 'our' is used to qualify 'God . . . Father' but not 'Lord'. Lohmeyer interprets this as significant for the meaning of the title *Lord*.[557]

---

[553] In I Cor. 1.2 'God' and 'Christ' are both named, but not in a comparable parallelism. I Cor. 1.1 and Rom. 1.7 mention only 'God', and Phil. 1.1 only 'Christ'. Gal. 1.2 and Philemon 1f. have neither.
[554] If this view corresponds to the facts, it provides one more argument for regarding I Thessalonians as the earliest of the Pauline letters known to us.
[555] Cf. Gal. 4.6; Rom. 8.15; cf. I Cor. 8.6.
[556] Cf. the original *dia*-phrases (see 19) and the closing greetings (see 20ab) etc.
[557] Lohmeyer, 'Probleme' 165–169, holds that the absence of the possessive emphasizes the great 'distance' between the *Lord* and believers. But he has to resort

But the reading at Gal. 1.3 which we take to be the original text and which has 'our Lord'[558] makes such a view impossible. For this passage shows that there is no difference in substance between the readings with and the readings without 'our'. On the other hand, there are formal considerations which may serve as an explanation, for arranged thus:

'Grace to you and peace   Χάρις ὑμῖν καὶ εἰρήνη
from God our Father   ἀπὸ θεοῦ πατρὸς ἡμῶν
and (the) Lord Jesus Christ'   καὶ κυρίου Ἰησοῦ Χριστοῦ

the salutation is perfectly balanced structurally, for each of the three parts contains three points of reference.[559] If we move ἡμῶν, this balance is destroyed. The balance of all the parts no doubt explains why the salutation in this form was preserved within the Pauline writings, as it were in stereotype fashion. This means that 'our', qualifying *Lord*, is omitted here for purely stylistic reasons, and its omission does not affect the meaning in the slightest.[560]

f. In terms of the ideas which it contains, the salutation comes very close to the pre-Pauline farewell formula.[561] In both, the (or our) *Lord Jesus Christ* is named as the one who stands in relation to the Church as the dispenser of grace. It is true that the wording of the farewell formula is 'the grace of the (our) Lord Jesus Christ . . .', whereas that of the salutation is 'grace . . . from the Lord Jesus Christ . . .', but both are concerned to name the author of this grace. The main difference is that the salutation names both God and the Lord Jesus Christ, while the farewell formula speaks only of the Lord Jesus Christ. This setting in parallel of 'God' and 'Lord' is only possible because the thought is of a unity in function between God and the *Lord*. Thus what is implicitly presupposed wherever Jesus is acclaimed as *Lord* is here made explicit.

g. A glance at the post-Pauline letters confirms our observation that the salutation in the opening designation of the Paulines does not represent a Christian formula which was in general use, but in

to arguments based on dualist metaphysics which are alleged to lie behind this. His arguments are not convincing.

[558] See n. 550.
[559] Lohmeyer himself stresses this, 'Probleme' 162.
[560] We reached a similar conclusion when we examined the farewell formula. See 20b.
[561] See 20.

its exact form is the work of Paul himself, for as a rule the deutero-Paulines differ characteristically from the Paulines in this respect.

II Thessalonians gives a definition of the recipient church which corresponds to that of I Thessalonians. The two *en*-phrases are used (i.e. 'in God our Father and in the Lord Jesus Christ'), but also the salutation is given in the form in which we find it in the other Paulines.[562] The same thing is found in Eph. 1.2. But in Col. 1.2 'the Lord Jesus Christ' appears to be secondary—an attempt to harmonize with the Paulines.

The authors of the Pastorals, who must have known the Pauline letters, have a phraseology of their own,[563] either (as in I and II Timothy) mentioning 'mercy' beside 'grace' and 'peace', and putting 'our' beside 'Lord' and transferring this to the end; or (as in Titus) substituting 'Saviour' for the title *Lord*.

I and II Peter, together with Jude, pray that grace and peace 'may be multiplied' and do not mention the author of these blessings. The epistle of James adopts the Greek form of the opening designation, and in the post-NT period this is found regularly in Ignatius.[564]

b. It is striking that Paul himself introduced the full titles including *Lord* into very few new contexts. One such context is the salutation. Another which might be mentioned is really another kind of *en*-formula.[565] The reason why Paul used these full titles is not difficult to discover. He uses them together in the opening designation of the letters because this requires a formal and dignified style, which in turn provides a suitable setting for the combined titles, for simply as a result of being combined, and also as a result of being used together in the liturgy, they have an im-

---

[562] On text-critical grounds 'our' is uncertain.

[563] Jeremias, *Die Briefe an Timotheus und Titus*, 1949, 5f., cites against this the fact 'that they (= the Pastorals) not only show the common and characteristic marks of the Pauline formula, but also in addition reflect precisely the stage of development which had been reached in the latest of the letters which preceded them' (among which he includes Eph. and Col.). He says that this is 'a weighty argument in favour of the genuineness of the Pastoral epistles'. This argument, if it referred simply to the overall pattern of the opening designation in the letters, might be admitted, for we have already recognized that the opening designation is a mixed form, based on Near Eastern and Greek models. But it is precisely with reference to the specifically Christian characteristics within this general frame that Jeremias' argument falls down.

[564] Thus Ignatius: *Eph., Magn., Trall., Rom., Smyrn., Philad.* The closing greeting, which again corresponds to the Greek formula, is usually ἔρρωσθε.

[565] This will not be discussed until later (see 51), for it needs to be compared with the formulae 'in Christ' and 'in the Lord' before we can judge its proper significance.

pressiveness of their own. But in those parts of the letters in which the style does not have to be particularly dignified Paul normally uses the simple title *Lord*. It is to these passages that we must now turn.

B. LORD

43. *'Lord' in Quotations of the Old Testament*

a. Paul quotes in his letters OT passages which contain the title *Lord*. In the texts quoted the title naturally refers to God. In the majority of instances Paul preserves this reference to God, but in a minority of instances, on the other hand, he applies the title to Jesus. This is not the place to discuss the entire range of problems associated with the fact that the name 'Yahweh' was no longer spoken in Judaism.[566] Since we are here concerned with Paul's use of OT quotations in Greek, we must simply assert that in the Pauline period, at public readings of the OT in Greek, 'Kyrios' was read instead of 'Yahweh', even though the tetragram still stood in the MSS of that period.[567]

Cerfaux,[568] in a very thorough exposition, has sought to discover which are the passages within the Paulines[569] in which the title *Kyrios* refers to God, and in which passages the title refers to Jesus. We can concur in large measure with his findings.[570] As a general rule the quotations in which the original meaning of *Kyrios* is preserved are fuller, and it is typical of them that they include

---

[566] On these problems see Baudissin, *Kyrios als Gottesname im Judentum und seine Stelle in der Religionsgeschichte*, 1929; and Cerfaux, 'Le nom divin "Kyrios" dans la Bible grecque', *Recueil L. Cerfaux* I, 1954, 113–36; ' "Adonai" et "Kyrios" ', *Recueil* I, 137–72; ' "Kyrios" dans les citations pauliniennes de l'Ancien Testament', *Recueil* I, 173–88.

[567] Cf. Schulz, *Johanneische Reden*, 3f.

[568] ' "Kyrios" dans les citations pauliniennes' 173–88; cf. also Foerster, *TWNT* III 1085.48–1086.33 (*Lord* 94–96).

[569] Cerfaux also includes II Thess. in his investigation.

[570] The following quotations refer to God: I Cor. 3.20; 14.21; II Cor. 6.17f.; Rom. 4.8; 9.28, 29; 10.16; 11.3, 34; 12.19; 14.11; 15.11. The following refer to Jesus: I Thess. 4.6; I Cor. 1.31 (= II Cor. 10.17); 10.21, 22; II Cor. 3.16, 18 (v. 16 is not an actual quotation but a Pauline formulation taking up the OT historical allusions. Cf. Hermann, *Kyrios und Pneuma*, 1961, 38, 57); Rom. 10.13. As against Cerfaux's arrangement, I would include I Cor. 10.26 in this second group.

expressions like 'as it is written',[571] or 'as God said',[572] and often mention the source,[573] thus making it quite plain that they are quotations. By contrast, the places at which *Kyrios* refers to Jesus merely give us fragments of quotations or isolated phrases which are not acknowledged as quotations.

This fact in itself probably means that the two groups do not have 'quotations' in the same sense. In the first group, where *Kyrios* refers to God, we can speak of quotations in the strict sense, for Paul draws upon LXX passages and uses its wording simply to support his argument. The choice of passage in such instances is Paul's own. With the fragments of quotations and the isolated phrases in which *Kyrios* refers to Jesus, however, it is otherwise. Here we find expressions which certainly (or at least probably) were current in Christian language before Paul's time, e.g. 'the table of the Lord', 'the glory of the Lord', 'to call upon the name of the Lord', 'to turn to the Lord', 'to provoke the Lord'.

Since these expressions are among the most useful in helping to reveal how Christians understood the title *Lord* we must examine a few of them in more detail.

b. 'Everyone who calls upon the name of the Lord will be saved' (Rom. 10.13) is a literal quotation of Joel 3.5 in the LXX (EVV 2.32). Paul has used it here to reinforce his own statement that '(the Lord) bestows his riches upon all who call upon him'. Without doubt this is the right text for the purpose, for the expression 'to call upon the name of the Lord' is itself derived from Joel 3.5 (LXX).[574] The same expression, again including 'the name' (*onoma*), is used at I Cor. 1.2 to designate the recipient Church, and in the non-Pauline writings it is found at Acts 2.21; 9.14, 21; 22.16. Clearly the expression belongs to pre-Pauline Christian terminology.[575] So this expression from the LXX must have been taken over, and the title *Kyrios* applied to Jesus, before

[571] E.g. I Cor. 3.19; 14.21; Rom. 12.19; 15.9.
[572] II Cor. 6.16.
[573] E.g. Rom. 9.25; 10.16.
[574] Even if the expression were derived from Ps. 98.6 rather than from Joel 3.5 (see Kümmel in his revision of Lietzmann, *Korinther* 166), this would make no fundamental difference to the reflections which follow. In either case the expression is a literal adoption of the wording of the LXX.
[575] Lietzmann, *Korinther* 5 calls it a 'customary designation'. But he is mistaken in interpreting this constant calling upon the Lord simply as 'daily prayer'. Cf. Bultmann, *Theology* I, 12.2, 125f.

Paul. Even in the pre-Pauline period the expression had become a way of describing Christians themselves as those 'who call upon the name of the *Lord*'. But this could only have happened in a church in which 'calling upon the *Lord*' was a characteristic activity and not simply a marginal one. It was only in the Hellenistic Gentile church that this condition was fulfilled. This would have to be admitted even by those scholars who think that the title *Kyrios* originated in the early Aramaic-speaking church.[576]

So it appears that the expression in question was taken over from the LXX because the title *Kyrios* was already used in a variety of ways in the Gentile-Christian church, largely because of the influence of the surrounding Hellenism. In this sense the application of the LXX *Kyrios* to Jesus marks the final stage, not the first, in the title's history within the Christian Church.

c. We reach a similar conclusion if we examine the expression 'the table of the *Lord*' from Mal. 1.7, 12, which in I Cor. 10.21 is applied to the Lord's Supper. There are two clear indications that Paul is here using the expression as a technical term. The first is that he takes for granted that the church will understand what he means, without further explanation, and the second is that he invents, in antithesis, the expression 'the table of demons'. Since the expression 'the table of the *Lord*' refers to the service of the Lord's Supper as a whole, it can only have been chosen when the celebration of the Lord's Supper and also the liturgical terminology associated with it had reached a developed form. But since *Kyrios* features prominently and in a variety of ways in the language associated with the Lord's Supper,[577] we may take it that in this respect, at least, the formulation of the eucharistic liturgy did not take place without the participation of the Hellenistic Gentile church. But this brings us to the same conclusion as we reached above, namely that it was the Hellenistic Gentile church which took over the LXX expression 'the table of the Lord', so that its introduction into the terminology associated with the Lord's Supper marks a fairly late stage.

d. The adoption of this LXX expression had two consequences which ought not to be overlooked. Firstly, it encouraged the use

---

[576] Thus e.g. Cullmann, *Christology* 195.
[577] Cf. 'the *Lord's* supper' (I Cor. 11. 20) and 'the *Lord's* death' (I Cor. 11. 26). See also 45 below.

of the title *Kyrios* on its own. It is not, of course, the primary cause of such a use, for *Kyrios* stands on its own in the acclamation. But in view of what we find in Paul's writings we cannot deny that LXX quotations facilitated the use of the title in this particular form.

Secondly, the application of the title to Jesus played an important part in the spread of the '*Kyrios*-idea' which had been so strongly influenced by the surrounding Hellenistic world. The statements from the LXX made a decisive contribution to the growth of the idea that Jesus is the Pantocrator. I Cor. 10.26 and Phil. 2.10f. reveal this very clearly. In this sense the influence of the LXX upon the formation of the Christian understanding of the title *Kyrios* is not to be underrated, even though we must acknowledge that it made itself felt only at a relatively late stage, i.e. in the Hellenistic Gentile church. On no account is it to be taken as the reason why the title was adopted as a christological designation.

Even though the LXX title *Kyrios* was applied to Jesus, the distinction between God and the *Kyrios* was not removed. The quotations from the LXX themselves make this plain, for in a majority of cases 'Kyrios' still means 'God'.

44. '*Lord*' *in Expressions which Introduce Quotations*

a. The expression 'says the *Lord*' is used in quotations from the LXX to mark God's speech.[578] In a few places Paul himself adds these words,[579] and it is clear that *Lord* signifies God.

There are other expressions used by Paul which have a similar form. I Cor. 7.10 has 'not I but the *Lord*'. With this we may compare v. 12: 'I say, not the *Lord*'. Other expressions which belong here are: 'we declare . . . by the word of the *Lord*' (I Thess. 4.15); 'I have no command of the *Lord*' (I Cor. 7.25); 'the *Lord* commanded' (I Cor. 9.14). In all these places the title refers to Jesus, and in all of them a word of the *Lord* is introduced with the same purport as in other places a quotation from the LXX would have, for it underlines the authority and validity of whatever statement

---

[578] Rom. 14.11; cf. II Cor. 6.18. In non-Pauline writings: Heb. 8.8, 9, 10; 10.16; cf. Rev. 1.8.
[579] I Cor. 14.21; II Cor. 6.17; Rom. 12.19.

is being made on any given subject. This, too, may have encouraged the use of the title on its own.

b. Of course, other explanations are not thereby excluded automatically. The expressions we have listed introduce statements
which give a decision on whatever subject is under discussion.
Now we must not fail to notice that all the passages we have
mentioned are concerned either with concrete ethical questions[580]
or with the delay of the parousia.[581] It is precisely in these two
contexts that the title *Lord* is preferred.[582]

If we enquire into the nature of these words of the *Lord*, a third
possible explanation suggests itself. For many reasons it is impossible to think that they could be actual sayings of the historical
Jesus.[583] Nor is it any more reasonable to suppose that the thought
here is of direct revelations made to Paul. It is much more likely
that these words of the *Lord* are the utterances of Christian
prophets, on the basis of which particular attitudes and customs
come to be established in the Church.[584] The title *Lord* in these
contexts could be due to the fact that the prophets' utterances were
regarded as making known the will of the Lord of the Church.

Although all these possible motives may have played some part
here and there, the one which best accounts for the occurrence of
the title *Lord* on its own is the LXX expression 'says the Lord'. It
is this expression which Paul echoed whenever he referred to the
utterance of a Christian prophet or even to a so-called saying of
Jesus, for it was this expression that he used elsewhere when
referring to OT passages.

Whether the use of this kind of expression is entirely due to
Paul himself or whether it had begun in the pre-Pauline church is
a question which cannot be answered with any certainty. But since
it occurs in passages where Paul is formulating freely, we have
included these passages in this present section, in which we are
considering Pauline usage.

[580] I Cor. 7.10, 12, 25; 9.14.
[581] I Thess. 4.15.
[582] See 47, 48.
[583] Only I Cor. 7.10 possibly points back to an actual or supposed saying of Jesus.
In content and in terminology I Cor. 9.14 points to a much later time. I Thess. 4.15
answers a question which was not a burning one in the earliest period but only in the
later Church.
[584] This is not so in I Cor. 11.23, for there the expression 'I received from the
Lord' is a rabbinical technical term signifying a chain of tradition leading back to
Jesus himself. Cf. I Cor. 15.3 and the remarks of Jeremias, *Eucharistic Words* 129.

45. 'Lord' in the Context of the Lord's Supper

a. In the context of the Lord's Supper the title *Lord* appears very frequently in the Paulines. The following is a summary of the expressions which occur:

I Cor. 10.21: the cup of the Lord; the table of the Lord.
I Cor. 10.22: Shall we provoke the Lord to jealousy?
I Cor. 11.20: the Lord's supper.
I Cor. 11.23: I received from the Lord.
    The Lord Jesus on the night when he was betrayed.
I Cor. 11.26: the Lord's death.
I Cor. 11.27: the cup of the Lord; the body and the blood of the Lord.
I Cor. 11.32: But when we are judged by the Lord . . .
I Cor. 16.22: If anyone has no love for the Lord, let him be accursed.

The general conclusion seems to be clear: the title *Lord* has a fixed place in the terminology relating to the Lord's Supper. But closer examination reveals that particular expressions came to be associated with the Lord's Supper at various stages in the development of the tradition. We must now turn to this problem.

b. The LXX expression 'the table of the Lord',[585] the expression which appears in two places '(the) cup of the Lord',[586] together with 'the Lord's Supper'[587] and 'if anyone has no love for the Lord'[588] are all pre-Pauline technical terms in the language of the eucharist. I Cor. 11.23b 'the Lord Jesus on the night when he was betrayed' is also certainly pre-Pauline, for it is with these words that the liturgy quoted by Paul begins.

On the other hand, three of these expressions containing *Lord* are clearly Pauline formulations: 'Shall we provoke the Lord to jealousy?' (I Cor. 10.22) is a sentence which echoes Deut. 32.21, but the title *Lord* is inserted by Paul. I Cor. 11.23a 'I received

---

[585] I Cor. 10.21b; see 43c.
[586] I Cor. 10.21a; 11.27.
[587] I Cor. 11.20.
[588] On this see Bornkamm, 'Anathema' 124f. and *TWNT* IV, 811.8–32, where historical parallels with the mystery cults are pointed out.

(παρέλαβον) from the Lord' is a rabbinical technical expression to which *Lord* has been added.

I Cor. 11.32 'When we are judged by the Lord we are chastened' is Paul's own expression.

The reason why Paul uses the title *Lord* in these three sentences is no doubt that he usually keeps to one christological title within any one section. But this is surely proof, albeit indirect, that the material in these passages actually requires the title *Lord*.

It is in the case of the two passages which remain to be considered that we have the greatest difficulty in deciding who was responsible for their formulation. As a whole, the verse which speaks of 'the death of the Lord' (I Cor. 11.26) must be regarded as a Pauline sentence,[589] though Paul does of course adopt the eschatological outlook which is a feature of the liturgy of the Lord's Supper. This prompts us to ask whether the mention of 'the Lord's death' might also be a liturgical reminiscence and therefore pre-Pauline. This expression shows that there has been a shift of emphasis in the latter part of the liturgy of the Lord's Supper, a shift away from eschatological anticipation to a recollection of the saving death of Christ, proclaimed verbally in the Lord's Supper.[590] This shift of emphasis might come equally from Paul or from the pre-Pauline Hellenistic church. But since we observe in Paul's theology a certain concentration upon the death and the resurrection of Christ, and since the verb 'to proclaim' (καταγγέλλειν) is evidenced many times in the Paulines,[591] we must regard Paul as the author of the expression 'the Lord's death'. Admittedly, the statement about the death is usually associated in the Pauline corpus with the title *Christ*, echoing the language of the pistis-formula. If in spite of this Paul uses the title *Lord* here, this illustrates yet again his habit of keeping to the one christological title within any one section.

In the case of I Cor. 11.27b, a verse which speaks of being guilty of profaning the body and blood of the Lord, it is even harder to judge. The expressions used can easily be identified as pre-Pauline technical terms associated with the Lord's Supper. The difficulty is that I Cor. 10.16, which is also about the Lord's

---

[589] Thus Bornkamm, 'Herrenmahl' 172f.; Jeremias, *Eucharistic Words* 164; and presumably also Käsemann, 'Lord's Supper' 130.
[590] Thus Jeremias, *Eucharistic Words* 164.
[591] I Cor. 2.1; 9.14; Rom. 1.8; Phil. 1.17, 18.

Supper, speaks of 'participation (κοινωνία) in the blood, or body, of *Christ*'. This sentence as a whole must be a piece of pre-Pauline tradition.[592] But what are we to say about the christological terminology?

The fact that language about the body and blood, obviously familiar in the context of the Lord's Supper, is linked in the one instance with *Lord* and in the other instance with *Christ*, leads to the following reflections:

1. It is hardly possible that these expressions could have been just as easily linked with one christological title as with another in the pre-Pauline period, for everything we have learned so far about the use of the titles in that period suggests that each particular title had its own particular setting. So we must assume that in the pre-Pauline eucharistic terminology it was either the body and blood of the *Lord* that was spoken of, and which Paul kept in I Cor. 11.27 but altered in 10.16, or the expression was originally linked with *Christ*, and was adopted by Paul at 10.16 but altered at 11.27.

2. Because the title *Lord* appears in a variety of expressions associated with the Lord's Supper in the pre-Pauline period, we would expect that the original expression spoke of the body and blood of the *Lord*. If this is so, it ought to be possible to discover why Paul altered the title. It is in fact possible to do this, for 'participation in the blood, or body, of *Christ*' (10.16) can only mean participation in the saving death of Christ.[593] For if we took this expression to mean 'participation in the eucharistic food', then 'cup of blessing' (v. 16a) and 'blood of Christ' would make a complete tautology. If on the other hand we took the expression 'the body of Christ' to refer, even in v. 16, to the Church, then we would be reading Paul's exposition in v. 17 back into v. 16. But this is impossible, because obviously 'the body of Christ' in v. 16 is parallel in sense to 'the blood of Christ'. But if the interpretation in terms of the saving death of Christ is the right one, it is natural that Paul should have linked 'body' and 'blood' with the title *Christ*, for the statement about the death is related to the pistis-formula in which *Christ* is firmly rooted. It is on this account that Paul has introduced *Christ* into eucharistic terminology which was originally linked with the title *Lord*.

---

[592] Cf. Käsemann, 'Lord's Supper' 109–12.
[593] Thus Bornkamm, 'Herrenmahl' 162–64.

c. We are now in a position to state our conclusions regarding Paul's use of the christological titles in the context of the Lord's Supper. The pre-Pauline church had already linked the title *Lord* with terminology relating to the Lord's Supper. Paul adopted this usage and included it in many formulations of his own. Only once were eucharistic terms linked with *Christ*, and this only happened because those particular terms could be taken to refer to the death of Christ, and were therefore in line with ideas derived from the pistis-formula.

d. Now we must ask why it was that the pre-Pauline church used the particular title *Lord* in its Lord's Supper liturgy. Two possible explanations are to be considered:

1. The prayer *Maranatha* clearly belongs to the liturgy of the Lord's Supper, as is proved by I Cor. 16.22; Rev. 22.20 and Didache 10.6.[594] Moreover Rev. 22.20 shows that in the Greek translation of the prayer the title *Kyrios* was used. From this point *Kyrios* made its way into the Lord's Supper tradition as a whole and its application spread. This title was in the last resort the *Mare-Kyrios* title which was associated with the idea of the parousia and thus established itself in the Lord's Supper liturgy. It continued to be associated with the Lord's Supper, even when the element of eschatological expectation, as a result of the advance of Hellenistic interpretations, became increasingly a merely marginal feature.

2. *Kyrios* in the Lord's Supper tradition is not genetically related to the *Mare-Kyrios* title. The former is to be understood against the background of the Hellenistic Kyrios-cults and is therefore related to the title *Kyrios* which is found in the acclamation.

The second explanation has the greater degree of probability, for *Maranatha* (as I Cor. 16.22 and Did. 10.6 show) remained untranslated in the liturgy of the Lord's Supper and so could have had no direct influence on the shaping of eucharistic terminology. Above all, we must not overlook the Hellenistic features in the eucharistic tradition as presented in the Paulines. These factors help us to understand how the emphasis shifted from eschatological expectation to a memorial of Jesus' death.

Thus in the Lord's Supper tradition the title *Kyrios* is a designation which was adopted by the Christian church because in some respects there were analogies with the Hellenistic Kyrios-cults.

[594] See 23ab.

46. 'Lord' and 'Spirit'

a. The link between 'Lord' and 'spirit' in the Pauline corpus is a very loose one and is found only in three passages.[595] We must bear this fact in mind as we examine these passages, in order to avoid either misinterpreting this link or overestimating it.

In connection with II Cor. 3.17 Bousset has said, 'What the apostles believed about Christ can essentially be summarized in a single sentence: "Now the Lord is the Spirit." '[596] Bousset admits that often the Spirit appears 'as a separate power side by side with Christ',[597] but this only serves to give added weight to II Cor. 3.17, where the 'supranatural Spirit' is identified with the 'Lord Christ'. Kümmel[598] rejects the view that *pneuma* and *Kyrios* are identified here and describes the sentence as 'a necessary exegetical digression'. Thus two opposing positions appear to have been taken up. More recent commentators, however, do not simply side with one or with the other, but attempt to examine the meaning of the sentence within its context, while defining more precisely what *kind* of identification is involved here.[599]

b. Let us analyse this sentence, at least as far as is necessary for our purpose. In II Cor. 3.16 there is an extemporizing reference to Ex. 34.34, and it is this reference which has determined the choice of the title *Lord* in v. 17. 'The Spirit' on the other hand is taken up from v. 6, where it is understood as the antithesis of 'the written code' (γράμμα).[600] This means that 'Spirit' and 'Lord' have been brought together in this passage by Paul himself. For the interpretation of v. 17 it is not only important to see why he did this, but also to bear in mind that in v. 17b the Spirit is described as 'the Spirit *of the Lord*' (τὸ πνεῦμα κυρίου), which makes it impossible to regard the two terms as completely identical.

---

[595] I Cor. 6.17; 12.3; II Cor. 3.17f. In Rom. 8.9 on the other hand 'spirit' is linked with 'Christ'.

[596] Bousset, *Kyrios Christos* 126. He maintains this, even though he admits (n. 1) that 'in its context the verse is merely a parenthesis'.

[597] Bousset, *Kyrios Christos* 142.

[598] Kümmel in Lietzmann, *Korinther* 200 (on II Cor. 3.17).

[599] Thus Schweizer, *TWNT* VI 415.34–416.29 (*Spirit of God* 59f.); Hermann, *Kyrios und Pneuma* 50f.

[600] With Schweizer, *TWNT* VI 416.7–11 (*Spirit of God* 59); Hermann, *Kyrios und Pneuma* 48; cf. also Ebeling, 'Geist und Buchstabe', *RGG* II, 1290f.

In v. 6 the antithesis between *gramma* and *pneuma* refers to the contrast between the old covenant and the new. The genitive is qualitative, and so *pneuma* describes the quality of the new covenant. In v. 12 the new covenant is characterized by the expressions 'hope' and 'boldness', for these are its gifts to mankind. At this point, having explained that for those who turn to the Lord the 'veil' is taken away, Paul might very well have returned to the idea of 'boldness', relating it directly to the *Lord*, and thus rounding off the entire argument of vv. 12–16. He does not do this, but turns instead to the other term which he has previously used to designate the new covenant, i.e. the Spirit. Without any change in sense, v. 17a could just as well read, 'Now the Lord is the new covenant'. For Paul is concerned to demonstrate the real connection which exists between the *Lord* and the new covenant, and therefore also (following Paul's line of argument) the real connection which exists between the *Lord* on the one hand and 'Spirit' or 'boldness' on the other. This shows clearly that v. 17a is not a mere aside, but is directly related to the whole train of thought in this chapter.

But from what we have said it is also plain that v. 17a cannot possibly mean, 'The Lord (i.e. as 'person'), however, is the Spirit (i.e. as 'substance')'.[601] With as much justification one might say that the new covenant is the Lord's 'substance'! Verse 17a refers primarily and simply to the fact that the *Lord* and the Spirit belong together. Both belong to the new covenant dispensation in which hope, boldness and liberty hold sway. Just as the *Lord* belongs to the realm of the new covenant, so he belongs to the sphere of the Spirit, but not as though he as the lesser power could be subsumed under the greater, for he is himself the supreme power by whom and through whom the new covenant and the Spirit are constituted. It is in this sense that v. 17b speaks of the 'Spirit of the Lord', where the genitive is of belonging or origin. This means that *Lord* and Spirit are not simply identical. The identification as made in v. 17a is to be understood as saying that the *Lord* belongs wholly and completely to the sphere of the Spirit, or in other terms, his place is entirely within the new covenant. So whoever has to do with the *Lord* certainly has to do with the Spirit also, and whoever has to do with the Spirit has to do with the *Lord* also. This is

[601] Thus Lietzmann, *Korinther* 113 *ad loc.*

what made it possible to speak of *Lord* and Spirit as identical. In v. 18 we find the phrase, 'this comes from the Lord who is the Spirit' (ἀπὸ κυρίου πνεύματος), which is too short to be interpreted in isolation. So we must return to v. 17, and this makes it clear that the phrase is not to be understood as apposition, i.e. as 'identification' in the strict sense. It could be paraphrased in two ways, either (in the manner of v. 17a) 'from the Lord who belongs wholly to the sphere of the Spirit, i.e. to the new covenant', or (in the manner of 17b) 'from the Lord of the Spirit'. It is impossible to discover which of these nuances predominates.[602]

This gives us, for our subject, two important conclusions:

1. Paul himself has linked the terms 'Lord' and 'Spirit' in this passage, which therefore cannot rank as evidence that there is any real connection between the ideas associated with the title *Lord* and the ideas associated with 'Spirit'.

2. The tenor of the argument within this particular section makes it obvious that I Cor. 3.17a does not give us the fundamentals of Pauline christology but merely a peripheral statement. As such it is not without weight, for it shows how Paul in his own way brought into relationship teaching about the *Lord* and teaching about the Spirit which were originally separate.

c. Examination of I Cor. 12.3 leads to a similar conclusion. Here the acclamation is cited as a criterion for judging whether a man possesses the Spirit. Paul himself introduces this criterion, for he is discussing the gifts of the Spirit, particularly the gift of ecstatic utterance. So here, too, the combination of *Lord* and Spirit clearly is attributable to Paul. Here, too, *Lord* and Spirit are closely related to one another, though not so as to suggest that they are identical. The reason why the acclamation is made in the 'Holy Spirit' is that the *Lord* belongs wholly to the sphere of the Spirit. Hellenistic ways of thinking about *pneuma* form the background to this statement. But there are unmistakable signs of Paul's own work in removing from the understanding of 'Spirit' the merely miraculous elements. This is done by bringing the ideas associated with *pneuma* into relationship with the *Lord*, who in turn is linked with *Jesus*. The title *Lord* had already been linked with *Jesus* in the pre-Pauline Hellenistic church, but the theological task of linking ideas about

---

[602] Hermann, *Kyrios und Pneuma* 56, wishes to combine both solutions and suggests the translation: 'from the Lord whom I experience as Spirit'.

pneuma with the Christian understanding of the title *Lord* was performed by Paul.

d. I Cor. 6.17 reads: 'He who is united to the Lord becomes one spirit with him.' The idea of 'the body' (σῶμα) lies behind Paul's argument here. The Christian is a 'member of Christ'.[603] Thus it is impossible that he should become the 'member of a prostitute', for the two things are absolutely exclusive. Just as he who consorts with a prostitute is 'one body' with her, so he who belongs to the *Lord* is one body with him. We would have expected parallel ideas to encourage parallel expressions, but Paul does not speak of being 'one body' with the *Lord* but of being 'one spirit' with him. Actually this way of speaking is only possible because the 'body' of the Lord belongs wholly to the sphere of the Spirit. His mode of existence is entirely 'pneumatic'.

What prompted this way of speaking is in all probability the word 'flesh' (σάρξ) in the quotation at v. 16.[604] Certainly it is not sexual intercourse as such that is referred to here, for 'one flesh' in the quotation means nothing other than what Paul defines as 'one body'.[605] But since 'being united' (κολλᾶσθαι) to the Lord and being united to a prostitute are mutually exclusive, it is natural that the latter should be described as fleshly. In sharp contrast to this, the 'body' of the *Lord* belongs to the sphere of the Spirit. It is this thought which determined the choice of the expression 'one spirit'. Thus here, too, the combination of *Lord* and Spirit is shown to be of Pauline origin. In this passage also the unity but not identity of the two is evident.

e. Our examination of these three passages has led to the same conclusion in each case. First, it is Paul himself who has brought together *Lord* and Spirit; and second, all these passages think of the two as belonging closely together but not as identical. This means that we cannot possibly regard these verses as giving us *the* key to Paul's understanding of the title *Lord*.

[603] The term 'body of Christ' does not appear here, but 'member of Christ' clearly means nothing other than a member of the body of Christ.

[604] Lietzmann, *Korinther* 28 *ad loc.*, must be right about this. But he is wrong when he puts all the weight on this contrast between 'body' and 'flesh' and stresses the difference between union with the *Lord* and sexual union. Schweizer, *TWNT* VI 417 n. 571 (abridged in ET), is right to oppose this interpretation. Hermann, *Kyrios und Pneuma* 63f., is equally right in emphasizing that 'the *tertium comparationis* is not the σάρξ-πνεῦμα relationship but the association denoted by the verb κολλᾶσθαι.'

[605] In this respect we must agree with Schweizer, *TWNT* VI 417 n. 571, when he writes, 'All three terms are thus interchangeable.'

47. 'Lord' in Statements about Practical Conduct

a. The title *Lord* occurs most frequently in statements about the practical conduct of the Church or of the individual.

By 'the work of the Lord'[606] is meant the kind of conduct which the *Lord* demands.[607] The phrase 'being anxious about the affairs of the Lord'[608] has the same sense: the unmarried can 'care' with undivided hearts about doing what the Lord requires. Synonymous with this is the expression 'to please the Lord'.[609] Whoever does this gives 'undivided devotion to the Lord'.[610] The expression 'to serve the Lord'[611] has clearly been influenced by the OT, and it is used in a passage which contains ethical instruction of the most varied kind.

The idea behind all these statements is quite clear. The *Lord* is the final arbiter, and it is under his authority that Christians conduct their lives from day to day. Of course, this definition tells us nothing as yet about what the actual content of Christian conduct is to be. If we make a survey of the passages of exhortation in which the title *Lord* occurs, we discover that it is very difficult to find any which give us evidence that the actual content of particular ethical instruction is directly related to the understanding of the title *Lord*. It is quite otherwise in cases where passages of exhortation are linked with the title *Jesus Christ*, for there the 'conformity-rule' brings concrete ethical propositions into direct relationship with the saving events.[612] But we find nothing like this where the title *Lord* appears,[613] for this title simply names the one who has

[606] I Cor. 15.58; 16.10.
[607] I Cor. 15.58 demands this sense, for there the exhortation 'be steadfast, immovable' and 'abounding in the work of the Lord' are parallel to one another.
[608] I Cor. 7.32, 34.
[609] I Cor. 7.32.
[610] I Cor. 7.35.
[611] Rom. 12.11 (τῷ κυρίῳ δουλεύειν), unless the reading with καιρός is preferred. Cf. Rengstorf, *TWNT* II 267.7–16, 270.28–272.38. I Cor. 10.9 'to put the Lord to the test' must also have been influenced by the OT (cf. Deut. 6.16 and Seesemann, *TWNT* VI 27.10–45).
[612] See 34a and n. 480.
[613] The sentence, 'What I am saying I say not with the Lord's authority' (οὐ κατὰ κύριον), cannot rank as an exception. It is true that one might regard this sentence as being related to the 'conformity-rule', but the course of development seems to have run from sentences modelled on the 'conformity-rule' to statements like Rom. 15.5

authority and in doing so it underlines the urgency and the obligatory character of his demands.

b. The same is to be said about sentences which are not really ethical instruction but statements of what the Church actually does. Thus *Lord* is found in the statements about the collection,[614] and about the Thessalonians' Christian manner of life.[615]

It is the *Lord* who enables the Church to grow in love,[616] who gives Paul his apostolic authority,[617] who assigns to Christians their tasks.[618] News about the apostle's travel plans is given with the conditional 'if the Lord wills'.[619] Finally, it is the *Lord* who gives Paul visions and revelations,[620] and to whom Paul addresses petitions concerning his illness.[621]

What is common to these passages is that they are all about the actual duties, activities or experiences of individual Christians, and with all these the title *Lord* is associated. There is no thought of the saving events of the past but only of being bound, in the specific actions of the present, to the *Lord*. He is thus not merely the authority to whom all are answerable for their every action, but also the one who has the power to give revelations, tasks, success, etc. Human existence is lived out in the presence of this *Lord* and with constant reference to him. Here we can see a connection with the formula 'in the Lord' (ἐν κυρίῳ), but we shall deal with that later on.[622]

c. Now we must discuss three passages which at first sight do not appear to be about ethical instructions or about what the Church actually does, but about the basic fact that both the Church and individuals belong to the *Lord*. Rom. 14.8 is instructive, for

(κατὰ Χριστὸν 'Ιησοῦν), and thence to *kata*-clauses which were linked with *Kyrios*, despite the fact that with the introduction of this title all trace of a concrete term of reference for determining the content of the demand disappears.

[614] II Cor. 8.5, 19.
[615] I Thess. 1.6.
[616] I Thess. 3.12f. In style and terminology this verse is comparable with the preamble in the Pauline letters. The similarity is due to the presence of expressions which have their origin in the language of worship. Cf. Dibelius, *Thessalonicher* 19 *ad loc.*
[617] II Cor. 10.8; 13.10.
[618] I Cor. 3.5; 7.17; cf. 7.25b, where *Lord* may have been carried over from v. 25a.
[619] I Cor. 4.19; 16.7.
[620] II Cor. 12.1; cf. I Cor. 9.1.
[621] II Cor. 12.8. By contrast, the Church's prayers and also a large proportion of personal prayers are addressed to God. Cf. Bultmann, *Theology* I, 12.2, 128.
[622] See 50.

there the fact that the Christian's whole life is governed by the *Lord* is expressed by saying that the Christian is 'the Lord's'. The verse does not stand in isolation but is to be understood as the climax of Rom. 14.1–12. The section begins with the question about eating meat (offered to idols)[623] and about the observance of certain (non-Christian) festivals. So Paul is here giving a decision on a question about practical ethical conduct.

His answer is neither 'Eat' nor 'Do not eat', but 'Do not despise' and 'do not judge'—an answer which directs the attention to the brother who has decided differently. Paul gives two reasons for his 'Do not judge'. The first is in v. 3, 'God has welcomed (the weaker brother).'[624] The second begins with the metaphor of the slave whose actions may be judged by no one but his master, his lord. As soon as the word 'lord' has been mentioned, Paul's thought turns to the *Lord* of the Church. It is he who judges the brother's decision, and he does so in a very positive way, for he will uphold him, so that he is 'able to stand'.[625] This statement draws its force entirely from the picture of the slave-master relationship. The idea of the heavenly *Lord* makes no significant contribution to this picture, except in the affirmation that this particular *Lord* will decide in his slave's favour. So here, too, the actual content of ethical instruction does not follow directly from the Christian understanding of the title *Lord*. The verses which follow emphasize merely that man in all his deeds and in all his omissions is confronted by the *Lord*, because his belonging to the *Lord* is something which embraces his life and his death, his whole self. So this passage does not take us beyond the general understanding of the *Lord* as the all-embracing authority over the life and the deeds of man.[626]

d. II Cor. 5.6, 8 are concerned with a specific question about

[623] Unfortunately we cannot be sure whether in v. 1 Paul has in mind ascetic tendencies which led certain people to refuse to eat meat at various times (thus Lietzmann, *Römer* 114, excursus on 14.1), or alternatively a group of Christians who refuse to eat because all meat purchased, as it were, on the market came from animals which had been ritually slaughtered and were therefore 'offered to idols' (cf. Michel, *Römer* 297, excursus on 14.1; he, too, leaves the question open).
[624] Cf. the similar argument in I Cor. 8.11; Rom. 14.15. In those two passages the argument is 'christologically' based, i.e. on the saving event of the death of Jesus. On this, see 34a.
[625] We cannot tell whether the future tense looks to the last judgement or to the end of the individual's present life. Vv. 10–12 certainly have the judgement in view.
[626] For a more detailed analysis of Rom. 14.1–12 see 57d.

what the nature of human existence will be in the resurrection. Life and death are here evaluated in terms of the thought which underlies the Pauline expression 'with the Lord'.[627] True, this expression does not actually occur in this passage, but the description of life as being 'away from the Lord', or of death as being 'at home with the Lord', makes it plain that here we have an instance of the σὺν κυρίῳ idea (the eschatological σύν), albeit only by implication. This naturally prompts us to ask how the title *Lord* is understood here. Does the title refer in the last resort to the *Mare-Kyrios* whose parousia is expected, or to the *Kyrios* who is acclaimed in worship as the one who has present dominion?

Here, unlike I Thess. 4.17, it is a question about the death of the individual and therefore not about the parousia.[628] This means that 'being absent from the Lord' during earthly life is not meant absolutely, as though here we were simply abandoned by the *Lord*.[629] So it is more likely that this is a borderline instance in which 'with the Lord' refers to the *Lord* who is acclaimed. But we cannot be sure about this. At all events the *Lord* is depicted here as ruler, and it is in relation to him that human existence, life and death, are evaluated.

e. I Cor. 6.13c reflects the idea that man's concrete earthly existence belongs to the Lord. Here again a practical question about ethics is asked, in this instance about fornication. Human existence, which Paul cannot conceive as anything other than bodily existence,[630] belongs exclusively to the *Lord*. Since to associate with a prostitute affects this same bodily existence, Paul sees only a sharp 'either-or'.[631] So here, too, it is the idea that man belongs absolutely to the heavenly *Lord* that decides the practical problem which is in question.

f. In conclusion we must summarize the principal features of the understanding of the title *Lord*, as expressed in the passages we have examined.

1. Since in every case the passages are about concrete questions, problems and instructions concerning the present life of the

---

[627] See 38.
[628] Cf. the similar passage at Phil. 1.23. On this cf. 38 and n. 540.
[629] Indeed v. 5 speaks of the Spirit as 'a guarantee'.
[630] Cf. Schweizer's article on σῶμα, *TWNT* VII.
[631] Essentially the same idea is present in v. 15, where 'bodies' are 'members of Christ'.

Church or of individual Christians, it is obvious that the *Lord* is thought of as one whose dominion is in the present.

2. The Lord is the authority, who makes claims upon every aspect of daily life. Reference to the *Lord* gives to ethical instruction a note of urgency and of obligation.

3. The power of the *Lord* is as all-embracing as his authority. There are no areas of human life which lie outside it.

4. These features show clearly that the understanding of *Lord* which is expressed here resembles the idea which lies behind the acclamation. Whereas the 'acclamation-*Kyrios*' was associated primarily with worship, here the relationship of the *Kyrios* is to the whole of life. There has been a development from the 'acclamation-Kyrios' to this present concept, which is wider in its scope.[632]

5. What is striking is that although the title *Lord* can be used to impart to ethical instruction and to discussion of practical questions a general sense of obligatoriness, it is impossible to derive from it any concrete ethical propositions. The idea of being confronted by, or belonging to, the *Lord* does indeed provide a kind of backcloth, but the actual content of ethical propositions is drawn from elsewhere, e.g. from the slave-master metaphor, or from the metaphor of the body, or from the idea of being 'with the Lord'. This distinguishes these ethical propositions associated with the title *Lord* from those which are associated with the title *Christ*, for in the latter the understanding of *Christ* directly influences the content of ethical instruction.

48. *'Lord' in Statements about the Parousia*

a. With only three exceptions[633] it is the title *Lord* which is linked in the Pauline corpus with the parousia.[634] Since the exceptions

632 Against Foerster, *Herr ist Jesus* 192, who regards 'the idea of service, coloured by eschatological notions' as 'the point of departure' in the development of the early Christian understanding of the title *Lord*. Certainly the 'idea of service' is present, even as early as the Pauline period, but nothing in the texts suggests that it is this idea which accounts for the title. Nor is there any trace of evidence that there was from the beginning a correlation between the terms *Kyrios* and 'slave'. (This is against Foerster, *Herr ist Jesus* 193, who supports his thesis by appealing entirely to Pauline and deutero-Pauline passages.) See 33a.

633 The exceptions, which give *Christ*, are: Phil. 1.6, 10; 2.16; cf. I Cor. 15.23. See 35.

634 With *Lord*: I Thess. 4.15, 16, 17; 5.2; I Cor. 4.5 (cf. 11.26); 5.5; cf. Phil. 4.5. With '(our) *Lord* Jesus (Christ)': I Thess. 2.19; 3.13; 5.23; I Cor. 1.7b, 8; II Cor. 1.14.

occur in Philippians, in which the title *Christ* predominates,[635] they are no doubt understandable. The evidence is so consistent that it cannot be regarded as accidental. So our task is to record it and interpret it.

b. On the one hand there are short expressions which denote the parousia, like 'the day of the Lord',[636] 'the parousia of the Lord',[637] 'the revealing of the Lord'.[638] On the other hand there are sentences which describe what will happen at the parousia, whether the descent, or the coming, or the meeting, or finally the nearness of the Lord.[639]

Whereas we find in the short expressions with the genitive both *Lord* standing alone and *Lord* with extended titles, in the statements which contain verbs we find only *Lord* standing alone. Since these statements are obviously Pauline formulations, they provide clear evidence that it was Paul's custom to put simply the title *Lord* in passages which do not require particularly distinguished style. But when a more formal style is required, we find that the fuller christological titles are preferred. Two instances of this are found in the preamble in I Corinthians, one in I Thess. 3.13 (a verse which in form and content corresponds exactly with the preambles), one in the farewell formula in I Thessalonians, and two in expressions concerning 'boasting',[640] one of which occurs at the end of the sentence. Since liturgical language is echoed in the preambles and the closing sentences of the letters, as well as in various expressions concerning 'boasting', we must conclude that the fuller christological designations are an indication of liturgical usage. It may be that Paul simply took these designations over as they stood, or it may be that in particular sections of his letters which on account of their position required a formal style Paul used distinctive language of a kind which was customary in worship. In either case we find that there is a connection between the distinctive and solemn language of worship and the use of the fuller christological titles.

c. The fact that the title *Lord* appears regularly in the context of

---

[635] The ratio (excluding the *en*-formulae) is 21:4, whereas e.g. in I Thess. it is 1:17.
[636] With *Lord*: I Thess. 5.2; I Cor. 5.5; with extended title: I Cor. 1.8; II Cor. 1.14.
[637] With *Lord*: I Thess. 4.15; with extended title: I Thess. 2.19; 3.13; 5.23.
[638] Only with extended title: I Cor. 1.7b.
[639] I Thess. 4.16; I Cor. 4.5b (cf. I Cor. 11.26); I Thess. 4.17; cf. Phil. 4.5.
[640] I Thess. 2.19; II Cor. 1.14. On the place of 'boasting' in worship, see n. 295.

the parousia leads us to suppose that the idea of the parousia and the understanding of the title *Lord* are related in some way. Certainly we have already shown[641] that what lies behind the acclamation and the situations associated with it is the idea that the *Lord* belongs to the present, and also the idea that he may be invoked by calling upon his name. Neither of these features are found in passages which have the parousia as their subject. So it is impossible to see any original connection between the notion of the 'acclamation-*Kyrios*' and the idea of the parousia.

But we may recollect that the title *Kyrios* was used when the *Maranatha* prayer was translated into Greek.[642] *Maranatha*, in its original sense, must be regarded as the prayer of the Aramaic-speaking church for the parousia, and so we must assume that the Greek translation has the same meaning. But because *Kyrios* was used in this translation, statements about the parousia also came to be connected with the *Kyrios* title, or more precisely with the *Mare-Kyrios* title.[643] We find abundant evidence of this connection in I Thessalonians and in I and II Corinthians, and the result of this has been that several scholars[644] have mistakenly supposed that the statements about the parousia represent the context in which the title *Kyrios* was first employed.

Considerations which we have already listed[645] show that simply to transfer to the *Kyrios*-concept as a whole the connection which exists between the *Mare-Kyrios* and the parousia is to go too far. If we distinguish between the *Mare-Kyrios* and the 'acclamation-*Kyrios*' it becomes possible to see things more clearly and to understand them. As a result of these considerations we take *Kyrios* in the statements about the parousia to be the *Mare-Kyrios*.

d. Finally we must note the fact that all the statements about the parousia which are linked with the title *Lord* come from I Thessalonians and I and II Corinthians. Since these are to be regarded as early, perhaps the earliest, Pauline letters, they indicate that Paul took over this usage from the pre-Pauline church. Certainly in the passages in question Paul is on the whole formulating freely,

[641] See 18e.
[642] See 23.
[643] On this whole section see 23de.
[644] E.g. Cerfaux, *Christ* 468f.
[645] See 23 ef.

but this does not mean that he is not dependent upon pre-Pauline usage in employing the title *Lord* in connection with the parousia. If in Philippians Paul associates the title *Christ* with statements about the parousia, this is not only a sign of an increasingly indiscriminate use of the christological titles, but also an argument for regarding Philippians as late.

e. In conclusion we must enquire particularly into the origin of the expression 'the day of the Lord'. At first sight one is inclined to regard it as an echo of the OT *yōm YHWH*. But since the phrase is used only twice outside the Pauline corpus[646] we have too narrow a basis to obtain a reliable answer to this question.

49. *'The Lord's Brother'*

a. Two passages mention the 'brother(s) of the Lord'.[647] The sense makes it quite clear that they refer to the actual brothers of Jesus of Nazareth. The problem is that it should be the title *Lord* which appears in these passages, for in this context the title cannot represent either the 'acclamation-*Kyrios*' of the *Mare-Kyrios*. It is very close to the *Kyrios* which occurs in narrative passages within the synoptic Gospels. But these, as a rule, belong to the latest stratum of the synoptic tradition, i.e. they are the editorial work of the particular evangelist,[648] and reflect a late use of the title, not the original one.

The same might conceivably be said of the expression 'the *Lord's* brother'. But this would not correspond with the way in which the title *Lord* is used generally within the Pauline corpus, for there we have seen how firmly particular titles are set in particular contexts. On this basis we would have to regard the expression 'the *Lord's* brother' as an inexact use of the title and attributable to Paul himself, for presumably the title could only have been used in this way when its original meaning had faded. But this does not tally with the way in which Paul uses the expression, for it appears in his writings as an expression which all would under-

---

[646] II Thess. 2.2; II Peter 3.10. In the second passage it occurs in the traditional phrase about the day of the Lord which comes as a thief (cf. I Thess. 5.2). See also note 500.

[647] Gal. 1.19 (James); I Cor. 9.5 (not named).

[648] Thus Taylor, *The Names of Jesus* 41 n. 4.

stand and which already had 'technical' significance.[649] If this is correct, then the expression must be pre-Pauline. Since it was no doubt necessary in the Jerusalem church to distinguish James 'the Lord's brother' from others of the same name, we may assume that the original Aramaic form of this expression arose in the Jerusalem church.

But which title stood in this original Aramaic form, and what did it mean? The most likely supposition is that this church spoke of the brother of the 'Rabbi' or 'Mare', the latter term standing not for the 'Marana' of the prayer *Maranatha* but rather for the respectful title by which the earthly Jesus was addressed.[650] 'The brother of the Lord' thus meant simply 'the brother of the Rabbi', and *Rabbi-Kyrios* at first had no christological significance whatever.

50. 'In the Lord'

a. The formula ἐν κυρίῳ occurs 29 times[651] in the genuine Paulines, i.e. about the same number of times as 'in *Christ*' or 'in *Christ Jesus*'.[652] In none of these 29 places can the formula be shown to belong to traditional material, and so we must regard it as a Pauline creation. It is striking that the article does not appear in a single instance. This shows that in the Paulines the expression is not used hesitantly and experimentally whilst seeking its final form but is used as a formula from the beginning. We find it as well in the body of sentences as at the end of sentences, so its position in the sentence does not tell us anything in particular about its use or its content.

The 29 instances are distributed among the various parts of the letters as follows: 1. In passages of exhortation—7 instances;[653]

---

[649] In Gal. 1.19 it is in apposition, which makes quite clear which James is meant; in I Cor. 9.5 it suggests someone who has a recognized status alongside the apostles.

[650] Thus the translation of this term 'Rabbi' or 'Mare' corresponds to the translation in the synoptic Gospels, where the original form of address 'Rabbi' is rendered by 'Kyrie'.

[651] I Thess. 3.8; 5.12; I Cor. 4.17; 7.22, 39; 9.1, 2; 11.11; 15.58; 16.19; II Cor. 2.12; Gal. 5.10; Rom. 16.2, 8, 11, 12a, 12b, 13, 22; Phil. 1.14; 2.24, 29; 3.1; 4.1, 2, 4, 10; Philemon 16, 20. (I Cor. 1.31; II Cor. 10.17 are excluded, for they are OT quotations going back to Hebrew *hālal b^e*, which means that ἐν in these instances is necessitated by the grammatical construction.)

[652] 'In Christ' 23 times, 'in Christ Jesus' 28 times. See 36ad.

[653] I Thess. 5.12; I Cor. 15.58; Gal. 5.10; Phil. 3.1; 4.1, 2, 4.

or in passages which, though not in the form of exhortation, discuss questions about practical conduct—5 instances.[654] 2. In personal messages—10 instances;[655] and particularly in lists of those to whom specific greetings are sent—7 instances.[656] So the formula does not occur in passages of theological argument, though the formula 'in *Christ Jesus*' occurs frequently in such passages.[657]

b. On the basis of this distribution we should expect to find, when we come to examine the passages themselves, that the formula is used both in imperative and indicative clauses which have as their subject the day-to-day life of Paul, or of individual church members or of the Church as a whole. This is exactly what we find.

Exhortations, both general and particular, are linked with the formula 'in the *Lord*'.[658] It is used to describe the character of relationships within the Church's fellowship[659] and also the whole of Paul's work as an apostle and all the activities associated with the Church's worship.[660] The specific personal greetings belong basically to this group, too.[661] Of course it is possible to be uncertain here and there whether 'in the *Lord*', e.g. in I Cor. 16.19, is to be taken with the verb 'send greetings', or whether it qualifies the object, e.g. in Rom. 16.11. But whichever way our decision may go in these cases the idea remains the same, because as a rule the recipients are described in terms of what they do, so that in any case the formula defines specific human actions.

c. At the same time, the recipients are also defined by means of participles and adjectives in connection with which the formula 'in *Christ* (*Jesus*)' could equally well be used, as in other places it

[654] I Cor. 7.22, 39; 9.1, 2; 11.11.
[655] I Thess. 3.8; I Cor. 4.17; II Cor. 2.12; Rom. 16.2; Phil. 1.14; 2.24, 29; 4.10; Philemon 16, 20.
[656] I Cor. 16.19; Rom. 16.8, 11, 12a, 12b, 13, 22.
[657] See 36ad. Cf. with our division Neugebauer, 'In Christo' (*NTS*), 134f.
[658] Examples of general exhortation: I Thess. 3.8; Phil. 4.1 ('stand fast in the Lord'); an example of a more concrete kind is 'rejoice in the Lord' (Phil. 3.1; 4.4). Similarly the exhortation to be of the same mind (Phil. 4.2) or to welcome a messenger (Rom. 16.2; Phil. 2.29) are linked with the formula 'in the Lord'.
[659] Thus there are brothers (Phil. 1.14; Philemon 16), overseers (I Thess. 5.12), or children (I Cor. 4.17) 'in the Lord'.
[660] The apostle's confidence in a particular matter (Gal. 5.10; Phil. 2.24), or his joy at a gift received (Phil. 4.10), usefulness (Philemon 20a), or success in missionary work (II Cor. 2.12), permission for the widowed to remarry (I Cor. 7.39), the right kind of hope for reward (I Cor. 15.58)—all are linked with this formula.
[661] I Cor. 16.19; Rom. 16.8, 11, 12a, 12b, 13, 22.

is in fact used.[662] The reason for the indiscriminate use of the formulae is partly that being similar they became interchangeable. But on the other hand it should be noted that all these passages occur in Rom. 16, which is of uncertain origin.

Finally we must mention here four passages of mixed content which do not speak of concrete acts or relationships, but which have more fundamental things in view and could thus equally well be linked with the formula 'in *Christ*'. In two of these passages Paul is speaking of churches which he has founded.[663] In I Cor. 11.11 the theme is that man and wife belong together 'in the *Lord*' and in 7.22 Paul speaks of being 'called in the *Lord*'.

d. These last passages are not true to type, and if we leave them out of account we get a relatively uniform picture of the formula's use. 'In the *Lord*' appears in the context of ethical instruction and of particular questions, relationships and actions in the life of the Church. So the Church (as well as each individual Christian) in all that it does and in all that it endures is aware of being confronted by the *Lord*, and knows that it is accountable to him. He is therefore the *Lord* who is present, and by his authority every Christian activity is governed.

We should notice that the formula is never used to describe activities which take place in worship. In the earliest period, of course, when the title *Lord* began to have a place in the Christian Church, it was used predominantly in worship. But it did not remain confined to the liturgical sphere but found its way into the most varied statements about the day-to-day life of men. This shows that the *Lord* was not regarded only as Lord over a particular area of human life but as Lord over its totality.

51. 'In the Lord Jesus (Christ)' and 'In Christ Jesus Our Lord'

a. We have been able to show that each of the two formulae, 'in the *Lord*' and 'in *Christ*', had a particular sphere in which it was regularly employed. We now have to ask to which of the two groups the expressions with combined titles belong. Of the three

---

[662] Cf. e.g. Rom. 16.8, 13 with Rom. 16.3, 9; or Rom. 16.11 with II Cor. 5.17.
[663] In I Cor. 9.1 he calls the Corinthians his 'workmanshipi n the Lord', and in v. 2 the 'seal of his apostleship in the Lord'.

places at which the expression 'in the *Lord Jesus*' occurs, two are in passages of exhortation,[664] and one on a personal message.[665] In I Thess. 4.1 a particular exhortation is made 'in the *Lord Jesus*', and Rom. 14.14 and Phil. 2.19 speak of Paul's conviction or hope 'in the *Lord Jesus*'.

This corresponds exactly, in terms both of form and content, with what we found in the case of the formula 'in the *Lord*'. Only in I Thess. 4.1 is it possible to explain the addition of the name *Jesus*, for *Lord Jesus* occurs in 3.11, 13. We have already noted that Paul usually kept to the same title within any particular section.[666] Plainly, the addition of the name *Jesus* to the title *Lord* does not alter the meaning in any way.

b. The expression '(in)[667] the *Lord Jesus Christ*' is found only in the opening designation of I Thess. (1.1). There it is used as a description of the recipient church. In other similar passages this function is performed by the expression 'in *Christ Jesus*'.[668] The reasons for the inclusion of the title *Lord* here are no doubt purely external ones. The first is that the full titles occur in the opening designations, where the style is somewhat formal, and the second is that, as we have observed elsewhere,[669] the influence of liturgical language no doubt accounts for the fact that the expressions 'God the Father' and 'the Lord Jesus Christ' are used in conjunction with one another.

c. The expression 'in *Christ Jesus our Lord*'[670] occurs in three places, all within passages of theological argument. Twice it qualifies God's gifts in salvation, and once Paul's 'pride'. In view of this we might have expected, at least in the first two passages, to find the formula 'in *Christ Jesus*'. But it so happens that in all three cases the expression comes at the end of the sentence, in two cases actually occupying the final position,[671] once in a short, summary definition, and once at the end of a section in which the style is exalted, almost hymn-like. Since the same extended expression is used with a *dia*-phrase at the end of chapters 5 and 7 of

[664] I Thess. 4.1; Rom. 14.14.
[665] Phil. 2.19.
[666] See note 30.
[667] 'In' occurs only in the preceding phrase, 'in God the Father'.
[668] See e.g. I Cor. 1.2; Phil. 1.1; cf. I Thess. 2.14, etc.
[669] See 21.
[670] I Cor. 15.31; Rom. 6.23; 8.39.
[671] In Rom. 6.23; 8.39 (in each case the final verse of the chapter).

Romans, we may take it as certain that it was considerations of style which prompted Paul to use the fuller titles instead of the shorter. So the very occasional *en*-phrases which have the fuller titles are to be understood entirely in terms of the more frequent shorter forms. The differences are readily explicable.

52. Conclusions

Our conclusions about Paul's use of the title *Lord* are as follows:

1. Where Paul is formulating freely he normally uses the simple title on its own. On the other hand, in passages in which the style is more formal and distinctive he prefers the more impressive combined titles. This reflects pre-Pauline custom, at least to the extent that the fuller titles were customary in a number of pre-Pauline liturgical expressions. Similarly, in some contexts (e.g. in terminology relating to the Lord's Supper, or in OT quotations or in expressions introducing quotations) Paul's use of the simple title on its own is a continuation of pre-Pauline custom.

2. Paul uses the title most frequently in ethical instruction or when dealing with actual conduct or with practical problems in general. Since it is in contexts such as these that the Pauline formula 'in the *Lord*' is employed, we must look to the statements and to the ideas expressed in them to give us the clue to the way in which Paul himself understood the title. These reveal immediately the basic features of his 'Kyriology'.

3. The *Lord* is the authority to whom men are accountable for their every decision. The Church, in every sphere of its life and in all its characteristic activities, is confronted by the *Lord*, as the individual Christian is also. Because the Church (and the individual Christian, too) belongs wholly to the *Lord*, there is no place for fear, but only for confidence and for joy. This is expressed by the fact that the *Lord* does not simply make demands but also gives success.

4. Since all day-to-day decisions are made within the limits of the present, we cannot help but see that the *Lord* is understood primarily as belonging to the present. Nowhere is any line drawn which leads back to the saving events in the past. The future does indeed come within view, at least when man's future is being

discussed. But the only statement made about it is that there is no limit, even in the future, to the power of the *Lord*, nor will the Church cease to belong to him. What is true of the *Lord* now must continue to be true.

5. All this means that the understanding of *Lord* which we have noted here is similar to that which the acclamation expressed. Certainly there is a difference which we should not overlook, for at the pre-Pauline stage of the tradition the 'acclamation-*Kyrios*' is associated only with activities which belong to the Church's worship. But Paul uses the title, with far greater emphasis, to qualify the 'secular' activities of daily life. It would be wrong to make a sharp contrast out of this, for in the last resort even ethical counsel has its place in worship. All the same, we are justified in saying that there has been a shift of emphasis.

6. Eventually the title *Lord* or the formula 'in the *Lord*' comes to be linked also with statements about the Church and about the blessings of salvation. Elsewhere in such contexts we find the title *Christ*, so that in this instance we may say that these two titles are used indiscriminately.

7. Finally, we find evidence in Paul's writings of the idea of the *Mare-Kyrios* which has been shaped by the notion of the parousia, and also of the *Rabbi-Kyrios* which comes to light in the expression 'the *Lord's* brother'. The latter originally had no christological significance, for it presumably translates the polite form of address, 'Rabbi'. In both these instances Paul has adopted pre-Pauline language.

III · SON OF GOD

53. Statistics

Apart from the six occasions[672] on which Paul quotes a *Son of God* formula or adopts its wording, there are nine passages [673] in which he uses the title *Son of God* in formulations of his own. In comparison with the passages in which the titles *Christ Jesus* or *Lord* occur, this is an infinitesimally small figure.

The title in its fullest form, '(For) the *Son of God, Christ Jesus*'[674] is found only at II Cor. 1.19 (in the nominative). *Son* alone is found only at I Cor. 15.28 (also nominative). The remaining seven passages give 'his *Son*', six times in the genitive, and only at Gal. 1.16 in the accusative.[675]

The expression 'his *Son*' refers back to God, and so we must now examine the way in which the mention of 'God' prompts the mention of 'his *Son*'.

54. Motives for Paul's Use of the Title 'Son of God'

a. The most important motive for choosing the title *Son of God* is revealed by the fact that the title almost always occurs immediately after 'God' has been mentioned.[676] The following three passages make this very clear, for in I Cor. 1.9 and II Cor. 1.18 the title follows immediately upon the phrase 'God is faithful',[677] and in

---

[672] Rom. 1.4; 8.3; 8.32; Gal. 2.20; 4.4f.; I Thess. 1.10. See 24a, 25, 26ab, 28a.
[673] I Cor. 1.9; 15.28; II Cor. 1.19; Gal. 1.16; 4.6; Rom. 1.3, 9; 5.10; 8.29.
[674] Whether the order should be 'Christ Jesus' or 'Jesus Christ' is a matter of opinion.
[675] I Cor. 1.9, where *Son* is in the genitive, has the full titles added ('the fellowship of his Son, Jesus Christ our Lord'), but this is due to the fact that it rounds off the preamble.
[676] This is true also of I Cor. 15.28; Gal. 1.16; Rom. 8.29. In these verses 'God' is not specifically named, but he is nevertheless the implied subject or object.
[677] The two other Pauline passages in which this phrase occurs (I Thess. 5.24; I Cor. 10.13) contain no christological reference.

Rom. 1.9 it follows the phrase 'God is my witness'.[678] In all these passages the emphasis is upon God, and for this reason the title *Son of God* appears in the christological statement which follows. So in the first instance purely formal considerations constitute the motive for using the title *Son of God*. But even so, this still gives us some indication of the range of meaning which the title carries in the Paulines. It is evident that for Paul this title signifies, above all else, that there is a very close relationship between Jesus, the bearer of salvation, and God. The nature of this relationship is nowhere discussed or formulated, but its reality is presupposed as self-evident.

In Gal. 4.6 Paul takes the title *Son of God* directly from the formula in v. 4 about the 'sending' of the *Son*, and he forms a similar sentence about the sending of 'the Spirit of his Son'. Here, too, the choice of the title is externally conditioned, for because the *Son of God* formula has already been used, Paul continues with the same title. This does indeed have an effect upon the content, in so far as the Spirit is now described as the Spirit of the Son of God. But passages in which the Spirit is associated with other christological titles should put us on our guard against over-interpreting this fact.[679] Thus the motive which has governed Paul's choice of the title here is an external one, based upon what has gone before.

In the case of Rom. 1.3 we might wonder which of the motives we have mentioned will have prompted the choice of the title *Son of God*. We might at first incline to suppose that Paul uses the title here in anticipation of the formula about the 'adoption' of the *Son* in v. 4, and in order to make the formula more complete. But it is just as likely that the expression in v. 1, 'the gospel of God', brought the title *Son of God* in its train. At all events, 'his', referring back to 'God', suggests that the second possibility is the more likely. But however that may be, it is again external factors which account for the title's occurrence here.

b. Our observations so far are confirmed when we look at the *content* of the passages in which Paul uses the title, for there are no

---

[678] Of the other verses in the Paulines which are similar to this I Thess. 2.10 and II Cor. 1.23 are without any christological reference, and in I Thess. 2.5f. and Phil. 1.8 we find the technical expression 'apostles of Christ' or the phrase 'the affection of Christ Jesus'.

[679] Cf. e.g. II Cor. 3.17b (with *Lord*); Rom. 8.9 (with *Christ*).

particular themes which call for the title *Son of God*, nor does its presence influence in any way the course of the argument. The contexts in which the title appears can be very varied; but whether Paul is speaking of reconciliation by the death of him in whom salvation was accomplished (Rom. 5.10), or whether he is speaking of the gospel (Rom. 1.1f., 9), or of the Damascus experience (Gal. 1.15f.), or of the predestination of Christians (Rom. 8.29), or of the events associated with the parousia (I Cor. 15.23–28), there is in all these contexts no intrinsic connection with the title *Son of God*. This is demonstrated by the fact that statements which correspond to all these are linked in other places with different christological titles.[680] So in view of the content of these passages it appears that the title *Son of God* has been introduced into them *ad hoc*.

c. Whether any idea of adoption or pre-existence lies behind Paul's statements about the *Son of God* is a question which cannot, strictly speaking, be answered, for there is no passage which gives clear evidence of either background. The title *Son of God*, which is now used simply in a general sense to designate the bearer of salvation, could come from either source. All the same, a sentence like Rom. 5.10 which speaks of the death of the *Son*, or like Rom. 8.29 which speaks of our predestination, would permit the assumption that for Paul the bearer of salvation had always been *Son of God*.[681] This is tending towards the idea of pre-existence, but we can hardly say more than that.

d. Thus our conclusions are these: Paul's use of the title *Son of God* depends primarily on external factors, in that it is prompted by what has gone before. It is no longer possible to derive from the title (as Paul uses it) any sharp definition of its meaning which would distinguish it in character from other christological titles. The only factor which clearly prompted Paul to choose this particular title is that for him the title suggests the Son's solidarity with God. So 'his *Son*' (= *Son of God*) in Pauline usage indicates the very close relationship between the one who brought salvation and God himself. Because, in Paul's thinking, it is this idea which is uppermost, he can insert the title into contexts which in

[680] Cf. e.g. I Cor. 15.3b (the death, linked with *Christ*); I Cor. 9.12; II Cor. 2.12; Rom. 2.16 (the gospel, with *Christ*); I Thess. 4.15, 16, 17; 5.2; I Cor. 1.7b, 8; II Cor. 1.14 (the parousia, with *Lord*); Phil. 1.6, 10; 2.16 (the parousia, with *Christ*).
[681] This is presumably implicit in Rom. 1.3 as well.

the pre-Pauline period (on account of their content) would have attracted a different title. So Paul's use of the title reflects a stage of development at which the original meaning of the title has already faded, and at which its contours have already been blurred as the result of the cross-influence of other titles.

55. The Function of the 'Son of God' Formulae within the Paulines

a. If the observations we have made so far are correct, then we should expect to come to a similar conclusion when we examine the reasons which prompted Paul to adopt the *Son of God* formulae. This is largely the case. Evidently the primary consideration in Paul's mind when he adopted any formula[682] was that his church would be bound to assent to it, simply because it represented a piece of tradition which was generally acknowledged. That is why he often uses formulae, either as the point of departure for his train of thought, or as the decisive argument in it, or as its climax. But now we must ask more particularly about the motives which caused him to adopt the *Son of God* formulae.

b. In Rom. 8.3 we get a reminiscence of the formula about the 'sending' of the *Son*, and it occurs within a passage of theological argument. It is used as the basis of Paul's argument that we have been set free from sin and death. But it is impossible to discover any essential reason why Paul should have chosen precisely this formula.

If we try to find out how Paul built upon the formula in the course of his argument, we discover that he has not done so at all. Instead, he uses ideas which have already been introduced, 'flesh' and 'Spirit', to interpret the significance of the saving events. The *Son of God* formula, beyond simply affirming the *fact* that the saving events actually took place, has no particular significance here.

c. The case is similar with the formula about the 'giving up' of the *Son*, which occurs at Rom. 8.32 within a passage of theological argument which is strongly interspersed with rhetorical elements. 'God' is mentioned in v. 31, and this is no doubt why the *Son of God* was inserted. Again, the formula does not get developed in

---

[682] This is true of all the formulae, not simply the *Son of God* formulae.

any way, for in v. 34 the pistis-formula is introduced (extended *ad hoc* by a statement about the exaltation of *Christ Jesus* and his intercession in heaven). This shows that in this passage the two formulae are completely interchangeable.

d. Gal. 2.20 is a somewhat different case. Here the formula about the 'giving up' of the *Son* is introduced into a discussion of the doctrine of justification, and the content of the passage shows us why. The baptismal statement about being crucified with *Christ* (v. 19) leads to the sentence '*Christ* lives in me' (v. 20a). This sentence, which refers to a present state of affairs, is liable to misinterpretation; therefore Paul explains it in such a way as to bring into prominence the fact that there is an eschatological proviso. The life which is earthly (ἐν σαρκί)[683] is pointed towards the life which is by faith (ἐν πίστει).

But the content of this faith is given, not in terms of the pistis-formula, but in terms of the formula about the 'giving up' of the *Son*. Had Paul chosen the pistis-formula, the statement '*Christ* lives in me' would have stood next to the statement about 'faith in *Christ*, who . . .'. It would then have been all too easy to interpret in a mystical sense. By adopting the formula about the 'giving up' of the *Son*, any such misunderstanding could be averted, for the title *Son of God* (which carried with it the statement 'who gave himself for me') emphasized fully the objective reality of him in whom faith is placed. So here the choice of this particular title turns out to be theologically motivated. But the theme of the formula is not developed in any way, for v. 21 takes us back immediately to the 'law/faith' theme which dominates the whole section.

e. In Gal. 4.4f. the formula about the 'sending' of the *Son* is introduced into a passage of theological argument. It is intended to show the reason for, and therefore also the reality of, our deliverance from domination by the 'elemental spirits of the universe'. The word 'heir', which first appears at 3.29, governs the whole section 4.1–7. Paul distinguishes two stages in the life of the heir. The first is the stage of minority, in which the heir is no different from a slave, and the second is the stage of majority, in which

[683] The expression as used here is not to be understood in terms of the fully developed Pauline understanding of *sarx*. Thus with Schweizer, *TWNT* VII 125.28f., and Schlier, *Galater* 64 *ad loc.*; similarly Lietzmann, *Korinther* 141 (on II Cor. 10.3) and *Galater* 17 (on 2.20), though in the latter instance he is not very clear.

which he becomes effectively the heir. For Paul, 'Son' is synonymous with this. Certainly the idea of 'Sonship' was provided in the
first instance by the formula itself, but clearly the tacit identification of Son and heir is what led Paul to introduce this particular
formula here, so that really its presence is due to the progression
of Paul's thought. In his exposition of the formula Paul's primary
interest is in the title 'Son' as a designation for Christians, and he
produces two pieces of evidence to prove that this designation
reflects their real status, for Christians possess the Spirit, and also
they are able to call upon God as 'Abba, Father'. Paul echoes the
formula, not only by speaking of the 'sending' of the Spirit, but
also by describing the Spirit as 'the Spirit of his Son',[684] and so the
effect of the argument is to establish a self-contained series of
relationships: God (the Father), his Son, and we who are the sons.
All that is necessary in v. 7 is to sum all this up, and to refer back
to the key word 'heir' with which Paul began. We must be careful
to notice that this series of relationships—God, Son, sons—
belongs entirely and only to Paul's own argument.

f. We cannot be quite sure what prompted Paul to insert the
formula about the 'adoption' of the *Son* into the opening designation of Romans at 1.3b. It may have been the Pauline expression
in v. 3a 'concerning his *Son*', but equally (if in v. 3a Paul were
consciously improving upon the idea of adoption as presented in
the formula) it may have been the expression in v. 1 'the gospel of
God'. In either case it would have been external factors which
influenced the choice of this particular formula. It is impossible to
say that the formula is developed in any way, for the christological
titles *Jesus Christ* and *Lord* are simply strung on to it. Of course,
this tendency to use the fuller titles in passages requiring distinctive style is natural here, since the formula occurs within the
opening designation. Nevertheless it is also a witness to the fading
of the original meaning of the titles concerned.

g. In I Thess. 1.9b, 10 the formula about the parousia concludes
the preamble. The theme of the preamble, i.e. the way in which the
Thessalonian Christians had received the gospel, is rounded off
by means of a traditional summary of the kerygma. Paul could
have chosen to refer to the pistis-formula here. Why he did not
do so, but added this other formula instead, is impossible to say.

---

[684] This reading is to be preferred to that of p[46].

Since the formula comes at the end of the preamble, it is natural that it is not developed in any way.

h. Reviewing the passages we have just discussed, we find that only in two places was the choice of a *Son of God* formula motivated by the content of the passages. In Gal. 4.4f. Paul is concerned to demonstrate that Christians have the status of 'sons', and in Gal. 2.20 the formula is used to guarantee the objective reality of him who gave himself and in whom our faith is placed. In the latter case, only a formula about the *Son* would have achieved this purpose. In both these instances the formula is introduced simply as part of Paul's own argument. In the other passages we can establish at the most only external reasons (as, for example, when 'God' has been mentioned in the immediately preceding verses) which may have prompted Paul to adopt a *Son of God* formula.

Only in one instance (Gal. 4.6) can we say that Paul has developed the formula, and even then only to the extent that Paul takes a few elements from the formula and combines them with ideas of his own.

Thus our investigations here have led to a result which is very similar to the result we obtained when we made our analysis of the Pauline passages in which the title *Son* occurs. This will help us to draw conclusions about the significance which Paul attaches to the idea of 'Sonship'.

56. The Status of the 'Son of God' Concept (in Paul's View)

What we have discovered as the result of our present investigation leads us to conclude that in Paul's view both the title *Son of God* and the ideas associated with it are of relatively minor importance. When Paul speaks of the *Son of God* he is simply referring in a general sense to him who brought salvation. When he quotes the formulae about the 'sending' or the 'giving up' of the *Son*, he regards them simply as alternatives to the pistis-formula, for both kinds of formula are about the saving events. Only in one respect does the term *Son of God* have distinctive significance in Paul's view, for it expresses literally, in a way that the other christological titles cannot do, the very close relationship between the bearer of salvation and God himself.

57. Reflections Arising out of 'Part Two'

a. We cannot summarize again all the results we have obtained in 'Part Two',[685] but simply point out in a short survey what is characteristic in the way Paul uses the titles, and then draw from our survey a few conclusions about the significance of the christological titles in Paul's writings, and of the themes with which the titles are associated.

What is striking about Paul's use of the christological titles is that he follows pre-Pauline custom to a very considerable extent. We find evidence of this, not only in the way he adopts formulae and expressions which were already in existence, but also in sentences in which he has formulated freely.[686] Paul, too, puts in any given context the title which, on the basis of its original meaning, is appropriate to that context. So with regard to the Pauline corpus as a whole it would be quite wrong to make the sweeping statement that the christological titles are used indiscriminately.

b. All the same, it cannot be denied that the use of the titles has become less precise in the course of development. This is revealed by the fact that the titles find their way into new contexts. True, at first these new contexts are closely related to those in which the titles were originally set. But since in certain fields the ideas associated with the pistis-formula are just as useful as ideas associated with the *homologia*, it is in such fields that indiscriminate use of the titles most quickly sets in. There are three particular fields in which we can watch this happen: 1. Statements concerned with the blessings of salvation; 2. Ecclesiological statements; 3. Passages of exhortation.

It is possible to think of the blessings of salvation either as issuing from the saving death and resurrection of *Christ*, or from the *Lord*, who in the present moment has the power to give and to demand.

It is possible to think of the Church as the assembly of those who believe that *Christ* died and was raised for them. But it is also

[685] All the places at which summaries are given can easily be found by consulting the table of contents.
[686] In practically every paragraph we could point out definite parallels in pre-Pauline usage.

possible to think of the Church as the assembly of those who recognize that the present power of the *Lord* makes demands upon them and governs them, and who are constituted a 'Church' by the very act of acclaiming this *Lord*.

Ethical instruction may on the one hand demand the kind of action which 'conforms' to the saving death of *Christ*; or on the other hand, by pointing to the authority of the *Lord*, it is seen to be universally binding.

Once both titles have come to settle in such areas as these, then the conditions are given for their becoming interchangeable and ultimately cut off from the background of ideas in which they originated. Widespread indiscriminate use of the christological titles is then bound to follow. But in the Paulines this stage is clearly not yet reached.

c. By comparison with the very considerable importance of the titles *Lord* and *Christ* the title *Son of God* plays a relatively insignificant part in Paul's writings. Evidently it has already lost much of its particular significance. Since Paul regards it as a title which may be used in connection with the saving events, it comes to approximate more and more to the title *Christ*. Both titles are found where faith and the blessings of salvation are discussed. The peculiar characteristic of the title *Son of God* is that it states quite literally what the relationship is between the bearer of salvation and God himself. This clearly determines the actual contexts in which it can be chosen, for almost without exception it is used only in places where 'God' has just been mentioned.

d. But now we must enquire whether there are any places in the Paulines at which we find evidence that the ideas associated with the titles *Lord*, *Christ* and *Son of God* have been worked in together.

1. Certainly there are places at which various titles are combined. One would not exactly describe the combination of *Lord* with *Jesus* (*Christ*) as rare. But this combination is the result of rhetorical, stylistic and liturgical requirements, and is therefore rather a matter of 'deploying the titles' than of working together the ideas which underlie them. The full designation containing *Lord*, for instance, means exactly the same as the title *Lord* standing on its own. In those parts of the letters which require a more ponderous style it is the fuller designation which is preferred, simply because it has greater weight itself. The same thing applies

in cases where other titles are added to the title *Son of God*.[687] All these are relatively superficial combinations.

2. Only with regard to Rom. 14.9 do we need to consider seriously the possibility that ideas which underlie the title *Lord* and ideas which underlie the title *Christ* have been worked in together. The verse forms part of the section Rom. 14.1–12, the first half of which we have already examined.[688] It deals with the question about eating meat (offered to idols). The title *Lord* was introduced into the course of the argument on account of the metaphor of the slave who is answerable only to his own 'lord'. Verse 6 says that whatever anyone decides in the matter of observing particular days or of eating or not eating, everything should be done τῷ κυρίῳ, i.e. 'for (or with regard to) the *Lord*'. And the sign that this is actually done is the giving of thanks (at meals). Thanksgiving is addressed, not to the *Lord*, but to God.

Verses 7 and 8 take this further. Absolutely everything, in life and death alike, is done 'for the *Lord*'. The reason for this is that the Christian belongs totally to the *Lord*, as well in life as in death. With this statement the climax of the argument appears to have been reached. The fact that we belong to the *Lord* is the reason why we live 'for him'.

But in v. 9 Paul takes the argument one step further still, for he gives the reason why the *Lord* should have the mastery over the dead and the living. He himself died and came to life again in order that he might have the lordship over the dead and the living. So Paul is using a statement from the pistis-formula as the basis for the *Lord's* dominion over mankind. Or, to put this another way, Paul uses ideas associated with the title *Christ* (i.e. ideas about the saving events of the past) as the foundation for ideas associated with the title *Lord* (i.e. ideas which are largely about the rule of the *Lord* within the confines of the present).

We must note what Paul's concern is in writing Rom. 14.9. It is not to give a theoretical exposition of christology, still less is it to indulge in christological speculation, but to show how it comes about that the Christian belongs to the *Lord* 'in life and in death'—a matter which concerns the whole of human existence. In terms of the ideas associated with the title *Lord* we can get no further

[687] Cf. I Cor. 1.9; II Cor. 1.19; Rom. 1.4.
[688] See 47c.

than saying *that* we belong in this way; but by contrast, in terms of the ideas associated with the title *Christ* we can say *why* we belong.[689] Because Paul wished to add to the fact *that* we belong the reason *why* we belong, the ideas associated with each of the two titles have been joined together. Thus the saving events, in terms of which the title *Christ* is understood, have become the basis of his status as *Lord*. More than this the passage does not say. But it is plain that when reflection proceeds beyond this point it associates Christ's lordship particularly with his resurrection, which is regarded as the act by which he who brought salvation is exalted as *Lord*. The hymn at Phil. 2.6–11 is evidence that this stage of reflection had already been reached either before or during the Pauline period. If Paul had been asked how he imagined the relationship between the saving acts and the status of the *Lord*, he would doubtless have answered in just these terms, namely that the resurrection represents the installation of Jesus as *Lord*. If we do not find this expressly stated in Paul's writings, this merely pinpoints the fact that christology is never itself the subject of argument. If it had been, Paul would have had to occupy himself with combining the several christological conceptions or with adjusting them one to the other.

e. Nevertheless, the enormous significance of the christological statements in the Pauline corpus cannot be overlooked. Their importance consists in the fact that particular christological propositions are employed in the course of Paul's argument as authoritative utterances with reference to which any problem in question may be decided. They represent the criterion by which Paul's own opinions, as also those of his opponents, are to be measured. They are capable of being criteria because they are recognized by Paul, by the churches, and by Christian opponents as propositions which represent common tradition. Whether in any given context a proposition about the *Lord*, or about *Christ*, or about the *Son of*

[689] This is done by taking the key words 'life' and 'death' and adapting the statements of the pistis-formula to suit the purpose of the argument. Christ's death and his coming alive again are what constitute his lordship over the dead and over the living, and therefore over us, whether we 'live' or 'die'. The argument appears to be crystal-clear and flawless. Nevertheless, on closer examination we discover that it will not hold. It is impossible to separate the saving events in such a way that Christ's death constitutes his lordship over the dead and his resurrection his lordship over the living. It is the death and the resurrection together which form the basis of his status as Lord. So we must regard this combination of 'anthropological' and 'christological' interpretations of the key words 'life' and 'death' as purely rhetorical.

God is used, this does not depend particularly upon the content or the sense of the title. The choice of a particular proposition depends far more on the question which is being dealt with in the discussion, for particular questions (according to the topic) each incline to favour particular forms of christology.[690]

This is why Paul could take first one, then another set of propositions, and thus to a very large extent adhere to the christological conceptions and formulations which he received from the pre-Pauline church. This is also why Paul, the great theologian, does not develop further the christological propositions which he inherited, for he was less concerned with these in themselves than with making use of them in thinking through soteriological, ecclesiological, ethical and other questions. So it is not in his christology that we find Paul's own theological achievement, but rather in the way in which he works up his subjects, drawing upon already existent propositions about *Christ*, *Lord* and *Son of God*.

[690] By this we mean that Paul does not have any general preference either for 'kyriology' or for 'christology'. He chooses elements from either, according to the topic with which he is immediately concerned.

PART THREE

Particular Problems

58. Procedure

There are in connection with the christological designations a few particular problems which have often been written about in commentaries and monographs. Since these problems are not confined, as a rule, simply to the pre-Pauline or to the Pauline material, we are devoting 'Part Three' of this essay to a discussion of them.

A number of scholars have already expressed their own opinions on these particular problems, and so our method will be to take one of these opinions, as we discuss each particular problem in turn, and to draw our own conclusions about it by analysing the material available.

I · JESUS

59. 'Jesus'—The Historical Jesus?

a. It is Foerster's opinion that when Paul uses 'the simple name Jesus . . . he is thinking especially of the "historical" Jesus'.[691] Schmithals defines in more detail, asserting that when Paul speaks of Jesus he has in mind 'Christ kata sarka', whom he 'distinguishes from the heavenly, spiritual Christ'.[692]

Our task in this section is to test these opinions by examining the material and taking into account such results as we have established already.

b. Ἰησοῦς or ὁ Ἰησοῦς occurs 17 times in the genuine Paulines.[693] The first thing we must do is to show in what kind of contexts this designation appears.

1. 'Jesus' associated with statements from the pistis-formula.[694]

In all these passages the question of the name used in them is part of the more general problem of the name or title which is used in the pistis-formula itself. For even though we must admit that the particular passages with which we are concerned do not reproduce exactly the wording of the pistis-formula, there can be no doubt that they are directly dependent upon that wording.[695] If we were right in supposing that the statement about the resurrection was originally linked with Jesus,[696] this would mean that in three of these passages its occurrence would be traditional and not due to Paul at all. Only in I Thess. 4.14a is Jesus the subject of the statement about the death, and therefore a deviation from the wording of the pistis-formula, which gives Christ in that context.

[691] Foerster, TWNT III 289.30–32.
[692] Schmithals, Gnosis 52.
[693] I Thess. 1.10; 4.14a, 14b; II Cor. 4.5, 10a, 10b, 11a, 11b, 14a, 14b; 11.4; Gal. 6.17; Rom. 3.26; 8.11; Phil. 2.10. In I Cor. 12.3 and Rom. 10.9 Jesus is named in the acclamation.
[694] I Thess. 1.10; 4.14a; II Cor. 4.14a (Kyrios is here judged secondary, on text-critical grounds; see 3h); Rom. 8.11.
[695] See 2–5.
[696] See 8e.

Thus in that particular passage *Jesus* has the same meaning as *Christ*.[697]

2. 'Jesus' as the object of faith and as the content of preaching.

In the two passages which come up for consideration here[698] Paul is formulating freely. In connection with the words 'faith' and 'preaching' the title *Christ* is regularly used.[699] So here again the name *Jesus* is simply an alternative to *Christ*, for there is no evidence of any difference in meaning.

3. 'Jesus' in statements about participation by Christians in the death and resurrection of Christ.[700]

The train of thought is similar to the thought in Rom. 6.3–11, that whoever shares intimately in the death of Christ will also share intimately in his life. Behind II Cor. 4.10–14 lies the Pauline σύν-phrase, as is shown most strikingly in v. 14, '(God) will raise us also with Jesus'. The only difference from Rom. 6 is that persecution, not baptism, is the situation in which Christians die with Christ, though the name *Jesus* is used in all these instances instead of *Christ*. Thus *Jesus* in this context means exactly what is usually meant by the title *Christ*.[701]

4. 'Jesus' in the acclamation.[702]

Since the acclamation is pre-Pauline, we cannot hold Paul responsible for the name *Jesus* in this context. *Jesus* denotes simply the one who is acclaimed as *Lord*. The antithesis of *Kyrios Jesus*, i.e. *anathema Jesus*, is to be understood in the same sense, as is also the expression 'the name of Jesus',[703] by which the title *Lord* is meant. One last passage presumably should be mentioned here, in which Paul proclaims *Jesus* as *Lord*, and in so doing he proclaims himself to be the servant of the Church διὰ ᾽Ιησοῦν.[704]

c. Thus the result of our examination of the passages which contain simply *Jesus* is as follows: where it appears in the context of the acclamation it means the person to whom the acclamation is made, who is in all likelihood the earthly Jesus. No thought is given in this context to the saving events.

---

[697] This would be true of the other three passages, should it turn out that our earlier supposition (see n. 696) was incorrect.

[698] II Cor. 11.4; Rom. 3.26.   [699] See 10 and 11.

[700] II Cor. 4.10a, 10b, 11a, 11b, 14b; cf. I Thess. 4.14b (if διὰ τοῦ ᾽Ιησοῦ is to be taken with ἄγειν).

[701] Similar ideas are in the background at Gal. 6.17, where Paul speaks of the 'stigmata of Jesus' which he bears on his body.

[702] I Cor. 12.3; Rom. 10.9.   [703] Phil. 2.10.   [704] II Cor. 4.5.

In the great majority of passages *Jesus* is associated with statements which are either taken directly from the pistis-formula or which represent extensions of the formula. In these passages *Jesus* takes the place of the title *Christ* which normally features in the context of the pistis-formula. *Jesus* means here the person in whom the saving events took place.

The opinions of Foerster and Schmithals which we mentioned earlier have therefore to be rejected. Their arguments would, of course, be quite valid if all that had to be considered were the name *Jesus* in the acclamation, yet Schmithals has deliberately left out of account the passages in which the acclamation occurs.[705] But the passages to which they refer tell against their thesis, for *Jesus* in these passages (which are connected with the pistis-formula) definitely does not mean simply the man, the 'historical' Jesus. It means the one in whom the saving events took place, and therefore not 'Christ *kata sarka*' but simply 'Christ' (without any qualification), the *Christ* whose title, according to the tradition which Paul received, indicated in summary fashion the one whose death and resurrection alike constituted the saving events.

d. Our conclusion (that in the Pauline corpus *Jesus* has the same meaning as *Christ*) is underlined by the fact that the name *Jesus*, coupled with *Christ*, is introduced into the same contexts as those in which the simple title *Christ* is found. If we leave out of account the *en*-formula,[706] we find *Jesus Christ* or *Christ Jesus* 33 times within the genuine Paulines, 4 times in statements from the pistis-formula,[707] 4 times as the object of faith,[708] 10 times in self-designations and designations of the Church,[709] 7 times associated with the blessings of salvation,[710] 3 times in statements about human conduct,[711] once in a statement about the parousia,[712] and 4 times in *dia*-phrases.[713]

---

[705] Schmithals, *Gnosis* 51. Foerster, *TWNT* III 289.30–40, mentions only Phil. 2.10, and he interprets the *onoma* as meaning the name *Jesus*.
[706] Cf. 36a–c.
[707] Rom. 8.11, 34; cf. I Cor. 2.2; Gal. 3.1.
[708] Gal. 2.16a, 16b; 3.22; Rom. 3.22.
[709] In the opening designations, except in I Thess. Also at Rom. 1.6; 15.16; Gal. 5.24; cf. Rom. 3.22.
[710] I Cor. 3.11; II Cor. 13.5; Gal. 1.12; Rom. 5.17; Phil. 1.8, 19; 3.12.
[711] Gal. 4.14; Rom. 15.5; Phil. 2.21.
[712] Phil. 1.6.
[713] Rom. 1.8; 2.16; 5.17; Phil. 1.11. Also in the post-Pauline doxology, Rom. 16.25–27.

One has only to compare this list with the headings of the chapter on Paul's use of the simple title *Christ*[714] to realize that statements with precisely the same content are associated sometimes with *Christ Jesus* and at other times with *Christ*. So from the way in which these designations are used we conclude that for Paul they have exactly the same meaning. The only difference between them is a stylistic one, for it can be shown that at the end of sentences and in sections of the letters which require more formal language the double title is preferred on account of its greater weight.[715] It would be a mistake to build this up to an absolute principle, but as a tendency it is undeniable.

e. By way of summary we may say that in terms of their content the designations *Jesus, Christ,* and *Jesus Christ* have exactly the same meaning in the Paulines. All are summary expressions indicating the one in whom the saving events, the death and the resurrection, took place. Thus they also indicate the object of faith and the content of preaching. Self-designations and designations of the Church, as also the blessings of salvation, are linked with these same titles. The titles are also found in statements which can no longer be easily classified under particular heads. In many of these statements it is difficult to discover any direct link with the saving events. *Jesus, Christ,* and *Jesus Christ* increasingly become mere names for the one who in the eyes of the early Christian Church is the central figure. Definite and clearly distinguished christological conceptions are not invariably associated with these designations, so that it goes without saying that at this stage and in these areas they are used with less and less discrimination, as the other christological titles are also.

[714] See 31–37. The fact that the last three groups were originally associated with the title *Lord* rather than *Christ* does not affect the comparison of *Christ* with *Christ Jesus.*

[715] The double title occurs 7 times in the opening designations, 3 times in the preambles, and 7 times at the end of sentences. Cf. the exactly similar result obtained when we compared the formulae 'in *Christ*' and 'in *Christ Jesus*'. See 36g.

II · 'CHRIST' – A MESSIANIC TITLE?

60. The Problem

There can be no doubt that *Christ* goes back ultimately to *m^{e}šīḥā*, the Aramaic designation for the Messiah, for it represents the exact translation of the Aramaic word into Greek. To the original translators, who must have belonged to the ranks of Hellenistic Jewish Christians charged with the mission to the Gentiles, the meaning of the title was fully understood. But of necessity it was incomprehensible to Greek ears, so that inevitably *Christ* was taken to be a proper name. So we are clear about the point at which the development began, and also about its end. But what stage in this development is represented by Paul's usage is a matter of some debate, i.e. it is uncertain to what extent *Christ* has the meaning of Messiah in Paul's writings, and to what extent it is simply the proper name of a particular person or of him who died and rose again for our salvation.

Various scholars have given their answer to this question. The reason why we are looking into the same question is that our own examination of the material available causes us to take issue with the various opinions which have been expressed.

61. 'Christ' in the Double Designation 'Christ Jesus'

a. Cullmann's view[716] is that 'when the title *Christ* precedes *Jesus*', this is proof that Paul is clearly aware 'that the word *Christ* is not a proper name.' Of course Paul knows that *Christ* represents the Aramaic 'Messiah' translated into Greek. We must not overlook the fact, either, that it was precisely because *Christ* originally signified a messianic title that it was possible for it to precede the name *Jesus*.

[716] Cullmann, *Christology* 133f.

But here we are concerned to discover how Paul himself used the word. Does *Christ* in the Pauline designation *Christ Jesus* really signify 'Messiah' in the fullest sense? In order to answer this question we must examine the way in which Paul uses the two expressions *Christ Jesus* and *Jesus Christ*. We immediately run up against the difficulty, however, that at many places the word order is on text-critical grounds uncertain. Therefore we have to bear in mind from the outset that in this matter it is possible to give only an approximate indication of Paul's usage.

b. Only in 42 of the 60 instances of the double title in the Paulines is the word order certain.[717] In the following table they are arranged according to their case. The figures in brackets represent instances in which the word order is uncertain, and which have therefore been placed in the column to which they are most likely to belong.[718]

	CHRIST JESUS	JESUS CHRIST
Nominative	– (1)	2 (1)
Genitive	6 (5)	4 (1)
Dative	— (—)	— (—)
Accusative	1 (1)	1 (—)
Prepositional phrases with gen.	— (2)	3 (1)
with dat.	25 (2)	— (1)
with acc.	— (3)	— (—)
Total:	32 (14)	10 (4)[719]

In discussing these figures the following points are important:

[717] The places at which the double title is found in the Paulines are listed in nn. 719 and 503.

[718] As a rule, these are the readings which Nestle gives in the text. It is appropriate here to stress yet again how great is the difficulty of reaching a decision on text-critical questions. In many instances there is scarcely any basis for an assured judgement, for the various readings are distributed quite haphazardly among the various codices, so there could be no justification for preferring the reading of one particular codex throughout.

[719] The instances with *Christ Jesus* are:
Nominative: —; (Rom. 8.34).
Genitive: II Cor. 1.1; Gal. 5.24; Phil. 1.1, 8; Philemon 1; (I Cor. 1.1; Gal. 2.16a; Rom. 1.1; Phil. 1.6; 2.21).
Dative: none.
Accusative: Gal. 4.14; (Rom. 8.11).
Prepositional phrases: with gen.: (ὑπό: Phil. 3.12; διά: Rom. 2.16).
with dat.: the *en*-phrases listed in n. 503, except I Cor. 4.17b; Gal. 5.6; 3.14; (I Cor. 4.17b; Gal. 5.6).
with acc.: —; (εἰς: Gal. 2.16b; Rom. 6.3; κατά: Rom. 15.5).

1. Only in two contexts does the double designation appear frequently, first in the *en*-formula and second in genitive constructions. It is not found at all in the dative, and only in isolated instances in the nominative and accusative. There seems to be no reason for this curious distribution. 2. We notice that in the two main groups, i.e. in genitive constructions and in the *en*-formula (which requires, of course, the dative), there is a marked preference for the order *Christ Jesus*. This is particularly so in the *en*-formulae. This suggests that the order *Christ Jesus* is influenced by the genitive and the dative cases. 3. But the genitive prepositional phrases appear not to confirm this supposition, for there are three instances which demonstrate clearly that in the *dia*-phrase the order is *Jesus Christ*. However, we saw earlier[720] that the more original form of the *dia*-phrase which contained the title *Lord* also contained *Jesus Christ*. So in that context we must regard the word order *Jesus Christ* as traditional. It is therefore natural that Paul, too, should adopt this order in *dia*-phrases. This particular usage does not contradict our conclusion that Paul generally prefers the other order in the genitive and dative cases. The ὑπό-phrase confirms this observation, for there (though admittedly we cannot be absolutely sure about the readings) *Christ* precedes.

4. In the accusative and in accusative prepositional phrases, too, *Christ* is normally placed first, but the passages are so few in number that we cannot establish any rule about this. 5. Only in the nominative does the reverse seem to apply, for there the order *Jesus Christ* is the rule. 6. Thus our general conclusion must be that Paul speaks of *Jesus Christ* in the nominative case, but in the oblique cases he puts *Christ Jesus*. *Dia*-phrases present a different picture because in them Paul is simply following the pre-Pauline, traditional word order. We now have to interpret all this.

The instances with *Jesus Christ* are:
Nominative: I Cor. 3.11; Gal. 3.1; (II Cor. 13.5).
Genitive: Gal. 1.12; 3.22; Rom. 1.6; Phil. 1.19; (Rom. 3.22).
Dative: none.
Accusative: I Cor. 2.2; (—).
Prepositional phrases: with gen: διά: Gal. 1.1; Rom. 1.8; Phil. 1.11; (Rom. 5.17).
with dat.: —; (ἐν: Gal. 3.14).
with acc.: none.
The post-Pauline passage, Rom. 16.25, 27, has not been taken into account.
[720] See 19ab.

c. The order *Jesus Christ* must be regarded as the normal one, for it corresponds to the Aramaic *yᵉšua' mᵉšīḥā*.⁷²¹ It is natural that the Greek translation should preserve the same word order in the nominative. But what is the explanation of the reversal of the word order in the oblique cases? The dative *en*-phrases give the clearest picture, though the genitive constructions, too, are clear enough. In the dative and in the genitive Ἰησοῦς has exactly the same form, but Χριστός, which is not a contraction, is inflected and therefore reveals clearly which case is intended. If *Jesus* is placed first in a genitive or a dative construction, it cannot in itself give any clear indication of its case; but if *Christ* is placed first in such a construction, it shows immediately and unambiguously which particular case is intended. What we find in the Pauline material suggests that it is Paul's custom to put *Christ* first in these cases, and we can only conclude that his purpose in doing so really was to avoid the ambiguity which would have resulted if he had allowed *Jesus* to precede. Thus 'the reason for reversing the word order is a purely grammatical one, for Ἰησοῦς in the oblique cases is ambiguous'.⁷²² This reason is a purely formal one, so there can be no justification for saying that *Christ* has a special meaning when it precedes *Jesus*. This means that it is impossible to regard *Christ*, so used, as signifying 'Messiah'.

This is about as far as we can get, for if we examine, from the point of view of content, the passages in which *Christ Jesus* or *Jesus Christ* occur, we find nothing which would serve to distinguish them.

62. *'Christ' with the Definite Article*

a. Other scholars believe that where *Christ* has the definite article it ranks as a messianic title. Conzelmann expresses this opinion with the greatest clarity when he writes, ' "Christ" is meant as a title when the definite article precedes it'.⁷²³ His thesis appears to be crystal clear: Χριστός is a proper name, ὁ Χριστός means 'the Messiah'. Only an examination of the material can show whether it is in fact correct.

---

⁷²¹ Lietzmann, *Römer* 23 (on Rom. 1.2) has already pointed this out.
⁷²² Thus von Dobschütz, *An die Thessalonicher*, 1909, 61 (excursus on I Thess. 1.1).
⁷²³ Conzelmann, 'Christenheit' 65; cf. Arndt and Gingrich s.v. Χριστός.

b. There are 60 instances in which *Christ* is in the genitive. Of these, 30 give *Christ* without article and 30 with the article. I Cor. 6.15 is an instance in which both forms occur together, so we shall use it as our starting point. It reads: 'Do you not know that your bodies are members of Christ (μέλη Χριστοῦ)? Shall I therefore take the members of Christ (τὰ μέλη τοῦ Χριστοῦ) and make them members of a prostitute?'

It is evident that both these genitive combinations have exactly the same meaning. But in the first case μέλη is the complement and therefore has no article. Similarly, *Christ* (in the genitive) is also without the article. In the second case, however, τὰ μέλη is the object (in the accusative) and has the definite article, and *Christ* which follows has the definite article also. So as a somewhat generalized working hypothesis we may say that in genitive combinations *Christ* appears without the article when the noun which governs the genitive has no article, but when the noun which governs the genitive has the definite article then *Christ* also has it. If we examine all 60 of the passages in which *Christ* occurs in genitive combinations such as these, we find complete confirmation of our hypothesis. Of the 30 cases in which *Christ* in the genitive has no article, in 29 it follows a noun which likewise has no article. The exception (Phil. 2.30) is inexplicable.[724] Of the 30 cases which give τοῦ Χριστοῦ, 27 are preceded by a noun with the definite article. We shall now consider the three exceptions.

In II Cor. 10.1 Paul entreats διὰ τῆς πραΰτητος καὶ ἐπιεικείας τοῦ Χριστοῦ. Now πραΰτης καὶ ἐπιείκεια is a hendiadys, so the article which appears before πραΰτης also determines ἐπιείκεια at the same time, so it is natural that the definite article should also precede Χριστός. This passage therefore conforms to the principle which we have discovered. II Cor. 13.3 is about the δοκιμή . . . τοῦ ἐν ἐμοὶ λαλοῦντος Χριστοῦ. Here the article belongs, not to *Christ*, but to the phrase which is in apposition to it, so that this passage really belongs to the group in which *Christ* without article follows a governing noun which is likewise without article. In I Cor. 11.3 Paul speaks of the κεφαλή . . . τοῦ Χριστοῦ. Here the definite article is to be explained as a repetition, for earlier in the sentence

[724] D and the *Koine* admittedly read with article, but this reading must be secondary. All the same it is significant that the article has been inserted in order to conform to normal usage.

we find ὁ Χριστός.[725] We shall discuss later the reason for the definite article with *Christ* in the nominative.

So the conclusion to be drawn from this whole discussion is that Paul puts the article with the genitive Χριστοῦ when the noun which governs the genitive also has the article. When the noun governing the genitive has no article, then Χριστοῦ likewise is left indeterminate. Since the reason for the presence or the absence of the article is a purely formal one, it is impossible to establish as a general principle that *Christ* with the article means 'Messiah'.

c. Only on four occasions does *Christ* in the dative have the article.[726] Here the presence of the article is not so obviously a purely formal matter as was the case with the genitive constructions. All the same, it is quite clear that in Rom. 14.18, δουλεύων τῷ Χριστῷ, the article does not indicate that *Christ* is understood in a messianic sense, for in v. 15 *Christ* is without the article, and there is nothing to suggest that the meaning is different from the meaning of *Christ* (with article) in v. 18. Moreover, passages which are similar in content to Rom. 14.18 are linked elsewhere with christological designations which make it plain that it is not the Messiah who is thought of particularly.[727] So we may not assume that in Rom. 14.18 Paul is speaking specifically of the 'Messiah'.

In II Cor. 11.2 Paul expresses his desire to present the Church as a pure bride τῷ Χριστῷ. Here again there follows in v. 3 an instance of *Christ* without article. Since we have no evidence that the idea of the bride of the Messiah formed any part of Jewish messianic expectation, we cannot see why Paul should wish to use the title 'Messiah' here.

There remain now the two instances in which we find the article in the *en*-formula. In I Cor. 15.22 the article has been inserted on the analogy of the expression ἐν τῷ Ἀδάμ. In the

---

[725] Dahl, 'Die Messianität Jesu bei Paulus', *Studia Paulina in honorem Johannis de Zwaan*, 1953, 85 n. 2, gives a different explanation of the article here, saying that κεφαλή is 'only formally indeterminate'. It is quite true that the sense makes clear that a particular 'head' is being spoken of here. Nevertheless it seems unlikely to me that an incidental consideration of sense such as this should have caused the insertion of the definite article before *Christ*. To regard the article simply as a repetition (and this is, after all, looking at it from a formal point of view) makes perfectly good sense.

[726] I Cor. 15.22; II Cor. 2.14; 11.2; Rom. 14.18.

[727] Cf. particularly Rom. 16.18.

preceding verses and in subsequent verses *Christ* is mentioned frequently, as a rule without the article.[728] Since there is nothing to suggest any change in meaning, we cannot regard *Christ* with the article as a messianic title.

The same is to be said of II Cor. 2.14. In v. 15 *Christ* occurs without article. It seems that the article has been inserted in order to echo the exclamation τῷ δὲ θεῷ χάρις τῷ . . ., and is thus conditioned by considerations of style. This means that in none of these passages in which *Christ* in the dative has the definite article may we regard it as representing the title 'Messiah'.

d. The same picture is presented by the passages in which *Christ* is accusative.[729] In all four passages *Christ* without the article appears almost side by side. Only in I Cor. 15.15 can the article be explained as a repetition. There is no convincing explanation of the article in the other passages. It is obviously due simply to variations in Paul's own style and usage.

e. In the nominative ὁ Χριστός is found seven times.[730] In I Cor. 1.13 it follows a whole row of names—Paul, Apollos, Cephas and Christ. This setting, together with the fact that *Christ* with the article follows immediately upon *Christ* without article, makes it impossible to suppose that ὁ Χριστός really means 'Messiah' here. *Christ* with the article is found three times in comparisons,[731] two of these three instances occurring in the context of the 'conformity-rule'. This latter has obviously had an influence in encouraging the insertion of the article. It is impossible to discover anything in the content of these passages which might have prompted Paul to put the article. Indeed, in Rom. 15.7f. we find *Christ* first with, and then without, article. This shows clearly that the presence or absence of the article is without significance and makes no difference to the sense.

The typological statement ἡ πέτρα δὲ ἦν ὁ Χριστός (I Cor. 10.4) is an exegetical affirmation in the style of Jewish exegesis.[732] Because of this resemblance we might at first be inclined to regard *Christ* in this instance as a messianic title. Yet the rock (Ex. 17 or

[728] In v. 16 in the acc. with article, vv. 16, 17, 20, 23 in the nom., v. 18 in the *en*-formula, v. 19 in the dat., all without article. Only in v. 23 is the article given in the expression οἱ τοῦ Χριστοῦ.

[729] I Cor. 15.15; Phil. 1.15, 17; 3.7.

[730] I Cor. 1.13; 10.4; 11.3; 12.12; Rom. 9.5; 15.3, 7.

[731] I Cor. 12.12; Rom. 15.3, 7.

[732] Cf. Gal. 4.24.

Num. 20) which is referred to here was never interpreted messianically in Judaism,[733] though other OT statements about the 'stone'
were so interpreted.[734] Considered from this point of view it is
quite possible that ὁ Χριστός in this instance, too, is simply a
proper name.

In I Cor. 11.3 the image of 'the head' is used to represent a
hierarchy of being, and at one level within this hierarchy is
ὁ Χριστός. The meaning is that *Christ* ranks 'above' ordinary
humanity, but there is nothing here which is particularly reminiscent of the ideas associated with Messiahship. It is therefore
impossible to decide whether *Christ* really means 'Messiah' here, or
whether it is not much more likely to be the proper name of this
figure who is 'between' men and God.

There remains one passage (Rom. 9.5) in which there is the
greatest likelihood that *Christ* means 'Messiah'. In this passage
Paul is listing the decisive dates and events in the history of God's
dealings with Israel—sonship, glory, the covenants, the giving of
the law, the worship, the promises and the patriarchs. All these
expressions denote advantages or privileges granted to Israel. At
the end of this list Paul mentions finally the *Christ* whose origin
according to the flesh was in Israel. Since Paul's concern here is to
make a list of the blessings of salvation granted to Israel during its
own history within God's purpose of election, it is natural that he
should speak of the coming of the Messiah.

A review of these instances in which *Christ* is given in the
nominative thus leads to the conclusion that in two places ὁ Χριστός
might possibly mean 'Messiah' in the literal sense, but only in one
of these is it relatively certain. The difficulty of making a judgement about these passages is that unlike the genitive constructions
they offer no formal criteria which prove convincingly that the
presence or absence of the article has nothing to do with the
question whether *Christ* is a name or a title. Only in a few instances
does consideration of the content and terminology of the context
make it possible to regard *Christ* with the article as in some degree
equivalent to 'the Messiah'. Nevertheless it would be quite mistaken, with this group, to regard the presence of the article as the
sure sign that *Christ* has the same meaning as the title 'Messiah'.

[733] See Cullmann, *TWNT* VI 96.42f.
[734] See Jeremias, *TWNT* IV 276.14–277.16.

f. The four places at which *Christ* with the article occurs in prepositional phrases[735] contribute nothing new. So we may summarize as follows:

1. In genitive constructions the reason for the presence of the article with *Christ* is a purely formal one and therefore has no bearing on the question whether *Christ* is a proper name or whether it represents the title 'Messiah'. 2. Sometimes in cases other than the genitive the article can be explained simply as a repetition and so has no bearing on the title question either. 3. In several places *Christ* with the article is preceded and followed by *Christ* without article, which shows that there can be no difference in meaning between the two. We cannot regard the article in these instances as an indication that *Christ* is used in a 'titular' sense. 4. Where there are no formal criteria for deciding the question, the context of the greater number of passages makes it clear that *Christ* with the article is used as a proper name. Only in a very few isolated instances is it either possible or probable that *Christ* is used with the sense of 'Messiah'. These conclusions show that it is not permissible to confuse the question of the article with the question of titles.

g. The use of the article with the name *Jesus* confirms our conclusion, for although *Jesus* is without any doubt a proper name, we find that in several places it has the article, and for precisely the same formal reasons which operated in the case of *Christ*.

Jesus in the genitive has the article when the noun governing the genitive also has the article.[736] If the latter is without article, then so is *Jesus* also.[737] Where the article occurs with *Jesus* in cases other than the genitive it can be explained as a repetition.[738] There is no obvious reason for the presence of the article in Rom. 8.11a.[739] But it is quite certain that the article does not turn the name *Jesus* into a 'title'.[740]

---

[735] II Cor. 1.5; 3.4 (*dia* with gen.); Rom. 9.3 (*apo* with gen.); Phil. 3.7 (*dia* with acc.).

[736] Gal. 6.17; II Cor. 4.10, 11.

[737] Rom. 3.26. An exception is Phil. 2.10, but the omission of the article corresponds to the style of the hymn.

[738] Thus I Thess. 4.14b; II Cor. 4.14 (where the title *Kyrios* is secondary. See 3h).

[739] The reading with article is to be regarded as the more original.

[740] The statement by Schmithals, *Gnosis* 51, 'that "Jesus" in Gal. 6.17 and Rom. 8.11 is not simply a proper name but a title, as is shown by the insertion of the article in each case' clearly begs the question, and in face of the evidence his statement does not hold.

This makes it clear that 'Ἰησοῦς and ὁ 'Ἰησοῦς are variants which differ only in form and not in content. Even when it has the article, *Jesus* still remains a proper name. Why should the same not be true of *Christ* also?

h. But now we must try to ward off a possible misunderstanding. Our exposition has not been concerned to prove that the definite article and the original meaning of *Christ* as a title have absolutely nothing to do with one another. Of course *Christ* was originally the translation of 'Messiah' and as such must have had 'titular' significance. The habit of putting the article with *Christ* presumably arose because *Christ* had this meaning. But as time went on *Christ* came to be regarded increasingly as a proper name, yet in spite of this the article was still used with it here and there. This was possible because the habit had already been formed, but equally because it was quite possible to use the article with the proper name. It is this stage which is reflected in Paul's writings.

63. 'Christ' as the Subject of the Sentence

Conzelmann mentions one final criterion for judging the title question. He says that ' "Christ" has titular significance . . . where "Christ" (without the name "Jesus") is the subject of the sentence'.[741]

To this group belong on the one hand the majority of the passages in which ὁ Χριστός appears in the nominative and which we have already examined,[742] and on the other hand certain fragments of the pistis-formula in which *Christ* is the subject of the statement.[743] Finally there are a number of passages of mixed content which also belong here. Conzelmann obviously has only the fragments of the pistis-formula in view. There can be no doubt that *Christ* is given in the pistis-formula because it represents the translation of the Aramaic term 'Messiah'. When the pistis-formula first came into being it meant, 'The Messiah died and was raised.' But these statements represent a completely new interpretation of Jewish messianic expectation.

To Hellenistic Jewish ears both the original titular significance

[741] Conzelmann, 'Christenheit' 65.
[742] See 62e.
[743] See 3 and 4.

of *Christ* and also the re-interpretation of its significance were equally clear. But for Gentile Christians this was not possible, for they had no knowledge or understanding of the titular significance of *Christ* or of its religious background in Judaism. They were bound to understand *Christ* as a proper name. Even if they were instructed about the original meaning of the term (which probably did happen in the earliest period), for them *Christ* would have been, in precise terms, simply the name of him who died and had been raised. In the Pauline period *Christ* was for Gentile Christians the name of him in whom the saving events, death and resurrection, took place. It was in this sense that *Christ* was understood by those to whom Paul's letters were addressed. They did not regard it as a title.

So all that remains is to ask how Paul himself understood *Christ* in the context of the pistis-formula. But this is not a question which can be answered with great clarity. Certainly Paul was a Jewish Christian and therefore was aware that *Christ* was originally the translation of the Jewish title 'Messiah', or at least it would have been possible for Paul to recollect that this was the case. But it is highly questionable whether, in his use of fragments from the pistis-formula, he intended always to reproduce the original connection between *Christ* and the title 'Messiah', while those around him did not do so. At all events there is nothing in the text to warrant such an assumption. This means that it is impossible to say, with regard to the Pauline period, that *Christ* means 'Messiah' when it is the subject of a sentence.

64. Summary

It is necessary now to review the preceding paragraphs, for our examination of all the theses which sought to establish general criteria for deciding whether *Christ* is used as a title has led us in every instance to a similar result. No such general criterion can be found, either in cases where *Christ* is placed first in the double designation *Christ Jesus*, or in cases where *Christ* has the article, or in cases where *Christ* is the subject of the sentence. Even though all these things, at the time when they arose, may have been connected with the fact that *Christ* was originally a translation of 'Messiah' and therefore had titular significance, nevertheless such a connection is completely unrecognized by the Gentile Christian church in the Pauline period.

In Paul's own case we may assume that there was some latent awareness of the original connection, but it is only quite sporadically that we find literary evidence of it. And this is only found by examining the context very thoroughly. It can never be found simply by applying general criteria based on formal, grammatical considerations.

65. A Survival of the Original Meaning of 'Christ'

We find, however, within the Pauline corpus a particular linguistic tradition which is pre-Pauline and which could never have arisen without the awareness that *Christ* was originally a title.

Paul speaks of *the Lord Jesus Christ*, of *our Lord Jesus Christ*, and of *the Lord Jesus*, but not of the *Lord Christ*. Similarly, Paul uses the formulae 'in the *Lord Jesus Christ*' and 'in *Christ Jesus our Lord*', but not 'in *Christ the Lord*' (ἐν Χριστῷ κυρίῳ). In all these instances *Lord* and *Christ* never stand immediately side by side.[744] In view of the variety of forms in which these expressions occur, and in view of the frequency with which they are used, this can surely not be accidental. Moreover, if we take into consideration that *Lord* is a title and that *Christ*, as a translation of 'Messiah', originally ranked as a title, it is natural that the two titles were not made to follow immediately upon one another. It remained customary to keep them apart, so much so that the custom was still followed, even when all awareness of the original significance of *Christ* as a title had disappeared.[745] So the custom survives as a witness to something forgotten.

[744] A certain exception to this is found at Rom. 5.21; 7.25, where the phrase διὰ 'Ιησοῦ Χριστοῦ stands at the end of the sentence and has had added to it the words τοῦ κυρίου ἡμῶν. These last three words are to be regarded as in apposition, and are due to the fact that a fuller and more formal style was required at the close of such sentences (cf. Rom. 6.23; 8.39). Thus the order of words here came about as a result of these particular requirements of style. Another exception is Rom. 16.18 (τῷ κυρίῳ ἡμῶν Χριστῷ). On this it needs to be said that the question of the authorship of Rom. 16 has not been completely decided. If it really were Paul who wrote this particular expression, then it remains as an inexplicable exception.

[745] The rest of the NT literature presents the same picture. The only exceptions are Col. 3.24 (similar to Rom. 16.18); Jude 25 (similar to Rom. 5.21; 7.25). The same is true of the Apostolic Fathers; exceptions are I *Clement* 49.6; 50.7 (similar to Rom. 5.21; 7.25); Ign. *Eph.* 7.2.

III · LORD

66. The Relationship between 'The Lord Jesus (Christ)' and 'The Lord'

a. There are two reasons for wanting to define the relationship between the full title ὁ κύριος (ἡμῶν) Ἰησοῦς (Χριστός) and the simple title *Kyrios*. The first is that our historical interest prompts us to ask which of the two reproduces the earlier usage. The second is that we would like to know why Paul himself at one time uses the full title and at another time the shorter title. We cannot help being struck by the fact that the full title 'the (our) *Lord Jesus (Christ)*' occurs only in a limited number of expressions, all of which were already in use in the worship of the pre-Pauline church. Particular examples which we could mention here are the farewell formulae, the *onoma*-phrases and the *dia*-phrases, as well as the expressions in which God is called the Father of the *Lord Jesus (Christ)*.[746] Besides these we also find a limited number of passages in which Paul imitates, as it were, liturgical expressions of this sort when he links the salutation, a few *en*-formulae and also several statements about the parousia[747] with the full title. The simple title *Lord*, on the other hand, is found above all in sentences in which Paul is formulating *ad hoc*. Here we should recall primarily the passages which contain the formula 'in the *Lord*', and also statements which are about the practical activities of the Church.[748] Of course, the title *Lord* on its own is to be found also in pre-Pauline expressions, notably in the language of the Lord's Supper, and in expressions such as those which served to introduce quotations from the OT,[749] for in these the title *Lord* is already used in a technical sense. We showed earlier[750] that the title *Lord* could only be used in this technical sense when the expressions containing the title

---

[746] Cf. also I Thess. 3.11 and the salutation in the opening designation, where 'God, the Father' and 'the *Lord Jesus (Christ)*' are mentioned side by side.
[747] For a more detailed treatment of these, see 42, 48 and 51.
[748] For precise details see 47 and 50.
[749] See 43–45.
[750] See 43bc.

had established themselves firmly in particular contexts. But only
those liturgical expressions which we mentioned first (containing
the full title) can be considered as examples of such pre-Pauline
expressions. This means, then, that within the Pauline corpus it is
the full title which represents an earlier stage in the development
of christological terminology than the simple title *Lord*.

b. If we ask what prompted Paul to use at one time the full titles
and at another time the simple title *Lord*, we arrive at the following
conclusion: the simple title occurs predominantly in those parts of
the letters in which Paul, for purposes of his own, is developing
arguments designed to settle questions of principle or of practice.

The full titles, on the other hand, are found primarily in those
parts of the letters which by virtue of their position have a distinctive and somewhat formal style. Examples are the opening
designation, the preamble, the farewell formula, and also passages
which form the conclusion of a particular part of the letter, and
which frequently have an elevated style. All these parts of the
letters contain many reminiscences of liturgical language, whether
because (as in the case of the farewell formula)[751] complete
sentences or sequences have been drawn from the liturgy, or
because individual liturgical expressions like doxologies, thanks-
givings, or expressions of praise have been employed. It is together
with these things that the full christological titles were also
adopted, for the titles, too, are among the stylistic features which
were drawn from the liturgy and taken up in the letters. The full
christological titles are well suited, in combination, to the solemnity of liturgical language, and that is why they are used in places
where Paul is writing in an elevated style.[752]

Thus the circle is complete. The full christological titles are used
in passages of distinctive style (i.e. interspersed with liturgical
elements) because they have sufficient weight to be well suited to
the style which is characteristic in these passages. But the full titles
have this weight because they are a combination of various titles
or names. But then this combination in turn owes its origin to the
canons of form which were operative in a liturgy striving for
solemnity of expression.

[751] Cf. particularly I Cor. 16.20b, 22–24.
[752] Cerfaux, *Christ* 505–8, gives a quite different explanation, saying that originally
the 'complete title' was associated particularly with the idea of the parousia, and that
all other examples are to be regarded as later deviations from this norm.

Thus the principle which governed the choice of one or other type of christological designation turns out to be one of style. In 'ordinary' parts of his letters Paul uses the simple title *Lord*, but in passages which on account of their position demand a more distinctive style he puts the full titles including *Lord*.[753]

c. The question of the relationship between the expressions 'the (our) *Lord Jesus*' and 'the (our) *Lord Jesus Christ*', and of their relative age, is a question which is much more difficult to answer, for they are both found in completely similar contexts. The following table will make this clear.

ὁ κύριος (ἡμῶν) Ἰησοῦς	ὁ κύριος (ἡμῶν) Ἰησοῦς Χριστός

A. In the passages listed on the right the full designation still has the character of a precise statement and has not yet become a merely stylistic combination.

1. Acclamation[754]	1. Acclamation[755]
2. 'Our *Lord*' in apposition[756]	2. 'Our *Lord*' in apposition[757]

B. In the following passages the use of the full designation goes back to clearly defined pre-Pauline usage.

1. Farewell formulae[758]	1. Farewell formulae[759]
2. *Onoma*-phrases[760]	2. *Onoma*-phrases[761]

[753] We shall illustrate this by noting how the title is used in connection with statements about the parousia. For even though it is the *Mare-Kyrios* idea which lies behind the parousia contexts, Paul still follows this same principle in choosing between one or another designation. Of the six instances in which the full titles are associated with statements about the parousia, two occur in the preamble (I Cor. 1.7b, 8), one in the farewell formula of I Thess. 5.23 (the similarity with corresponding sentences in the preambles is striking), one in a 'farewell' prayer at the end of a section (I Thess. 3.13—here, too, the similarity with sentences in the preambles is not to be ignored), one very obviously occupies a final position and in addition is associated with the idea of 'boasting' (II Cor. 1.14), and only one occurs in a passage in which practical questions are being discussed (I Thess. 2.19 here again it is associated with the idea of 'boasting'). The remaining parousia statements which are linked with the simple title *Lord* are all without exception found in those parts of the letters which are devoted to general discussion or argument.
[754] I Cor. 12.3; Rom. 10.9 (both without 'our').
[755] Phil. 2.11 (without 'our'). Cf. I Cor. 8.6.
[756] I Cor. 9.1; Rom. 4.24 (both with 'our'). Cf. I Thess. 2.15.
[757] II Cor. 4.5 without, Phil. 3.8 with 'our'. Also three times in *en*-phrases (each time with 'our'): I Cor. 15.31; Rom. 6.23; 8.39. Also twice in *dia*-phrases (with 'our'): Rom. 5.21; 7.25. In the last five instances the title *Lord* is added at the end in order to give more weight to the christological designation.
[758] I Cor. 16.23 without, Rom. 16.20b with 'our'.
[759] I Thess. 5.28; Gal. 6.18 (with 'our'); II Cor. 13.13; Phil. 4.23; Philemon 25 (without 'our').
[760] I Cor. 5.4a (presumably without 'our').
[761] I Cor. 1.2; 6.11 (both presumably with 'our').

3. God, the Father of the *Lord*[762]   3. God, the Father of the *Lord*[763]
4. *dia*-phrases[764]   4. *dia*-phrases[765]
5. Lord's Supper liturgy[766]
6. Parousia statements[767]   5. Parousia statements[768]
   (*Mare-Kyrios*)   (*Mare-Kyrios*)

C. In the following places Paul is formulating freely, though to some extent (e.g. in the salutation) he follows certain usages which were customary in the pre-Pauline church.

1. Blessings of salvation[769]   1. Blessings of salvation[770]
2. *en*-formulae[771]   2. *en*-formulae[772]
                                  3. Salutation[773]

We have already stressed that both these expressions already had a place in the language of the pre-Pauline church. More than this we cannot say with absolute certainty. Are they both completely equivalent variants, or is one of them the basic form from which the other developed?

Our first inclination might be to say that the expression which does not include *Christ* is the earlier, and that *Christ* came to be added later. But what we find in the Pauline corpus gives no basis for a stratification of this sort. Both expressions can be found in the early Paulines as well as in the late ones. So we must get assistance from reflections which take us beyond what the text alone can yield.

First we must notice that the designation 'the (our) *Lord Jesus*', like the '*Kyrios Jesus*' in the acclamation, represents a combination of the title *Lord* and the name *Jesus*. Here we have the Hellenistic understanding of the title *Lord* which in fact forms the background of the acclamation, and indeed of the majority of the firmly

[762] II Cor. 11.31 (without 'our'). Cf. I Thess. 3.11, where 'God our Father' is parallelled by 'our Lord Jesus'.
[763] II Cor. 1.3 (with 'our').
[764] I Thess. 4.2 (without 'our').
[765] I Thess. 5.9; I Cor. 15.57; Rom. 5.1, 11; 15.30 (all with 'our').
[766] I Cor. 11.23 (without 'our').
[767] I Thess. 2.19; 3.13; II Cor. 1.14 (all with 'our').
[768] I Cor. 1.7b, 8; I Thess. 5.23 (both with 'our'); Phil. 3.20 (without 'our').
[769] I Cor. 5.4b with, Philemon 5 without 'our'.
[770] II Cor. 8.9; cf. I Thess. 1.3; Gal. 6.14 (in each case with 'our').
[771] I Thess. 4.1; Rom. 14.14; Phil. 2.19 (all without 'our').
[772] I Thess. 1.1 (without 'our').
[773] I Cor. 1.3: II Cor. 1.2; Rom. 1.7; Phil. 1.2; Philemon 3 (all without 'our'); Gal. 1.3 (presumably with 'our').

established expressions containing *Lord*, so we must assume that the expression 'the (our) *Lord Jesus*' was formed in the Hellenistic church.

In the case of the other designation 'the (our) *Lord Jesus Christ*' this is even clearer. For this expression, too (like the acclamation '*Kyrios Jesus Christos*') consists of a combination of a title and names. But this means that at the time when the full designation was formed *Christ* had already become essentially a proper name. This stage can only have been reached on Hellenistic Gentile-Christian soil.

If both these fuller expressions were formed in the Hellenistic Gentile church, we may assume that they do not represent stages of development but simply variant forms. We might possibly have to take a different view of the case if there had ever been a time when *Jesus*, but not *Christ*, had been understood in the Hellenistic Gentile church as a proper name, for only at such a time would it have been possible to link the name *Jesus*, but not the title *Christ*, with the title *Lord*. But it is more than likely that such a time never existed, for when the title 'Messiah' was translated as *Christ*, the title as such was unintelligible to Greek ears and thus became simply a proper name. Even if we were to suppose that the first Greek-speaking Jewish-Christian missionaries explained the meaning of the translation *Christ*, it would still be doubtful whether the understanding of the term as a title could ever have been a really live understanding. So we must take it that from the beginning *Christ* was essentially understood as a proper name.

If these reflections reproduce adequately the facts of the case, then the two fuller christological designations represent not two successive stages of development but two variants on the same level within the tradition. As such, both in form and content, they are completely synonymous.

67. The Function of the Adjective ἡμῶν

a. The last of the particular problems which we have to examine is the one which relates to the adjective 'our'.[774] This is made the more difficult by the fact that at a number of places ἡμῶν is text-

[774] Notes 754-73 list the places at which it occurs.

critically uncertain.[775] If we compare the number of passages containing 'our' with the number of passages without 'our', the proportions work out as follows: 1. In the acclamation, 0:3; 2. In passages where *Lord* is in apposition, 8:1; 3. In the full designation, 22:30.[776]

It is impossible to find any other principle of classification, for 'our' can appear or fail to appear as well in the designation *Lord Jesus* as in *Lord Jesus Christ*. Contexts which in form and content are similar do not give a unified picture where the adjective 'our' is concerned. This makes it perfectly plain that for Paul the meaning is the same, whether 'our' is inserted or not.[777] But was this so at the pre-Pauline stage of the tradition? Is the designation which includes 'our' the earlier form, or is the designation which omits 'our' the earlier one?

b. Cerfaux connects the form which includes 'our' with the Aramaic petition *Maranatha*.[778] This is to assert that it is very early indeed. But on the basis of our investigations so far the most we could possibly say is that the actual title *Lord* in the parousia statements is related to the *Maranatha*. This means that the hypothesis put forward by Cerfaux can claim validity for these few statements about the parousia. It is improbable that these statements subsequently influenced the fuller christological designation (which, of course, had no connection with the *Mare-Kyrios* idea), for this would mean that the parousia statements, in their particularity, would have influenced statements of a different kind which in number and variety were far greater. It is much more likely that the larger groups exercised an influence on the smaller group, causing the title(s) used in statements about the parousia to be brought into line with the usage which was customary in other kinds of statement. Thus Cerfaux's thesis will not stand.

c. It is striking that in the acclamation, which set the pattern for the way in which the title *Lord* was used generally within the Gentile-Christian church, the adjective 'our' does not appear. If we bear this fact in mind, and then take into consideration also

---

[775] In a number of instances it is a matter of opinion whether one decides for or against it.
[776] Of the 20 places where 'our' is lacking, 6 occur in the salutation in the opening designations of the letters.
[777] Cf. 20b and 42e.
[778] Cerfaux, *Christ* 505.

that 'our' appears very frequently in the full christological designation, we are tempted to conclude that designations without the adjective 'our' represent an earlier stage in the development of the tradition than those which include 'our'. This is the opinion of Foerster,[779] who regards the development as a sign that the Church's understanding of the title *Lord* shifted away from the idea that the *Lord* is ruler over all to the idea that the *Lord* is ruler over the faithful. But against this, if we take note of the fact that of all the many instances in which Paul uses the title *Lord* on its own only one instance contains the adjective 'our',[780] we could just as well argue that the development took place in the opposite direction.

The overall picture is clear yet strange. At the beginning of a line of development we find the acclamation, which does not include 'our'. Pre-Pauline expressions of liturgical type include it quite frequently. When Paul puts the simple title *Lord* in formulations of his own, the adjective is missed out altogether.

How are we to interpret all this? If we put side by side the acclamation and the pre-Pauline expressions of liturgical type, it seems probable that they do not represent two different stages along a single line of development (whether of language or of ideas).

The difference between the forms which include 'our' and those from which the adjective is absent is much rather a difference of *function*. When the Church utters the acclamation, it is clear that the Church is really making a statement about the *Lord's* status *vis-à-vis* the Church. The *Lord* is acclaimed by the Church, in fact, as *its Lord*. The adjective is not included in the acclamation because the acclamation itself, simply by being pronounced, expresses exactly and directly what the adjective 'our' would express. Only in a later period does it become necessary, for polemical purposes, to reflect whether the *Lord's* dominion embraces the whole world or only the Church.

When *'our Lord Jesus Christ'* is spoken of in pre-Pauline expressions, the concern is not to establish the relationship which exists between the Church and the *Lord*. It is rather to bring something else, i.e. a particular act or a particular blessing, into

---

[779] Foerster, *Herr ist Jesus* 200.
[780] Phil. 3.8.

relationship with the *Lord*. The adjective 'our' is not inserted
with any polemical intent. It represents simply the first person
plural which is common form in confessional style.

Certainly it is the idea of the *Lord* as *Lord* of the Church which
is the dominant idea here. But it would be quite wrong to infer
from this any deliberate contrast to the idea of the *Lord* as the ruler
of the world. It was only at a later stage of reflection that there was
any awareness of this problem.

I Cor. 8.5f. is a classic illustration of this. Here Paul is speaking
of the relationship between the sphere of dominion of the *Lord
Jesus Christ* and that of other 'lords'. It is typical that the statement
that the *Lord* is the one *Lord* of all should stand side by side with
the statement that he is the one *Lord* 'for us'. His unique lordship
over all, as represented by the idea of his mediation at the creation
(derived from Wisdom speculation), is interpreted as his unique
lordship 'for us'—in view of the 'many lords' in the surrounding
Hellenistic world. It is probable that Jewish influences have led to
the statement about the *Lord's* unique dominion over all.[781] From
this stage onwards the problem of the scope of the Lord's
dominion—whether he is *Lord* over the world or only *Lord* over
the Church—becomes a live one which calls for an elaboration or
a balancing of the two ideas. For Paul the title *Lord* naturally
includes both ideas, and that is why the insertion or the omission
of the adjective 'our' is of no significance for him.

In the pre-Pauline period there is no difference in meaning
between expressions which contain 'our' and those from which
'our' is absent, for both types of expression describe the *Lord*
simply as the *Lord* of the Church.

68. In Conclusion

Thus we have reached the end of our inquiry. A résumé of 'Part
Three' is hardly necessary, for the problems discussed and the
conclusions reached are so varied that they cannot be conveniently
summarized.

[781] Cf. 43d.

ABBREVIATIONS

Abh. Th. ANT	Abhandlungen zur Theologie des Alten und Neuen Testaments
Arndt and Gingrich	See Bibliography under Bauer
Bl-Debr.	F. Blass, *Grammatik des neutestamentlichen Griechisch*, bearbeitet von A. Debrunner
BKW	Bible key words (translations of articles from *TWNT*)
BZNW	Beihefte zur *ZNW*
Did.	*Didache*
ET	English translation
EvTh	*Evangelische Theologie*
FRLANT	Forschungen zur Religion und Literatur des Alten und Neuen Testaments
HNT	Handbuch zum Neuen Testament (Lietzmann)
Herm. *vis*	Hermas, *Vision*
Herm. *sim.*	Hermas, *Similitude*
Ign.	Ignatius (Epistles: *Eph.—Ephesians; Magn.—Magnesians; Rom.—Romans; Smyrn.—Smyrnaeans; Trall.—Trallians; Philad.—Philadelphians*)
KEKNT	Kritisch-exegetischer Kommentar über das Neue Testament, begründet von H. A. W. Meyer
NTD	Das Neue Testament Deutsch, ed. P. Althaus and J. Behm, 1932ff.
NTS	*New Testament Studies*
NtlStud	*Neutestamentliche Studien für R. Bultmann* (BZNW 21), 1954
1 QSa	Dead Sea Scrolls: Rule of the Community (Appendix)
RGG	*Religion in Geschichte und Gegenwart*, 3rd ed., 1956ff.
SBT	Studies in Biblical Theology
TLZ	*Theologische Literaturzeitung*
TWNT	*Theologisches Wörterbuch zum NT*, ed. G. Kittel, 1933ff.
ZNW	*Zeitschrift für die neutestamentliche Wissenschaft*
ZTK	*Zeitschrift für Theologie und Kirche*

BIBLIOGRAPHY

BAMMEL, E., 'Herkunft und Funktion der Traditionselemente in I Kor. 15.11', *TZ* 11, 1955, 401–19

BAUDISSIN, W. W. GRAF, *Kyrios als Gottesname im Judentum und seine Stelle in der Religionsgeschichte*, 1929.

BAUER, W., *Griechisch-deutsches Wörterbuch zu den Schriften des Neuen Testaments*, 5th ed., 1958; ET of 4th ed., 1949: W. F. Arndt and F. W. Gingrich, *A Greek-English Lexicon of the New Testament and other early Christian literature*, 1952

BEYER, W., εὐλογητός, *TWNT* II 761.38–762.36

BIETENHARD, H., ὄνομα, *TWNT* V 242.9–283.15

BORNKAMM, G., 'Das **Anathema** in der urchristlichen Abendmahlsliturgie', *Das Ende des Gesetzes*, 1958, 123–32

— '**Herrenmahl** und Kirche bei Paulus', *Studien zu Antike und Christentum*, 1959, 138–76

BOUSSET, W., *Die Religion des Judentums im neutestamentlichen Zeitalter*, 1903

— *Jesus der Herr* (FRLANT 25), 1916

— *Kyrios Christos* (FRLANT 21), 1st ed., 1913 (2nd ed., 1921)

BRAUN, H., 'Der Sinn der neutestamentlichen Christologie', *ZTK* 54, 1957, 341–77

— 'Zur Terminologie der Acta von der Auferstehung', *TLZ* 77, 1952, 533–6

BULTMANN, R., *Die Geschichte der synoptischen Tradition*, 3rd ed., 1957; ET: *History of the Synoptic Tradition*, 1963

— πιστεύειν, *TWNT* VI 174.17–182.15; 197.34–230.28; ET: *Faith* (BKW 10), 1961

— *Theologie des Neuen Testaments*, 2nd ed., 1954; ET: **Theology** *of the New Testament* I, 1952; II, 1955

CERFAUX, L., ' "Adonai" et "Kyrios" ', *Recueil L. Cerfaux* I, 1954, 137–72

— ' "Kyrios" dans les citations pauliniennes de l'Ancien Testament', *Recueil L. Cerfaux* I, 1954, 173–88

— *Le Christ dans la théologie de St Paul*, 2nd ed., 1954; ET: **Christ** *in the Theology of St Paul*, 1959

— *Le culte des souverains* (Bibliothèque de Théologie, Série III, volume V), 1957

Bibliography

CERFAUX, L., 'Le nom divin "Kyrios" dans la Bible grecque', *Recueil L. Cerfaux* I, 1954, 113-36

— 'Le titre Kyrios et la dignité royale de Jésus', *Recueil L. Cerfaux* I, 1954, 3-63

COLPE, C., *Die religionsgeschichtliche Schule* (FRLANT 78), 1961

CONZELMANN, H., 'Was glaubte die frühe **Christenheit**?', *Schweizerische Theologische Umschau* 25, 1955, 61-74
  See also M. Dibelius, *Die Pastoralbriefe*

CULLMANN, O., *Die Christologie des Neuen Testaments*, 1957; ET: The **Christology** of the New Testament, 2nd ed., 1963

— *Die ersten christlichen Glaubensbekenntnisse* (Theologische Studien, ed. K. Barth, 15), 2nd ed., 1949; ET: *The Earliest Christian Confessions*, 1949

— πέτρα, *TWNT* VI 94.16-99.21

DAHL, N. A., 'Die Messianität Jesu bei Paulus', *Studia Paulina in honorem Johannis de Zwaan*, 1953, 83-95

— 'Der gekreuzigte Messias', *Der historische Jesus und der kerygmatische Christos*, ed. H. Ristow und K. Matthiae, 1960, 149-69

— '**Formgeschichtliche Beobachtungen** zur Christusverkündigung in der Gemeindepredigt', *NtlStud*, 1957, 3-9

DALBERT, P., *Die Theologie der hellenistisch-jüdischen Missions-Literatur unter Ausschluss von Philo und Josephus* (Theologische Forschung 4, ed. H. W. Bartsch), 1954

DALMAN, G., *Die Worte Jesu*, 1898; ET: *The Words of Jesus*, Edinburgh 1902

DIBELIUS, M., 'Jungfrauensohn und Krippenkind', *Botschaft und Geschichte* I, 1953, 1-78

— *An die Thessalonicher I, II. An die Philipper* (HNT), 2nd ed., 1925

— *Die Pastoralbriefe* (HNT), 3rd ed. rev. H. Conzelmann, 1955

— *An die Kolosser, Epheser, an Philemon* (HNT), 3rd ed. rev. H. Greeven, 1953

VON DOBSCHÜTZ, *Die Thessalonicherbriefe*, 1909

DODD, C. H., *The Apostolic Preaching and its Developments*, 2nd ed., 1944

DÖLGER, F. J., *Sol salutis* (Liturgiegeschichtliche Forschungen 4/5), 1925

EBELING, G., 'Geist und Buchstabe', *RGG*, 3rd ed., II, 1290f.

FOERSTER, W., *Herr ist Jesus* (Neutestamentliche Forschungen, ed. O. Schmitz, 2nd series, vol. 1), 1924

— 'Ιησοῦς, *TWNT* III 284.46-294.12

— κύριος, *TWNT* III, 1038-56, 1081-94; ET: *Lord* (BKW 8), 1958

FRIEDRICH, G., εὐαγγελίζομαι, εὐαγγέλιον, *TWNT* II 705.1-735.43

— '**Lohmeyers These** über "Das paulinische Briefpräskript" kritisch beleuchtet', *ZNW* 46, 1955, 272-4

Fuchs, E., *Christus und der Geist bei Paulus* (Untersuchungen zum NT, ed. H. Windisch, 23), 1932

— *Die Freiheit des Glaubens*, 1949

Fuller, R. H., *The Mission and Achievement of Jesus* (SBT 12), 2nd ed. 1955

Haenchen, E., *Die Apostelgeschichte* (KEKNT), 10th ed., 1956

Hahn, F., *Christologische Hoheitstitel. Ihre Geschichte im frühen Christentum* (FRLANT 83), 1963

Heitmüller, W., 'Zum Problem Paulus und Jesus', *ZNW* 13, 1912, 320–37

— *Im Namen Jesu* (FRLANT 2), 1903

Hermann, I., *Kyrios und Pneuma* (Studien zum Alten und Neuen Testament, ed. V. Hamp und J. Schmid, 2), 1961

Hommel, E., 'Maran atha', *ZNW* 15, 1914, 317–22

Jeremias, J., *Die Abendmahlsworte Jesu*, 3rd ed. 1960; ET: *The* **Eucharistic Words** *of Jesus*, 1955

— *Die Briefe an Timotheus und Titus* (NTD 9), 1949

— λίθος, *TWNT* IV 272.5–283.29

— παῖς θεοῦ, *TWNT* V 676.33–713.17; ET: *The* **Servant** *of God* (SBT 20), rev. ed., 1965

Käsemann, E., 'Anliegen und Eigenart der paulinischen Abendmahlslehre', *Exegetische Versuche und Besinnungen* I, 1960, 11–34; ET: 'The Pauline Doctrine of the **Lord's Supper**', *Essays on New Testament Themes* (SBT 41), 1964, 108–35

— *Das wandernde* **Gottesvolk** (FRLANT 55), 1939

— 'Eine urchristliche Taufliturgie', *Exegetische Versuche und Besinnungen* I, 1960, 34–51; ET: 'A Primitive Christian Baptismal Liturgy', *Essays on New Testament Themes* (SBT 41), 1964, 149–67

— 'Kritische Analyse von **Phil. 2.5–11**', *Exegetische Versuche und Besinnungen* I, 1960, 51–95

— 'Die Legitimität des Apostels', *ZNW* 41, 1942, 41ff.

— 'Liturgische Formeln im NT', *RGG*, 3rd ed., II 993–6

Klein, G., *Die zwölf* **Apostel** (FRLANT 77), 1961

— 'Maranatha', *RGG*, 3rd ed., IV 732f.

Kleinknecht, H., θεός, *TWNT* III 65.20–79.3

Klostermann, A., *Probleme im Aposteltexte*, 1883

Kuhn, K. G., μαραναθά, *TWNT* IV 470.5–475.29

Kümmel, W. G., See H. Lietzmann, *Korinther*

Kuss, O., *Der Römerbrief*, 1957ff.

Lietzmann, H., *Messe und* **Herrenmahl** (Arbeiten zur Kirchengeschichte, eds. K. Aland, W. Eltester, H. Rückert), 3rd ed., 1955; ET: *Mass and* **Lord's Supper**, Leyden, 1953ff. (incomplete)

— *An die* **Römer** (HNT), 3rd ed., 1928

Bibliography

LIETZMANN, H., *An die* **Galater** (HNT), 2nd ed., 1923
— *An die* **Korinther** *I und II* (HNT), 4th ed., rev. W. G. Kümmel, 1949
LOHMEYER, E., *Christuskult und Kaiserkult* (Sammlung gemeinverständlicher Vorträge und Schriften aus dem Gebiet der Theologie und Religionsgeschichte 90), 1919
— κύριος 'Ιησοῦς (Sitzungbericht der Heidelberger Akademie, Phil-Hist. Kl.) 1927–28 (cited as **Kyrios**)
— '**Probleme** paulinischer Theologie I', *ZNW* 26, 1927, 158–73
— *Die Offenbarung des Johannes* (HNT), 2nd ed., 1953
— *Die Briefe an die* **Philipper,** *Kolosser, und Philemon* (KEKNT), 8th ed. 1930
LÖVESTAM, E., 'Die Frage des Hohenpriesters', *Svensk Exegetisk Årsbok* 26, 1961, 93–107
MICHAELIS, W., *Einleitung in das NT*, 1946
MICHEL, O., ὁμολογεῖν, *TWNT* V 199.1–220.13
— *Der Brief an die* **Römer**, 12th ed., 1963
MICHEL, O., BETZ, O., 'Von Gott gezeugt', *Festschrift für J. Jeremias* (BZNW 26), 1960
NEUGEBAUER, F., 'Das paulinische **"in Christo"**', **NTS** 4, 1957/58, 124–38
— **In Christus.** *Eine Untersuchung zum paulinischen Glaubensverständnis,* 1961
NORDEN, E., *Agnostos Theos*, 1913
OEPKE, A., διά, *TWNT* II 64.22–68.8
— *Die Missionspredigt des Apostels Paulus* (Missionswissenschaftliche Forschungen, ed. C. Mirbt 2), 1920
— ἐν, *TWNT* II 534.1–539.35
PETERSON, E., ΕΙΣ ΘΕΟΣ (FRLANT 41), 1926 (cited as **Theos**)
RENGSTORF, K. H., ἀπόστολος, *TWNT* I 397.1–448.5; ET: *Apostleship* (BKW 6), 1952
— δοῦλος, *TWNT* II 264.8–283.38
ROBINSON, J. M., 'Heilsgeschichte und Lichtungsgeschichte', *EvTh* 22, 1962
— **A New Quest** of the Historical Jesus (SBT 25), 1959
— **Kerygma** und historischer Jesus, 1960 (expanded translation of the foregoing)
ROLLER, O., *Das* **Formular** *der paulinischen Briefe* (Beiträge zur Wissenschaft vom AuNT, ed. A. Alt und G. Kittel, 4th series, vol. 6), 1933
SCHETTLER, A., *Die paulinische Formel 'durch Christus'*, 1907
SCHLIER, *Der Brief an die Galater*, 12th ed., 1962
SCHMAUCH, W., *In Christus*, 1935
SCHMITHALS, W., *Die* **Gnosis** *in Korinth* (FRLANT 66), 1956
— *Das Kirchliche* **Apostelamt** (FRLANT 79), 1961

SCHMITZ, O., *Die Christus-Gemeinschaft des Paulus im Lichte seines Genetivgebrauchs* (Nt. liche Forschungen, ed. O. Schmitz, 1st series, vol. 2), 1924

SCHNIEWIND, J., *Euangelion* I (Beiträge zur Förderung christlicher Theologie, ed. A. Schlatter und W. Lütgert, 13 and 25), 1927 and 1931

SCHRENK, G., δικαίωσις, *TWNT* II 227.9–229.21; ET: *Righteousness* (BKW 4), 1951

SCHULZ, S., *Komposition und Herkunft der* **Johanneischen Reden** (Beiträge zur Wissenschaft vom AuNT, ed. K. H. Rengstorf und L. Rost, 5th series, vol. 1), 1960

— *Untersuchungen zur Menschensohnchristologie im Johannes-evangelium*, 1957

— '**Maranatha** und Kyrios Jesus', *ZNW* 53, 1962, 125–44

SCHWEIZER, E., 'Abendmahl im NT', *RGG*, 3rd ed., I, 10–21

— **Erniedrigung** *und Erhöhung bei Jesus und seinen Nachfolgern* (Abh. Th. ANT 28), 2nd ed. 1962; English version: **Lordship** *and Discipleship* (SBT 28), 1960

— *Gemeinde und Gemeindeordnung im Neuen Testament* (Abh. Th. ANT 35), 1959; ET: **Church Order** *in the New Testament* (SBT 32), 1961

— 'Die Kirche als Leib Christi in den paulinischen Antilegomena', *TLZ* 86, 1961, 241–56

— πνεῦμα, *TWNT* VI 387.26–453.20; ET: *Spirit of God* (BKW 9), 1960

— 'Zur Herkunft der Präexistenzvorstellung bei Paulus', *EvTh* 19, 1959, 65–70

— 'Anmerkungen zur Theologie des Markus', *Festschrift für O. Cullmann*, 1962

SEEBERG, A., *Der* **Katechismus** *der Urchristenheit*, 1903

— *Die* **Didache** *des Judentums und der Urchristenheit*, 1908

SEESEMANN, H., πεῖρα, *TWNT* VI 23.1–37.15

SMITH, M., ' "God's begetting the Messiah" in 1QSa', *NTS* 5, 1958/59, 218–24

STAERK, W., *Søter* I (Beiträge zur Förderung christlicher Theologie, ed. A. Schlatter und W. Lütgert, 2nd series, vol. 31), 1933

TAYLOR, V., *The Names of Jesus*, 1953

TÖDT, H., *Der Menschensohn in der synoptischen Überlieferung*, 1959; ET: *The* **Son of Man** *in the Synoptic Tradition*, 1965

WEINREICH, O., *Neue Urkunden zur Sarapis-Religion*, 1919

WETTER, G. P., *Der Sohn Gottes* (FRLANT 26), 1916

WILCKENS, U., *Die* **Missionsreden** *der Apostelgeschichte* (Wissenschaftliche Monographien zum AuNT ed. G. Bornkamm und G. von Rad 5), 1961

WISSMANN, E., *Das* **Verhältnis** *von* ΠΙΣΤΙΣ *und Christusfrömmigkeit bei Paulus* (FRLANT 40), 1926

INDEX OF MODERN AUTHORS

Numbers refer to footnotes

INDEX OF BIBLICAL REFERENCES

The figures in brackets indicate the number of the footnote in which the reference is to be found. Figures which are not in brackets refer to the paragraphs and subsections of the text.

1. OLD TESTAMENT (LXX)

Genesis
22.16   (404)

Exodus
34.34   46b

Deuteronomy
6.16   (611)
32.21   45b

Psalms
2.7   (370)

Psalms
51.13   (363)
98.6   (574)

Isaiah
45.23   15c
53.5, 12   5e, 26d, 27d
63.10, 11   (363)

Daniel
2.47   (350, 353)

Daniel
5.23   (350, 353)

Joel
3.5   17d, 43b (251, 574)

Malachi
1.7, 12   43c

Wisdom
9.10   (406)

2. NEW TESTAMENT

Matthew
3.6   (216)
3.7   (414)
8.20   (349)
10.32f   (231)
11.25   (215)
14.7   (221)
17.22   (393)
20.18f   (393)
24.24   (349)
24.27   (349, 414)
26.28b   (35)
26.29   (347)
28.19   (244, 247)

Mark
1.1   (119)
1.5   (216)
1.11   (370)

Mark
1.14, 15   (119)
3.19   (392)
8.31   (41, 84, 349)
9.7   (370)
9.31   (41, 52, 84, 393)
10.33   (52, 84, 393)
10.34   (41)
12.35–37   (372)
14.10, 18   (392)
14.24b   (35)
14.25   (347)
14.41   (393)
15.1   (393)

Luke
1.35   (370)
3.7   (415)

Luke
9.44   (393)
9.58   (349)
10.21   (215)
11.31f   (68)
12.8f   (231)
12.40   (349)
16.17   (68)
17.24   (68, 349, 414)
18.32   (393)
20.20   (393)
22.6   (218)
22.16, 18   (347)
24.34   (57, 62, 64)

John
1.20   (231)
3.16   26a (52, 53, 380, 397)